Towards a Contextual Grammar of English

The Clause and its Place in the Definition of Sentence

E. O. Winter
*Reader in Contemporary English Language,
Hatfield Polytechnic*

London
GEORGE ALLEN & UNWIN
Boston   Sydney

George Allen & Unwin (Publishers) Ltd,
40 Museum Street, London WC1A 1LU, UK

George Allen & Unwin (Publishers) Ltd,
Park Lane, Hemel Hempstead, Herts HP2 4TE, UK

Allen & Unwin, Inc.,
9 Winchester Terrace, Winchester, Mass. 01890, USA

George Allen & Unwin Australia Pty Ltd,
8 Napier Street, North Sydney, NSW 2060, Australia

First published in 1982.

British Library Cataloguing in Publication Data

Winter, Eugene
    Towards a contextual grammar of English.
1. English language — Clauses
I. Title
425   PE1385
ISBN 0-04-425027-4
ISBN 0-04-425028-2 Pbk

Library of Congress Cataloging in Publication Data

Winter, E. O. (Eugene)
    Towards a contextual grammar of English.

Bibliography: p.
Includes index.
1. English language — Clauses. 2. English
language — Sentences. 3. English language —
Discourse analysis. I. Title.
PE1385.W56   1982   425   82-11475
ISBN 0-04-425027-4
ISBN 0-04-425028-2 (pbk.)

Set in 10 on 11 point Times by Typesetters (Birmingham) Limited
and printed in Great Britain by Billing & Sons Ltd, London and Worcester

Contents

To my wife, Barbara, for all the unstinting generosity, the constant support and the strength of mind she has given me over the many years that I have been struggling with the subject matter of this book. To my family, whom I have often neglected as well.

Acknowledgements

I wish to express my deep gratitude to Norman Macleod for his detailed comments and requests for cuts to the original manuscript. Next, I wish to express my heartfelt thanks to James Monaghan, who not merely enabled me to appreciate Norman's comments but also enabled me to make further cuts, restructure and clarify the Introduction, 'The Nature of the Clause' (Sections 1–3), 'Adverbial Clauses with Subordinators' (Section 7) in particular, and 'The Proposed Complementary Definitions of Sentence' (Section 11). I greatly enjoyed the long discussions we had about various parts of the book which enabled me to make many other improvements to the manuscript. I also wish to thank Michael Hoey for his very helpful suggestions for changes.

Finally, I should like to express my thanks to Michael Radford for picking me up for some of the carelessness I showed in the manuscript and for some of the searching queries he made me answer. I particularly appreciated his suggestion of the word 'anywhereness' instead of 'ubiquitousness' to describe the intrusive nature of the interpolating clause.

Introduction

Preliminaries

The present study is an attempt to show that the foundations of a contextual grammar of English must be firmly based on an adequate definition of the sentence. The elements of a contextual grammar are built upon the relevant work of past and present scholars who have tackled the thorny problem of describing the English language as they find it. I wish to mention especially A. S. Hornby's description of the predictability of the verb patterns in English in *Guide to Patterns and Usage in English* (1954; 1975); A. A. Hill's impressive attempt to marry sound and structure in *Introduction to Linguistic Structures* (1958); C. F. Hockett's *Course in Modern Linguistics* (1956); G. C. Scheurweghs's *Present-Day English Syntax* (1959), a description of English by text example; R. Quirk's *The Use of English* (1968, revised); and, finally, D. Bolinger's *Aspects of Language* (1968, revised). Over and above these, the most important influence on the approach I have adopted here is C. C. Fries's *The Structure of English* (1952; 1957). It is sad that the full implications of his approach to syntax and morphology were never fully understood. This is particularly true of his illustration of the differences between grammatical and lexical meanings and their interaction with each other. This has led me to distinguish a third class of item, which I call vocabulary-3 words. These pattern like open-class lexical items but relate parts of the text in the same way as closed-system items such as subordinators. An example would be the word **reason**, which paraphrases and signals the same semantic relation as the subordinator **because** (Winter, 1977, p. 25).

One of the consequences of accepting Fries's signalling approach towards structural and lexical meaning was that I favoured a decoding approach towards research. It was above all Fries's discussion of the problems of defining the sentence that eventually stimulated me to having a crack at it myself after all these years. As readers of Fries will know, he eventually adopts the non-semantic definition of Bloomfield, though he makes it clear that Bloomfield's definition and a similar one by Jespersen (1924) are both built upon an earlier one by Meillet (1903). Meillet's definition in turn is presumably built upon the notion of independence in very much earlier grammarians who confused independence of the clause with 'completeness of thought', an understandable confusion. I quote the well-known Bloomfield (1926) 'independence' definition from Fries:

Each sentence is an independent linguistic form, not included by virtue of any grammatical construction in any larger linguistic form.

Fries notes significantly:

The basic problem of the practical investigation undertaken here is not solved simply by accepting Bloomfield's definition of a sentence. As one approaches the body of recorded speech which constitutes the material to be analysed (or any body of recorded speech), just how should he proceed to discover the portions of an utterance that are not 'parts of any larger construction'? How can he find out the 'grammatical constructions' by virtue of which certain linguistic forms are included in larger linguistic forms? What procedures will enable him to decide which linguistic forms 'stand alone as independent utterances'? (1952, pp. 21–2)

Fries resolves the purely grammatical problem by using the term *utterance unit* for 'those chunks of talk that are marked off by a shift of speaker' (Fries, 1952, p. 23). Fries divides utterance units into (i) single minimum free utterances, (ii) single expanded free utterances (both of which are sentences) and (iii) sequences of two or more free utterances. Elsewhere (Winter, 1979, pp. 95–133) I have discussed evidence in principle for this third category, and in particular his notion of a larger linguistic unit consisting of a 'situation' sentence followed by a 'sequence' sentence which contains a clear signal of its sequence. This signalling principle is illustrated by Fries's (A) (1952, p. 246) and my (B) examples:

Situation sentence	Sequence sentence
(A) Sunday we're going out in our boat for a picnic and we'd like to have you go with us.	*That* is *the* boat that is over near M— C—.

(B) Scratch any Quaker you meet – even the most solid and secure – and under the surface you'll probably find that he is not nearly so rigid as you expect about his religious beliefs and practices. *This is because* nobody tells him what to believe. (*Observer*, 23 January 1966, p. 24)

The sequence signals here are the pronominal heads as subject, the **that** in (A) and the **this** in (B), both of which refer back to parts of the preceding sentence and both of which answer **wh**-questions on their 'situation sentence in (A) 'What boat is that?' and in (B) 'Why is this?' The important linguistic point at this stage of our knowledge is that the meaning of their sequence sentences must be seen as a function of the meaning of their 'situation' sentences, so that together they form a semantically indivisible two-sentence utterance unit. (Please note that my term 'situation' is not the same as Fries's term here and does not imply that it comes first in sequence. For me 'situation sentence' refers to the semantics of a clause answering the question: 'What is the situation?')

Like Fries before me, my approach to the problem of defining the sentence is to examine the nature of the sentence in its utterance unit with its adjoining sentence. I also investigate the semantic as well as the syntactic boundaries of sentence. This means going outside the grammatical boundary of sentence as defined by Bloomfield and others, and attempting to work out the boundaries of a semantic unit for sequences of two or more sentences. I have already tackled this question elsewhere (Winter, 1971, 1974, 1977 and 1979) under the general heading of 'Clause Relations', the study of how we understand a clause or sentence in the light of other clauses or sentences.

Having considered utterance units of two or more sentences, I turned to re-examining the question 'What is a sentence?' Fortified by the solid description by Fries of its grammatical signalling, I now see the role of clause structure as the signalling of its contextual role as clause in the utterance unit or clause relation.

At present, the notion of 'sentence' is bedevilled by its conflation with the notion of 'clause'. There is no doubt whatever that much of the linguistic discussion of 'sentence' has centred on the tacit grammatical unit of independent clause. But, as we will note later, the grammatical unit of independent clause often contains other clauses, independent and subordinate. The definitions of sentence described by Fries do not account for the notion of clause, though traditional grammar has three kinds of grammatical sentence: simple sentence, complex sentence and compound sentence. Simple sentence is where there is just one clause which is also an independent clause; complex sentence is where there are two or more clauses, one of which is an independent (or main) clause and the other subordinate; and compound sentence is where there are two or more clauses, both of which are independent.

I propose to redefine the term 'sentence' to account for how it is used to communicate from a decoding point of view. The definition has to distinguish between two kinds of semantic boundary: the semantic boundary which coincides with the grammatical boundaries of simple sentence, complex sentence, and compound sentence, and the semantic boundary of the unit which coincides with two or more such sentences.

2 Problems of Defining the Sentence

I found that there were five main problems in tackling the definition of 'sentence':

(i) How to reconcile the notion of 'sentence' with the various communicative functions of 'clause', for example subordinate clause, independent clause, question clause, etc.

(ii) The confusion of sentence and clause in talking about matters of clause structure. Quirk *et al.* (1972, pp. 34–50), and many others, speak of subject, verb, object, adjunct, etc., as *sentence structure*.

(iii) No single definition of 'sentence' could cover the communicative function of clause in both its grammatical and semantic aspects as clause.

(iv) The difference in contextual meaning between independent clause and subordinate clause which had to be taken into account by the definition. I have already noted the essence of this difference in Winter (1977, p. 45), but it requires further description to meet the requirements of a comprehensive definition. This essence is the Prague School's notion of functional sentence perspective in which the sentence offers 'given' and 'new' information.

(v) An adequate definition has to account for the contextual role of subordinate clause as a basic function of (independent or main) clause, and ought not to treat subordination as something somehow 'included' or extraneous to the sentence.

I resolved problem (i) by deciding to use the term 'sentence' for the clause in its communicative function, namely the independent clause, by distinguishing between the various functions of the clause, and by contrasting independent clause with question clause. Problem (ii) can be resolved by only using the term 'clause' to speak of *clause structure*. Problem (iii) was resolved by settling for the notion of a composite definition, all of whose parts should apply.

Problems (iv) and (v) are closely related. We cannot fully describe independence without subordination since, as we will later note, their contrast in grammatical status corresponds with a contrast in their information status or the status of knowledge which their clauses signal. The Prague School's notions of 'given' and 'new' information certainly apply here, but it is not enough to account for the communicative function of clause. What we need to know as linguists is what kind of information is 'given' or 'new'. My resolution of this particular problem is to distinguish between two kinds of fundamental information that any clause gives: this is the information of the clause which answers the **wh**-question – 'What do you **know** (about X person, event, state, etc.)?' – and the information of the clause which answers the **wh**-question – 'What do you **think** (about X person, event, state, etc., that you know about)?' (cf. discussion of the use of the question criterion on pages 7, 8, 19).

I decided that we should re-examine the contextual role of independence and subordination in these terms, but found that the main obstacle to any successful attempt at defining the sentence was the greater structural and semantic complexity of subordination over independence. I accordingly decided to concentrate the focus of this work on describing the problems of subordination, contrasting subordination with independence whenever possible, with the eventual view of synthesising subordinate clause with independent clause in the definition.

As will be seen, the problem of subordination is not merely one of how it is signalled – by conjunction, verb morphology, etc. – but of what kinds of subordinate clause there are and what kinds of contextual function they have *as structures which are somehow contained within the grammatical boundary of (main) clause in its sentence function*. One particular theoretical problem is the role of postmodifier-like independent clauses which interrupt the structure of the (main) clause. I call this kind of interruptive process *interpolation*, and see it as a form of *interjection*. Interpolation is treated as a kind of adverbial adjunct function and is described along with what is traditionally regarded as subordinate clause. I found it necessary to compare and contrast interpolation with the other postmodifier-like function, apposition, since the two functions can have similarities in their structural manifestation, and can merge their meanings in a multiple relation.

In brief, the key to working out a definition of sentence is that (i) it must be a composite one which accounts both for the basic meaning of the clause and for the contextual role of independent clause and subordinate clause in the sentence, and (ii) in doing so it must account for subordination as a basic function of (main) clause. The descriptive strategy is to concentrate on describing the subordinate clause in its environment of main clause.

3 Problems of Description

In redescribing the various kinds of subordination, it will be noted that there are two extremes in the amount of description. The relative clause is barely touched upon except in relation to its communicative role. In contrast, the adverbial clause has a very much more detailed description. This requires explanation. The problem about relative clause is the existence of relative-clause-type grammar, for example noun clauses such as the **what**-clause where the **what** element is both indirect question and nominal head, as in 6.4.1 below.

The adverbial clause, on the other hand, constitutes the central problem in studying subordination in English. The main problem lies in its mobility within the main clause and, more particularly, in what semantic changes follow changes of its position relative to its main clause in terms of 'given' and 'new' information. I have taken the simplest course in adopting the three basic positions in the clause as in G. C. Scheurweghs (1959), namely front-position, mid-position and end-position. I found that the only way we could discuss the meanings of these changes of position was to present the adverbial clause and its main clause in their larger contexts. The approach adopted towards describing these positions in the clause was to describe front- and end-position separately and compare them in respect of their contextual meanings, and then describe the mid-position separately and contrast it in turn with front- and end-position.

The main criterion for examining the use of adverbial clause was for us to use the question criterion in order to establish what was 'given' or 'known' to the adverbial clause. Of the two positions, front- and end-position, end-position has the more severe problems in establishing the meaning of the adverbial clause. The analysis used is described below under 'Methods and Problems of Analysis'.

The most controversial of the subordinate structures is the category of *interpolation*, which I treat as a kind of special adverbial adjunct to the host clause. Here the crucial point to reconcile is the idea that a grammatically independent clause can be subordinate because it is included within the grammatical boundary of its host clause.

4 Methods and Problems of Analysis

The strategy of my presentation is to use traditional grammatical categories wherever possible, extending them in respect of the semantics of their contextual functions, and to present my own categories where the need arises. With very rare exceptions, the material used in this study is from written English, and the term 'sentence' is used in the first instance for the orthographic sentence: 'that which is between full stops', whether there is one clause or more clauses, that is, whether it is a simple sentence, a complex sentence or a compound sentence. Wherever I required a one-clause sentence example of English I have used Scheurweghs (1959) which, although it seldom uses examples of more than one sentence, cites their provenance so that interested readers could turn up their larger contexts.

In this study of the English clause, when we speak of grammar or parts of the sentence, we speak of the *clause* and *clause structure*. While acknowledging that speech is primary, I regard written English examples as being sufficiently close to the facts of living language to be taken seriously as evidence for our discussions of clause. I also regard the intonation of speech as equally important with the other devices of grammar described in this study. I would even insist that in further developments of a contextual grammar of English the elements of this grammar must be married to their appropriate places within the intonation system of English, probably using a system compatible with the type proposed by Brazil *et al.* (1980). Whatever the differences between written and spoken English, they are not serious enough to invalidate my arguments about a contextual grammar based on examples of written English.

The main problem of analysis was that I felt that I could not count on a knowledge of clause relations (as described in Winter 1971, 1974, 1977 and 1979), but would have to confine myself to the larger clause relations which I have called *situation* and *evaluation*, and *hypothetical* and *real*. The phenomenon of clause relations in English is still in the process of being described and analysed with the ultimate objective of marrying it with the grammar of the English clause. To compensate for the limited use of clause relations, I have for instance depended upon the notion of topic development in analysing adverbial clause placement (7.2) as it enabled me to link the adverbial clause and its main clause to its immediately adjoining context of sentences. Instead of clause relations, I depend on certain mutually predictive semantic categories of the clause such as affirmation and denial as part of the hypothetical and real relation, situation and evaluation clause, unspecific and specific clause, and 'know' and 'think' clauses. In addition, I wish to use the notions of topic development, Interpolation clause, and the question criterion. Examples of these categories and concepts now follow in a general description of my analytical procedure.

The use of the question criterion to examine meaning in syntax is an application of the approach proposed by Anna Granville Hatcher in two articles in *Word*, Volume 12 (1956): first, the proposal itself in 'Syntax and the Sentence' and then its application to the analysis of Spanish in her monograph, 'Theme and Underlying Question'. In the first article she proposes to use questions in the search for more specific relationships between meaning and form in language. She noted then that the appeal to question-and-answer in establishing the point of a predication was not unknown to grammarians, though it had only been used sporadically up to then. This still seems true today.

We take the pragmatic view that for every clause there must be a question to which it represents an answer, and that this requirement should be applied to the parts of the clause as well. We take the clause in its context of adjoining clauses and ask ourselves, 'What question does the clause under consideration answer of its adjoining clause or clauses in this particular context?' This refinement of the requirement for a clause to represent an answer to a particular question of a particular clause in the context is necessary because, out of context, any sentence can represent answers to as many questions as it has parts.

For example, in the well-known made-up example in (C) below, the semantics of context would differ according to what parts of the clause were already 'known' or 'given' by its preceding context, and what parts were presented as 'new' or 'not hitherto known'. This kind of semantics relates the decoder's state of knowledge.

(C)   I persuaded John to leave. (Chomsky, 1965, p. 22)

Following Quirk *et al.* (1972, p. 396), we take the approach that the question provides what is true, or presupposed as true, and asks for new information. The different state of information for each part of the clause would correspond to different questions which ask for 'new' information to be supplied for what is presupposed as already true. The answers to these questions would correspond directly with their intonation in spoken form. For example, if the stress was on the infinitive verb **leave**, then the question for it is: '**What did** you persuade John **to do**?', where the parts in bold type show that the question demands the lexical realisation of its to-finitive clause as something like **to leave**. Other questions can refer to subject: '**Who** persuaded John to leave?'; to main verb: '**What did** you **do** to John?'; to object: **Who** did you persuade to leave?'; to the verb **persuade** as opposed to any other verb, such as **force**: '**How did** you **get** John to leave?' The sentences that contain answers to these questions would have the stress on the new information of their replies.

A written example like this would imply at least all the contexts that are open to the questions. However, in context, the adjoining sentences, especially the preceding sentence(s), would narrow down to a specific question to which the sentence under consideration would represent a reply, as in (D) below:

(D)   Mr Baldwin promised to resign if the Cabinet refused his request. It did refuse and he did not resign.

Here, the first sentence is the hypothetical and the second sentence is the real member of the hypothetical and real relation. The hypotheticality is linguistically signalled by the verb **promise** which makes explicit that he is promising, not resigning. The second sentence co-ordinates an affirmation clause and a denial clause. Notice that the compound sentence here answers a compound **yes/no**-question: 'Did it refuse his request and did he resign?' – (yes) it did refuse, and (no) he did not resign. Now notice in particular that this question for the real member, the question for the truth of what actually happened later, is basically a 'know' question, because we could preface it with a steering question: 'What do you **know** about the subsequent events: did the Cabinet (actually) refuse his request and did he (actually) resign?'

The semantic categories of *situation* and *evaluation* clause are unfamiliar and require some explanation. The awkward member to grasp at first is the *evaluation* member. *Evaluation clause* may evaluate either a *basis* or 'fact' or it may evaluate a *situation* which need not be a *basis*. In (E) below, the first clause is an evaluation clause which is also a denial clause, and the second clause is a basis for the evaluation by denial.

(E) There is no justification for the widely held idea that monkeys spend much of their time 'flea catching' — they are, as it happens, particularly devoid of all forms of ecto-parasites. (*New Scientist*, 1 August 1967, p. 236)

We can regard the first clause as a **no**-reply to an evaluation clause asked as a **yes/no**-question: 'Is there any justification for the widely held idea that monkeys spend much of their time "flea catching"?' The second clause answers the **wh**-question: 'How do you **know** this (is true)?' The first clause evaluates the widely held idea that monkeys spend much of their time 'flea catching'.

The notion of situation must be clearly seen as 'linguistic situation' or linguistic representation of real situation. Basically, there are three kinds of situation, two of which are linguistic. The first is the non-linguistic real-world situation, also called context of situation. The second is the strictly selective linguistic representation of this real-world situation. The clause or clauses here answer the question: 'What is the situation (that is relevant) here?' The third is the chunk of preceding text whose overall structure is taken as linguistic situation to be evaluated by clause: 'What do you **think** of the situation here?' This is textual evaluation, as in (F) below, where the evaluation clause is in bold type. The preceding description of the situation for **Abortion** constitutes the textual situation which it is evaluating.

(F) But events move slowly. Abortion has been a dilemma, a scandal, a racket and a tragedy for so long that it produces in most people a stultifying sense of ill-omen and despair that inhibits action, not encourages it. Every day the phones ring, the curtains are drawn, the lies are told, the money changes hands, the women breathe again. **One day it may look barbaric, but for the moment it's our natural condition.** (*Observer*, 24 October 1965, p. 8)

Notice that the second sentence is an evaluation of the situation for abortion, and that the third sentence fills out the typical detail of the real-world situation for abortion. This detail represents 'know' information in contrast with the 'think' information of the fourth sentence. Notice finally that the last sentence answers the **wh**-question: 'What do you *think* of the situation for abortion as it is described here?'

Next, we consider the semantic category of *unspecific* and *specific clause*. The linguistic principle at its simplest is that *unspecific clause* requires *specific clause(s)* to provide the intelligibility of some or all of its clause's lexical choices. Sometimes we can have a special operations clause which requires the whole of its predicate to be specified next, as in (G) below, or part of its clause to be fully specified next, as in (H) below. The key linguistic concept in unspecific and specific clause is the notion of *lexical realisation*; that is, certain items of the clause may be lexically realised outside its sentence or clause boundary so that we have to take the clause and the adjoining clause as a single semantic unit for the understanding of both clauses. (See Winter, 1977, pp. 57–73.)

In (G) below, the cataphoric substitute clause **did something else as well as finger evidence** anticipates the compatible lexical realisation which follows in the very next sentence. The anticipatory element is printed bold.

(G)   Bullet 399 and Frame 313 aside, the Warren Commission **did something else as well as finger evidence.** Incidental to the matter of the report it also gave a horrific picture of a floating, rootless, footloose society in America drifting aimlessly and apparently endlessly from bedsitters in the South to rented rooms in Texas. And this seemed to be a vital clue to Oswald's or for that matter Jack Ruby's character. (*Guardian*, 30 January 1967, p. 7)

One way of understanding what lexical realisation means is to see it as an answer to a **wh**-question: 'What is this something else that the Warren Commission did as well as finger evidence?' The substitute clause **did something else** signals a startling piece of information which is compatible with fingering evidence.

In (H) below, the first sentence is an unspecific clause in respect of the specific meaning of the nominal group (taking) **unpopular measures**. The next two sentences specify **against whom** the unpopular measures are being taken.

(H)   Mr HEATH is more convincing in presenting himself as the Prime Minister who would really get tough in taking unpopular measures (which is perhaps one reason why he is lagging behind Mr Wilson in popularity). This is true of his policies towards the trade unions. It is also true of his plan to introduce an element of discrimination in welfare benefits so as to concentrate them where they are needed most. (*Observer*, 27 March 1966, p. 10)

I see the second and third sentences as *affirmation by example* where the examples are assumed known to the readers. The question which the writer seems to be anticipating is the **yes/no**-question: 'Isn't this true of his policies towards the trade unions?' Similar considerations apply to the third sentence. The linguistic point about **yes/no**-questions is that we have a fully formed clause which represents what is presupposed to be true, but which requires confirmation one way or the other.

These are just two examples of the many kinds of unspecific clause there are in English, but they suffice to illustrate the principle. I have ignored examples of the use of the conjunction **More specifically** since the principle of unspecific clause can be illustrated without examples like these.

Next, the category of interpolation requires some explanation, as I regard it as a very important category of adjunct in the description of the clause in English. Interpolation is otherwise known as *parenthesis* or *aside*. We are interested in the semantics of interpolation as a special adjunct function whose distinguishing feature is its interruption of the (main) clause with evaluative material. In (I) below, there is an interpolation by independent clause whose syntactic boundary is shown by the two dash signs. It interrupts the syntactic relation between the indirect and the direct object of the verb **tell**.

(I) However, the authorities tell me – **and I think now that I believe them** – that there isn't really any need to lose sleep over him. (See 9.5)

What interests us in the semantics of the English clause is that parenthesis is not any old irrelevant intrusion into the clause, but has its own meaning as intruding adjunct. Here the writer is commenting on the direct object. As an evaluation clause it answers the **wh**-question: 'What do you now think of what the authorities are telling you here?'

Perhaps the most controversial part of the present study of the English clause is the idea that the fundamental information of the clause consists of a complementarity between 'know' and 'think' information. The notion of 'know' and 'think' clauses is a notion about the superordinate verb in the **wh**-question which could elicit them. I regard the relation of situation and evaluation as offering 'know' and 'think' information respectively, but of being a special case of 'know' and 'think'. The other case of 'know' and 'think' clause is important in understanding the role of modal verbs. Modal verbs superimpose a 'think' upon 'know' verbs. The difference between the modal verb group **can make** and the zero modal verb group **is being grown** is illustrated by (J) below.

> *Fungus food ready for the hard sell*
> (J) A fungus that **can make** a protein, as good as the animal product, from carbohydrates **is being grown** by Rank Hovis McDougall Ltd. It is hoped that it will be possible to turn the new food source into marketable foodstuff within the next five years . . . (*New Scientist*, 29 May 1970, p. 29)

First note that it is not a fungus that makes a protein, etc. but it is *evaluated* as a fungus that has the ability to make protein. Second, notice that the verbal group **is being grown** as a definite clause simply signals that the process of growing is known to be happening right at that moment; not having a modal verb like **can** it is non-evaluative or non-speculative. The verb **hoped** is 'think' as are the remaining clauses in the **that**-clause subject which follows it. The future tense auxiliary **will** is evaluative in the sense that it *speculates*.

This area of the semantics of the verb has still to be developed and cannot be ignored. We could begin by concentrating on studies of the superordinate verbs of **wh**-questions; for instance, we could ask ourselves whether 'think' verbs will distinguish between verbs like **persuade** and **expect**.

Finally, the notion of *Topic* needs some explanation. In working out how questions relate the semantics of adverbial clauses to their preceding or adjoining context of sentences, we need the notion of topic in its simplest form. This notion does not mean the lexical participants or actors, etc. in the clause, but *what is predicated of these participants*.

In (K) below, we see the use of a substitute clause whose function is to pick up the preceding topic of **having to use force in Rhodesia**, complete with the participant **Britain.** Here we have the **if**-clause picking up the topic for the change of topic which follows in the second co-ordinate main clause to the notion of **discharging a duty it still owes to Rhodesia's African population.**

> (K) It may be that Britain will have to use force in Rhodesia. If **it does so**, it will not be to please any other member of the Commonwealth but to discharge the duty it still owes to Rhodesia's African population. Now that most of what was the British Empire has been dissolved, there is a tendency among people in Britain to assume that what happens in the rest of it is no longer our responsibility. This is an escapist attitude. (*Guardian*, 11 November 1965, p. 10)

Using the adverbial clause of the next sentence as the basis for our **wh**-question, we can see it as an answer to the question: 'What has happened to this sense of duty **now that most of what was the British Empire has been dissolved?**' Thus we see that this sentence and the last sentence develop the topic of **our duty** as the responsibility which we can no longer assume away.

When an adverbial clause is in end-position, its topic is most likely to be developed as the next immediate sentence in its paragraph. In (L) below, the preceding topic is **research in management**, with the **because**-clause introducing a change in topic from being invalid to what is wrong with it.

(L) The other sort of investigator is practical enough, but can hardly be called a scientist at all. Dr. V. L. Allen once remarked that nearly all the research in management that there had ever been was invalid from the start, **because it had asked the wrong questions.** For example, if you were studying absenteeism, the practical question you might want to ask was obviously 'why do people stay away from work?'. But the real scientific problem that underlay it might be a more general one: 'Why do people go to work in the first place?' (*TES*, 11 November 1966, p. 1153)

The two sentences which follow the **because**-clause develop its topic of the wrong question, with the clause connector **For example** signalling this clearly.

In studying adverbial clause placement, we note that in front-position, as in (K), the adverbial clause picks up the preceding topic, while in end-position, as in (L), its topic is picked up by the next immediate sentence in its paragraph. The notion of topic is crude and the use of questions as criteria requires further development as do most other considerations in grammar where we are interested in contextual semantics. However, there is no avoiding the use of topic and question criteria if we are to tackle questions of contextual semantics.

I have not pursued every avenue in either topic or question and hope the reader will fill out his own knowledge and develop this approach further. There should be no surprise at this after over twenty years of general neglect of simple matters of observation of language use.

5 The Outline of the Discussion

The work is in four main parts as described below, culminating in the tripartite definition of the sentence.

5.1   *The Nature of the Clause* (Sections 1 – 3)

My basic strategy here is to tackle the question of what is a clause? before turning to the question of the subordinate clause in its environment of independent clause. The clause is dealt with in three sections: (Section 1) sentence distinguished from clause, introducing the notion of parsing or the signalling approach developed from C. C. Fries; (Section 2) the clause as the sole device of lexical selection, introducing the idea of the clause as a representational vehicle *whose meaning is more than the sum total of its parts*; and (Section 3) the grammatical status of the clause, introducing the contextual difference between independence and subordination.

5.2   *Subordination in English* (Sections 4 – 9)

Here the strategy of description is to work from the very familiar to the less familiar notions of subordination. The approach is to consider as candidates for subordination any clauses or structures that are included within the grammar of the clause. Subordination is divided into six groups: (1) the relative clause, (2) the two kinds of noun clause, (3) the adverbial clause, (4) problems of non-finite clauses which do not have subordinating conjunctions, (5) apposition, and (6) interpolation as controversial super-adjunct for the clause.

Having described the problems of subordinate structures and some of the solutions to these problems, I next sum up subordination in contrast with independence and take into account the contextual roles of clauses other than subordinate. This is required to round out the description of clause in preparation for the attempt to define the sentence.

5.3   *Subordination and Non-Subordination* (Section 10)

After summarising and concluding upon the role of subordinate clause, it is necessary to consider, albeit very briefly, the contextual role of special operations clauses of which cleft and pseudo-cleft clauses are just two among many. The chief point about special operations clauses is that they are not basic clauses, but special grammatical operations upon basic clause structure; that is, instead of having lexical participants at subject, object or complement in a clause which has a lexical verb, they have grammatical operators which signal the particular contextual role of their clause in some way; details and examples are given at 10.3.4, 'The Marked Special Operations Clause'.

Having described the roles of subordinate clause, independent clause and clauses other than subordinate, we consider the assumptions about context which are based upon the foregoing description of clause in order to lay the final foundations for the definition of sentence.

5.4 The Complementary Definitions of Sentence (Section 11)

This section is in two parts, Section 11.1–11.6, 'The Proposed, Complementary Definitions', and Section 11.7 and 11.8, 'Rephrasing the Definitions as Requirements'.

In Section 11.2, we begin by looking at the clause as organiser in a word-based grammar. Starting with the notion that the minimum context for the word to have meaning as a word is a clause – that is, the notion that the meaning of a word is a function of the other words of its clause – we fan outwards, building up the requirements for this clause in turn to have meaning as a clause. As with words, the meaning of a clause is a function of its adjoining clauses, and so on into larger constructions. This setting out of the requirements for linguistic situation for our clause brings us finally to our definitions of sentence.

The strategy for presenting the definitions of sentence is to work from the familiar to the less familiar of the definitions discussed by C. C. Fries. There are three definitions of sentence, forming a composite whole. Definition 1 starts with the well-known Meillet/Bloomfield/Jespersen requirement of structural independence as the first part and introduces the requirement of semantic completion as the second part. Definition 2 starts with the well-known Prague School notions of 'given' and 'new' information, introducing the notion of communicating what is not known in terms of what is, with the further distinction between 'know' and 'think' information. Definition 3 starts with the less well known definitions of sentence by John Ries and Karl Sunden and develops further the idea that the sentence expresses its content's relation to reality.

In Section 11.7, we emerge with a set of three main requirements for the kind of sentence we want from our encoder, and in Section 11.8 conclude the discussion of definitions of sentence by applying the composite requirements to a well-known problem in linguistics today, the linguistic status of idealised examples of sentence.

Part One

The Nature of the Clause

Sentence and Clause in English

1.1 Sentence and Clause

The central problem of working towards a contextual grammar of English is our lack of an adequate description of the contextual role of clause in the notion of sentence, and especally of the contextual contrast between subordination and independence for the clause. This description is necessary as a preliminary to finding a definition of the sentence which will account for the real-world use of the clause in our daily communication, whether spoken or written. Familiar categories will have to be used in unfamiliar ways because they are being applied in a contextual description of clause and sentence. For instance, independent clause is seen as 'sentence' while question clause is not seen as 'sentence', but as a demand for 'sentence.'

While many traditional and modern grammarians conflate the notions of clause and sentence, I follow Halliday (1961, pp. 253-4) and Pike and Pike (1977, p. 482), who distinguish them. In Halliday's old rank analysis, a sentence consists of one or more clauses, and I wish to further specify that at least one of these clauses must be an independent declarative (including imperative and exclamatory) clause. In contrast, question clause is not regarded as 'sentence' but as a specially incomplete clause which demands propositional and gram- matical completion as independent clause or part of independent clause. This follows from the complementary definition of sentence presented in the final part of this book. We ignore the single-clause sentence (simple sentence) where the sentence function is represented by a single independent clause such as (1) below, which can be seen as an answer to a question like: 'What kind of claim was the claim of the councils?'

(1) The claim of the councils was a reasonable one. (Scheurweghs, 1959, p. 53)

The distinction between sentence and clause reflects the distinction between a whole and its parts. The simplest possible solution to the problem of conflating the terms 'sentence' and 'clause' is to examine how these two terms might be used in analysing those sentences where there is more than one clause.

What all clauses have, in common is that they have the well recognised syntactic constituents of subject and predicate with or without adjunct, or just predicate with or without adjunct. (We will take it for granted that the notion of Quirk *et al.* (1972, p. 42) of S V, S V O, S V C, S V O O, and S V O C requires supplementing for pre-positional structuring, for example 'He **talked to** her', in which the verb **talk** has the fixed phrase structure of **talk to,** and 'He **questioned** her **about me**', in which the prepositional phrase **about me** is part of the structure of the verb **questioned**. Such considerations require the analysis of S V prepositional 'object' and S V O prepositional 'object'). If we examine sentences, we find one or more clauses of different kinds of grammatical status, as in (2) below, where there are three:

(2)   It *is* possible that the contrast between the classical drama of England and the classical drama of France, to which reference **has** already **been made, can be accounted for** by the differences of audience. (Scheurweghs, 1959, p. 275)

Before we analyse the three clauses, we note a refinement to the analysis of S V O C A by Quirk *et al.*: the structure of the main clause can be represented as Si V C Sii, where Si is the use of anticipatory **It,** V is the verb **is,** C is the adjective **possible** as complement, and Sii is the **that**-clause as real subject of the clause which ends the sentence. Looking at the three clauses, we find that they are all finite clauses; one independent clause is represented as (a), a subordinate declarative type clause is represented as (b), and a relative clause is represented as (c). Both (b) and (c) and contained within the clause grammar of (a), with (b) as the **that**-clause subject which in turn contains (c):

(a)   **It** is possible   (b)
(b)   **that**   the contrast between the classical drama of England and the classical drama of France, (c) can be accounted for by the differences of audience
(c)   **to which** reference has already been made.

The difference in grammatical status between the three clauses can be seen in how they are grammatically signalled. First, according to the Meillet/Bloomfield/Jespersen definition of sentence to be discussed later in this section, only (a) can stand alone as sentence, provided that it has the **that**-clause of (b) as part of its clause structure which fulfils the anticipation of clause subject by the item **It**. Taking the clause (a) in some detail, the grammatical item **It** immediately followed by finite present tense verb **is** confirms that the item **It** is the grammatical subject of an independent clause whose predictable pattern is of the **It is possible that**-clause kind. As A. S. Hornby (1954) has shown, this pattern is one we can predict for the adjective **possible**, so that this adjective reinforces the prediction of a **that**-clause structure to follow it. Secondly, neither clause (b) nor clause (c) can stand alone as they are both signalled as subordinate clauses which are part of clause (a)'s structure. In clause (b), the subordinate **that** signals that there will be a declarative type clause as the real subject which fulfils its prediction by anticipatory **It**. Within the structure of clause (b) itself, we note that clause (c) interrupts the syntactic relation between its subject and its predication; more specifically, the subordinator (to) **which** signals that a non-defining relative clause will postpone the predication. Notice how this corresponds directly with the use of the punctuation by commas.

Taking Fries's (1952, p. 56) point that a sentence is the synthesis of its structural and lexical meanings, there are three clauses here whose structural and lexical meanings are synthesised in the larger structure containing them all. It follows that, in discussing the grammar and semantics of parts of this sentence, we must take account of the particular clause each part is in and in turn relate this clause to the other two. For instance, the nominal group **the contrast between the classical drama of England and the classical drama of France** must be taken as S of the **that**-clause; the interrupting relative clause **to which reference has already been made** comes in between the nominal group subject and its predication **can be accounted for**, etc. Secondly, in analysing our clauses within their sentence, we must take seriously the function words when we work out our clause boundaries. It therefore makes sense to keep a clear distinction for 'sentence' as the finished whole and 'clause' for focusing on matters of grammar and semantics within the sentence.

However, in speaking of the grammar of the clause within its sentence, we have the paradox that the clause itself does not exist except as a generalisation that all clauses have subjects and predicates, with or without adjuncts; or simply predicates, with or without adjuncts. Taking a simplified form of clause (b) above as **that the contrast can be accounted for by differences of audience**, we note that this exhibits just one of the many kinds of grammatical status which its clause elements can take, that is, the subordinator **that** signals the enclosure of what might otherwise be taken as independent declarative clause: **the contrast can be accounted for by the difference of audience**. As independent clause, it would have a different context. Again, if we nominalised the elements of the clause as **the differences of audience which can account for the contrast**, we would have the same clause elements but yet another context meaning. Here the unique clause meaning is used to identify the nominal head **the differences of audience**. The conclusion to be drawn here is that, although we have the same clause elements throughout, we can only speak of the particular contextual meaning imparted to the clause by its grammatical status as clause.

We come closest to recognising the changes of grammatical status for the clause when a particular clause structure is repeated by substitute clause. Consider the change of clausal meaning for the clause elements **they (the rugby tourists) retaliated** in (3) below. Note the first appearance of the clause elements in the **if**-clause (if **they had** not **retaliated**) and the change of subordination to **when**-clause for the second appearance of these elements (when **they did**):

(3)   It seems, then, that he must have been direly provoked, to lash out as he did. The reaction, unfortunately, was the opposite of what he had hoped: instead of civilising their methods, New Zealanders saw the attack as a challenge to their toughness. . . .
   As soon as it became clear that Neanderthal methods were the order of the day, the Lions showed themselves to be lively fighters. The trouble was that, once violence erupted, the tourists were bound to lose face; if **they had** not **retaliated**, they would have been branded as cissies; when **they did**, they were condemned as thugs. (*Sunday Telegraph*, 7 August 1966, p. 11)

The point of this extract is that the clause **the tourists retaliated** is presented as a fact which the paragraph is evaluating. It is presented as negatively hypothetical by the **if**-clause, and then re-affirmed by the **when**-clause as true (real). The contrast between the hypothetical action and the real action by the tourists is made explicit by the same clause elements according to the grammar of their subordinate clauses.

If we return to the text discussed on p. 8 (D), we can note that the relations we looked at there in terms of hypothetical and real and affirmation and denial can be seen as being realised by changes of grammatical status for the elements of the two clauses.

(4)   Mr Baldwin promised to resign if the Cabinet refused his request. It did refuse, and he did not resign.

The signals of hypothetical in the first sentence, the verb **promise** with its concomitant non-finite verb and the **if**-clause, are replaced by the denial **he did not resign**. This is an independent declarative clause instead of the previous non-finite clause (Mr Baldwin) **to resign**; it answers the question: 'What did he later actually do: did he resign?'

The answer is 'No, he did not resign.' The affirmation function of the clause can be seen in the change from the **if**-clause elements (if the Cabinet refused his request) to the independent clause **It did refuse**. Notice here that the clause is not the unmarked **It refused** but the marked **It did refuse**. (This is marked because the operator **did** is not grammatically required).

The point of the last example is to illustrate an important fact about the unique lexical elements of a particular clause. This is that, while we all accept the notion of subordination or *downgrading* (Hill, 1958, p. 357), we are not so familiar with the converse contextual process: the *upgrading* of the information of the clause. This is the change from the subordinate clause status of (Mr Baldwin) **to resign** to the independent clause status of **he did not resign**, and from the subordinate clause status of **if the Cabinet refused his request** to the independent clause status of **It did refuse**, where there is a deletion of the object **his request**. Both changes involve *replacements* of one grammatical status with another *for the same clause*. Only by noticing that we have the 'same' grammatical elements in contrast with each other in the clauses of succeeding sentences can we begin to account for the contextual semantics of this replacement. (See discussion of replacement in Winter, 1974, pp. 211–16.)

At this stage of our knowledge, it is only when an individual clause is significantly repeated within or without the sentence boundary that we, as linguists, realise the contextual meanings of independence (as in the upgrading discussed above) and subordination (downgrading). In studies of replacement relations between clauses, we study both upgrading and downgrading of the information of the clause within and without the sentence boundary. If we provisionally define the term 'sentence' as potentially the largest grammatical unit built around one or more independent declarative clauses which may or may not have one or more subordinate clauses, then we must use the term 'clause' for all the clauses within the sentence. However, as an abstraction the clause needs to be specified according to its grammatical status, for example question clause, independent clause and subordinate clause. These general terms are themselves further specified according to their contextual function, for example the distinction between **wh**-question clause and **yes/no**-question clause.

So far we have established a definition of sentence as consisting of one or more clauses, at least one of which is an independent declarative clause. The term 'clause' can be used to describe the minimal structure of the sentence, the simple sentence, but normally we will be concerned with sentences of more than one clause. The notion of clause is an abstraction for what all clauses have in common; namely, the constituent functions of subject and predicate, with or without adjunct, or simply predicate with or without adjunct. These constituent functions contribute to the composite meaning of the sentence via the grammatical status of the clause. The notion of a clause as an abstraction of syntactic relations is best seen where we consider how a clause changes its contextual meaning when it changes its grammatical status, for example from subordinate clause to independent declarative clause in (4) above. In the systematic repetition of the clause, we see how the 'same' clause can change its contextual meaning from one sentence to another.

To understand and communicative function of sentence, we need to compare the contextual meaning of independent declarative clause with that of the question clause. The independent declarative clause informs us of something; the question clause demands information about something. We might just note that passages of written English are very largely sentences as defined here, and very seldom raise questions. The punctuation by full stop very often corresponds closely with the grammatical definition of the sentence. This is very convenient for our analyses of the written examples upon which this book is based. In our discussion of examples, sentence will nearly always mean written sentence.

1.2 The Nature of the English Clause

It has long been a commonplace in linguistics to use a scrambled sentence as an easy way to illustrate an unlikely ungrammaticality, for example **Cat mat the on sat the** for something trivial like **The cat sat on the mat**. All this example does is to illustrate what happens when all the syntactic signals of a sentence are violated: there is no expected sequence of subject (the cat) followed by a predicate (sat on the mat); nor are the determiner signals obeyed by their predicted noun heads **cat** and **mat**. In such short examples, there are sufficient semantic cues in the nouns for us to re-assemble the sentence as **The cat sat on the mat**, and not the much more unlikely **The mat sat on the cat**. There should be no linguistic mystique about this example. We know that inanimates don't sit on anything except in the metaphorical sense (this is simply another way of talking about personification, which we are familiar with in traditional discussion of poetry). More simply, we know that sitting on mats is something which cats do. Thus, in tackling this sentence, we bring our knowledge of the world, our world, to bear on our decoding attempts.

What seems to have been very rarely discussed in linguistics is the fact that it is possible to devise scrambled sentences of up to at least 30 words, and consider the implications of these larger scrambled sentences for theory. Consider (5) below (16 words).

(5)   A repression always likely of totalitarian into government activity nearly measures suspects against extreme subversive alarms.

If subjects rewrite this sentence so that it makes sense to them, using all and only the words of the example to reconstruct it, then they will all produce the following solution to the puzzle. In doing so, they will be painfully aware that in trying to make sense of (5) they must convert the unfamiliar into the familiar; that is, they must at least try to rewrite it in a familiar sequence of English words. I show the adjective **extreme** in brackets in three possible alternative slots of the clause:

(6)   (Extreme) subversive activity nearly always alarms a totalitarian government into (extreme) measures of (extreme) repression against likely suspects.

The following linguistic points are to be noted in the above example:

(i) The scrambled sentence is by definition utter linguistic chaos because its words are randomly sequenced; that is, none of its structural signals are obeyed and there are no sequential cues of clause. A clue to the extent of this chaos for the mind can be seen in the fact that we cannot employ our intonation system normally on reading it out aloud.

Nobody who knows his Fries would be surprised by this point.

(ii) The 16 words of the example do not mean 16^2 possibilities but only one possibility. The only freedom we have is the placing of the intensifying adjective **extreme** in one of three premodifying slots in the clause, but the syntactic pattern of the clause remains unshakeable.

The combination of predictable grammatical patterning of the clause, and the lexical collocation of word with word in an implied context of political discussion, ensures that we eventually adopt the version in (6) as making sense to us. By making sense to us I mean that all the structural signals of the clause are fulfilled. The significance of this last point is examined below in 1.3.

(iii) Following Hornby (1954) and Scheurweghs (1959), we note that the solution to the puzzle depends upon the fact that the verb **alarms** itself has a predictable clause pattern, which we show thus:

$$
X \quad \begin{array}{l} \text{frightens} \\ \text{alarms} \\ \text{terrifies} \end{array} \quad Y \ \textbf{into} \ \text{(taking)} \ Z \ \text{(measures)}
$$

It is this clause pattern which provides the X, Y and Z slots for us into which to fit our collocational groups of words: X = the nominal group **subversive activity** as subject; the paired **nearly always** as adjunct; Y = the nominal group **a totalitarian government** as object, and the prepositional structure **into Z** which is predicted by the verb **alarms** where **Z** is filled by the complex nominal group (extreme) **measures of repression against likely suspects** as its 'object'. (Adapting Quirk *et al.* (1972)'s S V O C A, this would be an example of the basic clause structure of S V O prepositional 'object'.) The tendency for particular verbs to have predictable clause patterns is very strong in English and cannot be ignored in studies of English syntax. Between them, Hornby and Scheurweghs constitute an adequate working description of verb patterns in English. For a more up-to-date approach to English verb patterning, the reader is invited to consult Makkai (1972), whose work is particularly comprehensive in describing verb-particle constructions, – **do away with**, etc.

(iv) As with the successful decoding of **the cat sat on the mat** above, the reader has to bring his knowledge of the world to bear on his decoding attempt to find out what he doesn't know. He cannot just decode the words of the puzzle as such, though morphologically and grammatically he could complete it in time. He must bring something more to the operation; he must relate the words to each other in significant groupings and relate these in turn to what he knows about them in his real world in reconstructing not only the sentence itself but what it represents as a selection of lexical items out of the larger situational context which the sentence represents.

The linguistic point I am making here is that, in order for the reader to confirm this sentence as a plausibly true generalisation about the political behaviour of totalitarian governments in their fear of opposition, he needs to know something about the larger situational context which provides him with particulars which enable him to confirm it as true. The reader 'fills in' by bringing the 'given' particulars in his reconstruction of the sentence as a generalisation of these particulars. Thus the reader brings to the generalisation presented as 'new' in (6) his 'given' (what is known to him from the larger context about the expected behaviour of totalitarian governments).

The grammatical status of independent declarative clause presents the generalisation as 'new' to the reader; that is, it presents the information as if it were not known or not thought of in this way before. The main point is that (6) is more than simply the sum total of its words; it represents the synthesis of the 'given' information in the reader's (much, much larger) real-world knowledge with the new information actually presented by the words of (6) itself. We could indeed see (6) as a selection from this much much larger whole. We are interested in the clause as a device of lexical selection from this larger whole. Every sentence, however simple, has to be filled in in this way if we are to understand it contextually.

For a sentence to communicate something meaningful to the decoder, quite apart from the very unreal exercise of making up sentence examples to illustrate a linguistic point, the sentence must present a synthesis of 'given' and 'new' information. This synthesis of 'given' and 'new' information by the decoder is nothing new. (This communicative notion goes back to V. Mathesius's 1939 notion of functional sentence perspective in which the given or known acts as a starting-point for the core of the utterance to which the speaker adds new information. See F. Danes (1974, pp. 106–7). What we need is to develop the notion more into our analysis of elements of the **wh**-question clause. The use of the question criterion enables us to show what is 'given' and what is new to the sentence from the decoder's point of view. Taking only the **wh**-question here, we note that the lexical elements of the **wh**-question clause present what is 'given' (or presupposed as true according to Quirk *et al.*, 1972), and it asks for the 'new' as its reply as in (6): 'What effect does subversive activity have on a totalitarian government in its treatment of (likely) suspects?' The predication of the declarative independent clause reply presents the new information.

(v) Taking up the simpler matter of morphological signals, we note that one of the problems in solving the puzzle is that there are at least three morphological candidates for the all-important main verb of the clause: **alarms**, **measures**, and **suspects**. The possible confusion out of context is that these words can also be noun plurals. However, only one (**alarms**) fits the predication pattern.

(vi) A detailed signalling analysis based on Fries's frame and slot approach reveals the interaction between the morphology and the predictive syntax of the clause, on the one hand, and the 'filling in' by the reader with his knowledge of the world, on the other.

1.3 Parsing the Clause: New Style

We now examine what steps we take in the process of parsing the sentence word by word. We consider (6) as a sentence out of context in this demonstration analysis. It is important to say this because if we were parsing a sentence in context we would be carrying forward the context provided by the preceding sentences, and this would be reflected in the parsing of its conjunctions: the subordinator, the sentence adjunct, the lexical items which paraphrase conjuncts, co-ordinating conjunctions, etc. At this stage of our argument, we can only cope with the simple sentence examples of the kind used by linguists for so long, using only our knowledge of the real world which the sentence implies.

The parsing is set out in 16 steps to account for the 16 words of the example. For the convenience of analysis, the example is repeated:

(6)   Subversive activity nearly always alarms a totalitarian government into extreme measures of repression against likely suspects.

The procedure is very simple and very strict: we take each word starting with the first word. We consider what each word is signalling, follow it up, and do not move on until we have accounted for what it is signalling. We build up our sentence group by group or phrase by phrase as we go along.

(i) As the first word in the clause, the word **subversive** has the affix **ive** which signals adjective, and as adjective first word it signals that its nominal group head follows. This is what Quirk calls the grammar of premodifier to head. This is one of the slots in the frame described by Fries for class-3 words. Simplifying all this into a pushdown question, we ask the question **subversive what**? We at least have the notion of **subversion**.

(ii) The affix **ity** of the lexical head **activity** signals noun and confirms that we have completed the prediction of a noun head. This is the **what** of **subversive what**? The head is sufficient to complete the nominal group boundary and present our subject, but until we see the next word we don't know that this boundary is complete.

We now know that the sentence is about **subversive activity**, but don't know whether it is doing something, having something done to it, being identified, being defined, being characterised, or whatever.

(iii) The presence of the adverbial item **nearly** greatly reduces the chance of choosing a postmodifying structure for the nominal head **subversive activity**, and in doing so, confirms that its nominal group boundary has stopped here. The affix **ly** in the item **nearly** signals adverb. We don't know whether **nearly** is a premodifier until we see the next word **always**.

(iv) The adverb **always** as premodified head for the adverb **nearly** completes the structure of group at the typical adjunct slot (in between subject and verb) in the clause. With this head, we complete the meaning of the adverbial element in which the item **nearly** limits the meaning of the item **always** from **always** to **nearly always**. With this completion of our adverbial structure, we now expect our main verb.

(v) The finite verb **alarms** confirms that we have reached our expected main verb: we now know that it is something which **subversive activity nearly always** does. The affix **s** confirms that the subject of this verb is **subversive activity** by signalling concord with it. It also signals present tense (the generalising present or non-past) and in doing so signals finite verb and hence main verb. Most important of all, this signalling taken in conjunction with the stages (i) (ii) (iii) and (iv) confirms that we have now reached the main verb of our clause, and this in turn confers the grammatical status of independent clause for this and what structure follows it. As a transitive verb, the verb **alarms** raises the pushdown question **alarms who?** This object must be compatible with the meaning of the subject and the verb.

At this point, however, we have the rest of the structure of the predicate predicted for us: we know that the structure **X alarms Y** may have a prepositional 'object' so that we expect a Y object to be potentially in a close grammatical relationship with a Z prepositional phrase 'object' in the basic clause structure of **X alarms Y into Z** (measures). We are now ready for the idea of an object in relation with something else.

(vi) The indefinite article **a** signals that a noun head of some kind compatible with the subject and the verb will follow, and in doing so it signals the start of the nominal group boundary of the object. the noun head answers the pushdown question **a what?**

(vii) The affix **ian** in the item **totalitarian** signals either adjective meaning or noun meaning for this word, the latter being markedly less likely. As adjective immediately following the indefinite article **a**, it does not fulfil the prediction of a noun head, and this signals it as a premodifier. As premodifying adjective, it reinforces the prediction of a noun head to come, **a totalitarian what?**

(viii) The affix **ment** in the word **government** signals the meaning of noun for this word and our prediction of noun head is fulfilled, thus completing the nominal group boundary up to the noun head position. There is still the possibility of postmodification, but this is ruled out by the next word.

(ix) The preposition **into** which is predicted as part of the basic clause structure of **X alarms Y into Z** now confirms that we have reached the end of the nominal group boundary of object in (viii). It signals that the boundary of the clause will probably end with the completion of its nominal group structure **X alarms Y into what?**

(x) The slot immediately following the preposition **into** is a nominal slot which restricts the adjective **extreme** to the role of premodifier which signals the start of its nominal group boundary. As premodifier, it signals that its noun head will follow – the pushdown question **extreme what?**

(xi) The affix **s** as plural in the word **measures** signals that it is the predicted noun head. So far we have fulfilled the requirements for the noun head but now have the question of its postmodification. As an abstract noun which requires lexical realisation in order to be fully understood, the noun **measures** asks for the composite pushdown question **measures of what against whom?** Here we can assume the more explicit structure in which the noun **measures** collocates with the verb **take** as in **X takes measures against Z**.

(xii) As postmodifying preposition to the noun head **measures**, the preposition **of** signals that its nominal group will complete its grammatical structure as preposition.

(xiii) The affix **ion** of the word **repression** signals noun head and our prepositional phrase structure is minimally complete; that is, the head would suffice grammatically here. We now have the double-headed nominal group **measures of repression**, in which the noun head **repression** answers the pushdown question **measures of what?** This now raises the second part of the composite question **measures of repression against whom?**

(xiv) The predicted preposition **against** signals that the structure of the larger nominal group **extreme measures of repression** is being continued, and will be completed by its nominal group structure. At this point, we have the pushdown question to answer **against whom?** The reply to the **whom** bit will complete the prepositional phrase boundary.

(xv) Although the **ly** typically signals adverb, our knowledge of English tells us that the affix **ly** in the word **likely** signals adjective, and as first word after the preposition **against** it signals premodifier whose noun head is to follow: the pushdown question is **against likely what?**

(xvi) Finally, the affix **s** as plural for the last word **suspects** signals noun, and with this fulfilment of a noun head our immediate nominal group boundary is complete, and with it, the boundary of our larger nominal group is also complete. With this completion of the larger nominal group **extreme measures of repression against likely suspects**, the prepositional structure of the item **into** is now complete, and our sentence boundary has been reached.

Strictly speaking we could say that there was a stage (xvii). Having fulfilled all the grammatical cues in our clause, we have an independent clause whose syntactic boundary is complete, and with this completion of the boundary we have the clause in its communicative role as sentence. We now take the sentence as a whole and see it as a generalisation about the political behaviour of a totalitarian government. The important point is that the grammatical status of independent declarative clause means that it presents its information to be taken on trust as true and as new to the decoder. These last two separate points will be further developed when we come to the composite definition of sentence.

1.3.1 Discussion of the Parsing Procedure

The apparently slow parsing of the above sentence in which we follow up each word lineally in no way represents the efficiency and great speed with which we would actually hear or read it. I have taken for granted the high-speed triggering of our habitual patterns of the clause and the nominal group here, which are undoubtedly part of the collocational and colligational grouping of words which must go on. The grouping of words into uniquely different groups and sets should be obvious to those who have tried to unscramble the puzzle sentence here by the patterning which is forced upon them when they try to make sense of the puzzle by re-ordering its words.

What makes this parsing analysis seem laborious at first is that we consciously go through stages which are largely unconscious. These stages are the autonomous grammar of the clause elements and the highly predictable lexical collocations (for example **(take) measures of Z against somebody**). We go through each of these predictable patterns as if we actually think each piece out anew each time when it seems quite clear that each of these patterns are preassembled entities into which we fit creative lexical choices. By autonomous grammar I mean the automatic functioning of something like nominal group structuring, where the presence of a determiner like **the** signals the coming of a noun head, and the coming of this noun head completes the minimum grammar of the nominal group, though not necessarily the minimum semantic requirements of the noun itself – this is the function of the postmodifier structure of the nominal group. Perhaps the most important unit of autonomous grammar to be added into S V O C A analysis of the clause is the ubiquitous prepositional phrase. Besides being a common structure of A, the prepositional structure is a predictable postmodification for verbs (**talk to, discuss** X **with** Y, etc.), adjective heads (afraid **of the dark**) and nouns (measures **of extreme repression**). The appearance of these prepositions signals the coming of their nominal group structures. This grammatical autonomy of the prepositional structuring is to be contrasted with the grammatical cueing by the semantics of the lexical verb, where the choice of the lexical verb predicts the clause pattern which follows it and, along with this pattern, the semantic nature of its object(s), prepositional 'objects', complement or adjunct.

The parsing procedure demonstrated here is the nearest we can approach to the problem faced by the decoder in listening or reading, provided that we never lose sight of the assumption that the decoder has to bring his knowledge of the world to bear on the decoding. The prime problem in decoding is, as I have suggested, relating what is given with what is new information. If we stick rigorously to the parsing procedure as signalled by the clause, we come up inevitably with the structure of independent declarative clause, the structure upon which the definition of sentence by Bloomfield/Jespersen depends. We work our way through the structure of 'sentence' from the beginning to the completion of its syntactic boundary, using its clause and clause constituents only. Clearly defined structural boundaries are a very necessary part of the meaning of the clause(s) in their sentence, and have to be taken into account in any grammar of English. The theoretically most important aspect of sentence is a clear description of the function of independent declarative clause versus question clause.

1.3.2   Consequences of the Signalling Approach

The signalling approach is based on how the decoder 'fills in' the meaning of the sentence from the signals it contains and from his own knowledge. This involves examining the sentence word by word from beginning to end. More specifically, we act the part of the decoder who is seeing the sentence for the first time. We are concerned with how the structure unfolds from the initial signals in its clause or clauses to the fulfilment of these signals as their structures are completed. In written language, this means parsing from left to right; in spoken language, this means parsing the structure in time sequence as we hear it unfold. For convenience, we assume that the decoding process for hearing is the same as for reading but bear in mind the all-important difference between hearing and reading, that hearing has the vastly greater signalling advantages of sound, pitch and juncture, etc.

The analysis is at first sight rather like the traditional parsing method of school grammar in which the pupils parse a sentence for its subject, verb, object, subject complement, etc. It differs in three very important respects.

(i) It is very much more closely tied into all the structural signals of the clause, the use of determiners, morphological prefixes and suffixes of nouns, adjectives, verbs and adverbs, verb concord, the nature of function words like conjunctions of all kinds and the all-important prepositional phrase, pre- and postmodification of nouns, adjectives, verbs, adverbs, and so on. In principle we are concerned with the signalling role of any word in the clause, whether it signals backwards in its sentence or beyond its sentence to a preceding sentence, or whether it signals forward within its sentence or beyond its sentence to a sentence which follows it. (We have already discussed an example of forward signalling within the clause. In example (2), we noted the role of anticipatory **It** as signalling that its real subject would be a clause of some kind and this clause would follow its predication **It is possible**). In short, we are concerned as decoders with the syntactic environment of the clause and how its various signals might relate it to its adjoining clause in the sentence, or to the clauses in adjoining sentences.

(ii) In the kind of parsing we are doing here, we see that the sole purpose of the signalling is to indicate clearly the syntactic (and hence immediate semantic) boundary of the constituent functions of the clause, so that we work from the syntactic boundaries of S V O C and A, etc., right through to the final syntactic boundary of the clause which completes the boundary of our sentence where there is more than one clause.

(iii) Unlike the school grammar approach which was concerned largely with the constituent structures of S V O C and A, and with notions such as adverbial clause, adjective clause and noun clause in apposition, we are in principle concerned with both the semantics and the grammar of all the grammatical entities which we, as decoders, have to take in from the first word of our sentence to the last word or structural element which completes it grammatically. It should be obvious that the longer the sentence, the more decoding work there is to be done in order to keep the main outline of the sentence in mind as a grammatical entity whose grammatical completeness forms essential semantic units.

There is a very important theoretical difference between the decoding and the encoding approach which needs emphasising here. This is that as decoders we are concerned strictly with the sequence of words as they unfold to us as hitherto unknowns which we reconstruct according to our knowledge of the real world which it represents. The assumption which we make is that until the grammar of the clause is completed as sentence we do not fully comprehend its meaning as sentence. For the encoder, however, we assume that he or she 'knows' what they are talking about; otherwise they would not be able to encode their clauses, though we must concede that the encoder is governed by what he or she perceives as new to us.

Take the role of one of our most important syntactic signals in the clause, the determiner whose most common and frequent items are the definite article **the** and the indefinite article **a**. In the clause, it is the noun heads of the clause that tell the decoder what the encoder is talking about. The role of the determiner is both syntactic and semantic. Greatly oversimplifying, they are syntactic in that they signal the start of the nominal group boundary in the clause; they are semantic in that they tell the decoder something about the contextual semantics of the noun head, that is, whether it has already been introduced or 'known' (hence the article **the** or the pronominal **this**), or whether it is being introduced for the first time at this point in the context of utterance (hence the article **a**). It is in this contextual contrast between definite and indefinite article that the hearer listens for one of the cues of what is known to him and what is new to him in the clause. The articles are vital to his proper understanding of the clause and this understanding consists largely in his reconciling and synthesising that part of the subject which is known to him with that part of the subject matter which is being presented as new to him. As we shall later see, the role of independent clause status enters into this balance between the known and the new in the clause.

Having established some idea of the importance of the articles to the semantics and the syntax of the English clause, we can now rephrase the difference between the encoding and the decoding approach to syntax. As decoders, we hear the article first and this signals that a noun head of the relevant contextual semantics is following to complete its grammar as a nominal group structure. As encoder, on the other hand, we must 'know' the contextual nature of the noun head which we are producing before we can choose either the definite or the indefinite article in order to signal its referential relation to the context of utterance shared with us by the decoder.

If we take signalling seriously, then we have to show that syntax is an indispensable part of the semantics of the clause in context. This is more than simply reaffirming Fries's point that structural and lexical meanings are indivisible. We have seen from the 16 steps on 16 words that each word has to be considered for its predictive grammar in the clause structure to come. At the last resort, we have to take the structure as we find it, and at this stage of our knowledge, we have to be sure that we have accounted for all the fundamental semantics of lexis and grammar in synthesis. By taking a decoding approach (signalling), we can at least get to grips with the facts of meaning more reasonably.

There are two central points in the parsing procedure adopted here. The first point, already noted, is that we base our parsing on the structure of the clause so that if there is more than one clause in the sentence we parse each clause in turn until our grammatical structure is complete. The second even more important point is that our parsing procedure is motivated towards establishing the centrally significant clause or clauses upon which the communicative function which we call sentence depends; this is the main finite verb upon which the independence of the clause depends. Thus in (7) below, we ignore the first finite verb **are** and take the verb phrase structure **must be represented in** as main verb because of the signalling by the subordinator **although**. This conjunction signals that its clause boundary will delay the start of the main clause structure:

(7) **Although** most of us are unaware of these rules, they must be represented in our brains. (*Observer*, 9 April 1967, p. 21)

The comprehension point here is that while we are parsing this sentence, we are building up the sentence word by word or structure by structure only completing our picture when the last signal of the clause has been fulfilled – the fulfilling of the preposition **in** by its structure of the nominal group **our brains**.

We could say that our parsing process is complete when all the grammatical signals or cues are fulfilled in producing an independent declarative clause or clauses, together with any subordinate clauses which they may have. By grammatical signals or cues, I mean all the structural signals of the constituent boundaries of the clause according to the kind of structures occupying them, plus the completion of our clause constituents S V O C A according to the choice of lexical verb element, etc. In fulfilling all the grammatical signals along with their lexical semantics, we meet the syntactic requirements of the Meillet/Bloomfield/Jespersen definition of sentence, but we do not meet the contextual requirement by the clause-relating process whereby the clauses in one sentence are semantically related to the clauses in adjoining sentences of the utterance. What this means is that the Meillet/Bloomfield/Jespersen definition does not take into account the semantics and the grammar of the clauses in adjoining sentences, especially the preceding sentences.

Our major tool in getting at the semantics and grammar of the clauses of adjoining sentences is the use of the question clause, especially the **wh**-question. One of the most important parts of English grammatical signalling is the contrast in information between the question clause and the independent declarative clause. A contextual grammar of English must be built around the grammatical contrast between these two kinds of clause.

The Clause as Sole Device of Lexical Selection

2.1 Introduction

We have so far discussed the clause as an abstraction of what all clauses have in common; that is, they have in common the constituent functions of subject and predicate with or without adjunct, or predicate with or without adjunct. The important difference between the abstract notion of clause and real clause is that our abstract clause is a generalisation of the autonomous grammatical behaviour of the constituent parts which signal clause structure, while real clause is a clause which is committed to precise signals of its grammatical status. As an abstraction of typical structural behaviour, our clause is a fiction which we never actually see or hear.

Imagine the ghost clause **He-saw-me-there** as an idea of something which might have happened to me in the recent definite past. This is only a vague idea in the mind until it has executive function as explicit in its grammatical status as a real clause of some kind. By grammatical status, I mean whether it is a question clause, an independent clause, or one of three kinds of subordinate clause. Once this happens to the clause we are committed to presenting its status as true in some way. Consider the following four different kinds of grammatical status as an illustration of this point.

First, as a **yes/no**-question, **'Did he see me there?'** asks for confirmation as true for the fully formed (ghost) clause. The reply 'Yes, he did' confirms it as true. The independent declarative clause **He saw me there** presents the clause as true in having happened in the past. We no longer have the ghost clause which forms the basis of the **yes/no**-question, but the kind of clause we take as sentence. Second, the **wh**-question **'When did he see me there?'** presents the clause he saw me there as true and asks for information about **when**, for example **He saw me there yesterday**, so that **yesterday** is our only new information. Third, the cleft sentence question **'Is he the one who saw me there?'** asks for confirmation of the role of subject for the known clause represented by the subordinate clause **who saw me there**. Fourth, the non-finite clause as object in **He wanted to see me there** could be the answer to the question 'How did he feel about seeing me there?'

We have here four different kinds of grammatical status for the same clause elements **he, saw, me** and **there**. All four kinds of clause have the same lexical choices for subject (**he**), verb (**saw**), object (**me**) and adverbial adjunct (**there**), but in addition they share the grammatical pattern of participants **he** and **me** as organised by the verb **saw** with the circumstantial adjunct **there**. The unique lexical and grammatical patterning of these items carries with it its own semantics, which remains constant under the addition of the clause contextual relations signalled by the grammar of question, cleft sentence or non-finite clause.

It follows from this that when we speak of lexical choice we can only mean the lexical choice which is made within the constituent functions of subject, predicate and adjunct, etc., in clauses which have the contextually appropriate grammatical status. This is a strict requirement for their presentation as true, but it does not prevent us from seeing that it is the clause constituents themselves that are the vehicles of lexical choice. So whatever the grammatical status of the clause pattern **he–saw–me–there**, each one of the lexical choices is made with respect to the others in this clause, for example the verb **saw** is being made as a lexical choice for the subject **he** and the object **me** is made as a lexical choice with respect to the subject and verb **he saw**.

The notion of lexical choice means the selecting of items from the open-ended vocabularies of nouns, verbs, adjectives and adverbs as head as well as their pre- and postmodifying structures. Lexical selection at its most simple generally means selecting lexical items as constrained by the autonomous grammar of the constituents of clause and its grouping elements (for example pre- and postmodifying grammar). I am ignoring the selection of those closed-system words which signal structural relations for lexical choices, for example the articles **a** and **the** signalling noun head to come, but the principle of selection for lexical items still applies.

Having established what is meant by lexical selection or choice, we now have to consider the theoretical implications of lexical selection for our clause. The question we cannot avoid asking is this: what relation does the clause as a communicative vehicle of selection bear to the real-world referents from which it selects its lexical items?

2.2 The Clause in Discourse Structure

We begin with a well-known commonplace in communication studies. This is the idea that communication is by definition imperfect if only because we can never say everything about anything in a message. Apart from the physical impossibility of ever doing so, there are very powerful constraints of time and energy on both sides of the message. The more detail there is, the more time and energy required by both speaker and listener or reader. In our message, we do not say everything possible but simple settle for very much less than everything on a priority or relevance basis; that is, we choose something, from the larger whole of everything, which is relevant to the purpose of our communicating the message.

Consider a common tripartite structural relation in sentence 3 of (8) below, where the three parts express de Gaulle's problems with his allies in respect of his policies.

(8) (1) De Gaulle has taken the opposite course. (2) He has chosen to strike out on his own. (3) In the past **he** has found **his allies** at worst unreliable, at best unsympathetic to **his policies**. (4) He got no help from them during the Algerian war, though there was little open criticism. (5) He got no help in building up his nuclear force. (6) Indeed, far from providing him with technical knowledge (as was done for the British) the United States went to the other extreme and signed a test-ban treaty with the Soviet Union which made the French appear as the odd man out in the eyes of the world. (7) In addition, de Gaulle's plans for reorganising NATO on global lines received short shrift in London and Washington. (*Guardian*, 5 November 1965, p. 10)

Sentence 2 informs us of de Gaulle's solution to the problems of his policies presented by sentences 3–7. These five sentences are answering the question: 'Why has he chosen to strike out on his own?' Sentence 3 replies to this question by a previewing evaluation of the problem of his policies with his allies, as presented by sentences 4–7. These last sentences provide particulars of what help, etc., his allies did not give him.

The important point for us here is that sentence 3 itself cannot be fully understood until we get details of the problem in sentences 4–7, though by the time we have read sentences 4 and 5 we have a fair idea of the problem. Here we see the lexical selection for the clause in sentence 3 evaluating (or judging) the series of lexical selections for clauses outside its sentence boundary in sentences 4–7.

There is an important similarity of principle which needs to be understood here. I am saying that the lexical choice for the clause in sentence 3 is based on the lexical choice which is being made for the clauses in sentences 4–7. This is what is meant by saying that we can only fully understand what sentence 3 is evaluating on reading the lexical detail of sentences 4–7, the lexical detail to which it refers. In its turn, the lexical selection for the clauses of sentences 4–7 is being made from the vast amount of information which is available to the writer about de Gaulle's many problems with his allies. Here the writer has not told us all but just enough for us, as readers of the *Guardian*, to understand what these problems are. Summing up, sentence 3 refers largely to the information (the lexical selections) of sentences 4–7, and sentences 4–7 in turn refer largely to information chosen from the real world about de Gaulle's problems with his allies. Here is a sketch which illustrates the direction of lexical choice for the clauses.

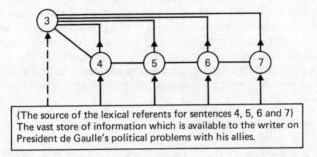

(The source of the lexical referents for sentences 4, 5, 6 and 7) The vast store of information which is available to the writer on President de Gaulle's political problems with his allies.

2.3 How the Clause Communicates Information in Sentences

When we say that sentence 3 refers to sentences 4–7, this is not intended as a mere statement of the fact that sentences 4–7 are next in sequence, but rather that the referents for the lexical choice for the clause in sentence 3 are to be found in sentences 4–7. The writer has based his lexical choice for sentence 3 on the 'raw material' of the clauses in sentences 4–7. Crudely speaking, this is a proportion of one to four sentences. In the clauses of sentences 4–7, however, the writer is going outside the text into the real world: he is choosing his lexical referents from the vast store of information about de Gaulle's political problems with his allies. He has obviously thought about the significant lexical selection for four different areas of the problem and has represented each area by a single sentence. The proportionate reduction in the amount of information here must be incalculable, but the fact of choosing to say something from a much larger store still remains.

The reader must know about a person called de Gaulle to appreciate the significance of the passage as seen by the writer. The sentence represents the tip of an iceberg of knowledge which the reader brings to bear on these sentences when he decodes them. The greater the representational compression of the real-world information in the text, the greater the need for the abstract 'filling in' by the reader in order to reconstruct the larger whole for himself. What is true of these sentences is true of all sentences; there is only a difference of degree rather than kind. The speaker or writer has to select from a larger store of choice and has to confine his or her lexical choice to a reasonably short clause of some kind.

We have had to discuss independent declarative clause as the executive form of clause. What we still need to discuss about the clause is that it has fairly stringent requirements as to the amount of lexical selection which the decoder will tolerate. This makes its representational role even more representative than real. In its independent clause form, the clause is often inadequate information as clause and often requires to be lexically realised by adjoining independent declarative clauses to be fully understood. A single example will suffice to illustrate what is meant by lexical realisation. Take the first independent clause of the independent clause pair in (9) below:

(9)   **Something** of significance **did**, however, **happen** in the middle of all this: a television camera was admitted into the chamber of the House of Commons for the first time. True, it was simply to record part of the ceremonial state opening. But, in a sense, the breach has at least been made. (*New Statesman*, 22 April 1966, p. 562)

The first clause here cannot be understood without the lexical referents provided for its signalling items by the second clause; that is, the second clause provides the lexical particulars of something of significance happening in the middle of all this. Linguistically, we understand the first clause by what is lexically realised for it by the second clause. The important thing to learn about clauses is that, although many of them will be grammatically complete as clauses, they may nevertheless be lexically inadequate and require the appropriate lexical realisation from another clause. The linguistic property of being unspecific is not confined to the indefinite pronouns like **something (happening)** but is a general semantic characteristic of many lexical items in the clause. For instance, in the grammar of nominal group, the abstract noun **type** has to be lexically realised by the noun to which it refers, for example **type of car**, as we see in the use of the pushdown question **Type of what?** (see Winter, 1977, pp. 81–6). We now develop the notion of unspecific and specific between clauses below.

2.4   The Crucial Contrast in Lexical Realisation between Non-Question Clauses and Question Clauses

We have already noted the difference in contextual meanings for the 'same lexical selection' for the ghost clause **he–saw–me–there**, when we varied the grammatical status for this clause in 2.1. We now take up the contextual notion of lexical realisation and refine it by considering two separate sets of linguistic contrasts: the first between the non-question clauses of independence and subordination; the second between non-question clause and question clauses.

2.4.1

Where the lexical selection of the non-question clause is completed by a particular kind of grammatical status as either independent or subordinate, we speak of the clause as being lexically realised and ready for communication as completed clause. The definition of completed clause is that it constitutes a grammatically satisfactory answer to a **yes/no**-question or a **wh**-question clause. However, we must distinguish between two kinds of lexical realisation for completed clause. We have already introduced the semantic category of unspecific versus specific clause for examples (G) and (H) on pp. 10–11 and for the first and second clause of the first sentence in (9) above. We now take up the difference between unspecific and specific completed clause.

The relation between unspecific and specific is best understood by considering unspecific and specific in turn. Unspecific clause by definition is inadequate information which although understood in the abstract requires to be further specified by a specific clause. The function of specific clause is to fulfil the lexical meaning of unspecific clause in terms of the relevant specifics so that unspecific clause is now fully understood. A typical relation between lexical unspecific and lexical specific is to be seen in the semantic relation between **a fatal cave accident** and its specification as **a man was drowned while swimming in underground waters**, in (10) below.

> (10) Are caving and climbing risks insurable? If so, have clubs any systems of getting their members insured?
>   Luckily, caving accidents are very rarely fatal. According to the Mountain Rescue Committee's accident report for 1964 . . . only six caving accidents were reported last year, as against 147 accidents on the hills. There was only **one fatal cave accident; a man was drowned while swimming in underground waters**. (*Guardian*, 7 December 1965, p. 8)

We start by noting the environment for the sentence under discussion. First, the lead sentence of its paragraph **Luckily, caving accidents are rarely fatal** is an evaluation clause whose disjunct, the item **luckily**, implies a **no**-reply to the **yes/no**-question clause of the preceding paragraph. The second and last sentences in the paragraph provide the basis for this evaluation, with the last sentence providing the significant part of the basis itself. Secondly, taking the last sentence, we note that there are two signals of significant specific clause to come: the presence of existential **There** and the unspecific nominal group as its real subject (only **one fatal cave accident**. The second clause constitutes an answer to the last question: 'What kind of fatal accident was it?' With the answering of this last question we complete the particulars of the basis for the evaluation clause in the lead sentence. The contextual mechanics of unspecific and specific clause are described in more detail in Winter (1977, pp. 67–78).

The theoretical question which arises here is: Why have unspecific clause when we can go directly to specific clause? I suggest that unspecific clause can be indispensable as that which provides a generalising or superordinate context or situation against which the nature of the specific clause is understood. The practical point is that unspecific clause in all its forms is very common and cannot be ignored. We need to study more precisely what it is that signals unspecific.

Finally, putting it at its most simple, completed clause provides information whose clause is grammatically complete. The significance of grammatical completeness will become clearer when we discuss the first requirement for the composite definition of sentence. The theoretical point we must insist upon is that completed clause is a response to incomplete clause and that for every completed clause there must be a corresponding incomplete clause.

2.4.2

In contrast with the completed clause of non-question clause, we have the incomplete clause of the question function whose finalised grammatical form is completed clause. The communicative function of incomplete clause is to demand information by means of two kinds of completion to yield completed clause which presents the kind of information required. The first and simplest to grasp is where we have a grammatical signal that the lexical selection of its clause is not yet complete for the particular constituent of the clause indicated by the **wh**-item. This is the **wh**-clause of the question system which asks for open-ended lexical choice. The purpose of the **wh**-question clause is twofold: first, it presents the lexical realisation it already has as its 'known' or presupposed as true, and, second, the **wh**-item signals the grammatical nature of what it wants to be made known. For instance, the **wh**-question clause 'What did he do to her?' expresses a knowledge of some kind of relation between him and her but demands a verb to make the nature of this relation known in a completed clause, for example 'He insulted her', where the lexical selection of a verb like **insulted** answers the **wh**-question clause. The primary function of the **wh**-question clause is to demand the completed clause version of its incomplete clause in respect of the lexical selection required for its 'missing' constituents S, V, O, C, A and prepositional 'object'.

The second notion of incomplete clause, less easy to grasp, is where we have the signal of interrogation by the fronting of the verb element, as in the first clause of (10) above, 'Are caving and climbing risks insurable?' which has the S V C analysis of V S C?' where V = **are**, S = **caving and climbing risks** and C = **insurable**. Unlike the **wh**-question clause, the **yes/no**-question clause is a fully lexically realised clause whose grammar of communication is incomplete until it is answered by a completed clause in the form of independent declarative clause. The reply clause either confirms it as true – (Yes) they are insurable – or denies it as true – (No) they are not insurable. The grammar of the **yes/no**-question clause is the grammar of the hypothetical whose resolution is by the grammar of the real, the grammar of independent declarative clause which satisfies the question. Where the **yes/no**-questions are not directly answered by their independent clause forms or proxies as in the first two clauses of (10) above, we speak of the two questions as hypothetical clause or incomplete clause. Hypothetical clause or incomplete clause means that until we have a completed clause offering its real the communication is incomplete in that the lexical realisation of hypothetical clause remains unconfirmed.

It should be pointed out that non-answered **yes/no**-questions like those in (10) are just one kind of hypothetical clause. We can also have completed clauses which also signal hypotheticality. When they do, they raise the **yes/no**-question for their real members as we saw for (D), which is repeated below:

(D)   Mr Baldwin promised **to resign if the Cabinet refused his request**. It did refuse and he did not resign.

The **yes/no**-question which the second sentence as the real member answers is: 'Did it (subsequently) refuse his request and did he resign?' – (yes) it did refuse and (no) he did not resign. It should also be pointed out here that affirmation and denial are part of the grammar of real, a knowledge of which is important in studying the semantics of negation.

Taking the two kinds of incomplete clause as **wh**-question clause and **yes/no**-question clause, we must again insist that for every such incomplete clause there must be a completed clause, whether or not the completed clause is expressed linguistically. A study of English grammar must be a study of the relation between incomplete and completed clause.

2.5   Conclusions

Our whole approach to the contextual semantics of the English clause is based upon the contrast in information status described above for independent clause with or without subordinate clause as completed clause in 2.4.1 and question clause as incomplete clause in 2.4.2. If the clause is a device of lexical selection, then the grammatical status of its lexical realisation is crucial. What this means is that potentially every lexical selection is evaluative or subjective; that is, the writer or speaker has had to choose it on some priority principle or other over other lexical items which he might otherwise have chosen. The significance of this point about the evaluation implied by choice is that one of our important categories of clause relation is that of evaluation clause. This is the clause which is wholly devoted to evaluation as seen in the **wh**-question clause which it answers: 'What do you think about X, event X, state X, quality X, the person X, etc.?'

The Contrast in Grammatical Status between Clauses

3.1 Introduction

So far we have considered two important sets of contrasts between clauses in English. The first was the contrast in lexical realisation between unspecific and specific, in which the function of the specific clause was to realise the meaning of the unspecific clause in full. The second was the contrast in grammatical completeness between completed clause (independent clause and subordinate clause) and incomplete clauses (**wh**-questions and **yes/no**-questions), in which incomplete clauses demanded completion by completed clauses as their final grammatical form. Now we take up a third contrast between clauses and this is the contrast between independent clause and subordinate clause in respect of their information status as 'new' and 'known' or 'given'.

What is fundamental to the notion of context is the relation of 'given/known' to 'new' information, and the fact that the internal grammar of the clause itself, regardless of its grammatical status as a whole, will have signals of 'given/known' and 'new' for its words or groups of words in their syntagmatic relations.

In this section, we are going to consider in some detail the contrast in information status for the clause implied by the grammatical difference between independence and subordination. Of the two kinds of clause status, much of this book is devoted to the problem of describing subordinate clause because the contextual relation between independent clause and subordinate clause is the key to tackling a composite definition of sentence. A study of the grammatical cues of subordination is very important to the parsing procedure which we apply when we work out the boundaries of the clause within the sentence. Six kinds of subordinate clause are discussed.

We now consider the contrast between the state of information presented by the independent clause and by the subordinate clause.

3.2   The Contextual Meanings of Independent Clause and Adverbial Clause

We begin with what is already well known about the grammatical difference between independent clause and subordinate clause. This is that it is self-evident that independent declarative clause can stand alone and make sense and subordinate clause cannot stand alone and make sense without some kind of main clause to which it is grammatically attached. We take it for granted that the two kinds of clause are indissolubly linked in their semantics. What is not so well known, however, is the contextual difference between independent clause and (adverbial) clause with respect to the state of information which they each present. We start with the meaning of independent clause. Basically, we try to tell people something they don't already know, but this needs to be qualified.

Imagine that you are speaking to a group of people here in Britain some years after the Conservative Party has won the election, with Mrs Thatcher becoming Prime Minister. You tell them:

(11)   Mrs Thatcher is Prime Minister.

If your audience want to be rude, they will say 'So what! We know that! Tell us something we don't know!' or 'Why are you telling us this (now)?' Such a response indicates clearly that the role of declarative independent clause is that of presenting the clause on the assumption by the encoder that the decoder does not know (including 'appreciate the status of') this information about Mrs Thatcher. In the hours just after the public announcement of the Conservatives' winning the election, the grammatical status of independent declarative clause would have been perfectly appropriate for telling this same group of people the news if you were sure that they had not heard it before you did. What was 'given' to this audience then was the knowledge that Mrs Thatcher as Tory leader was competing with Mr Callaghan, the Labour Prime Minister in office at the time of the election.

It should be clear from this discussion that the meaning of this independent clause differs contextually for the same audience from being 'given' (Mrs Thatcher as Tory candidate) and 'new' (Mrs Thatcher becomes Prime Minister) to 'given' (Mrs Thatcher as past Tory candidate) and 'new' (Mrs Thatcher now Prime Minister). To sum up, immediately after the election this utterance tells the audience something they didn't know in terms of something they did know; the utterance now simply tells them something which they already know, and is hence not acceptable as independent clause without any change or addition of information. Informally, they are no longer interested in hearing the sentence now. One kind of boredom is to be told something which we already know and don't want to hear in any detail.

However, for the information status of the clause **Mrs Thatcher is Prime Minister** to be acceptable as information to this particular audience now, their knowing it must be acknowledged, either by a change of grammatical status from independent to subordinate clause, or by some other explicit indication of this. Let us take subordination first. If you subordinate the clause **Mrs Thatcher is Prime Minister**, the information becomes acceptable in terms of what new information is offered by its declarative independent clause:

(12) **Besides** being Prime Minister, Mrs Thatcher is **President of the National Cats Club**.

The fact that Mrs Thatcher is Prime Minister is now acceptable in its adverbial subordination by the **besides** -ing construction; this presents what we already know about Mrs Thatcher with an explicit cue that the main clause will present compatible particulars about Mrs Thatcher which are new to us now. Mrs Thatcher being President of the National Cats Club is news indeed because it is simply not true; you are hearing it for the first time because I have made it up for the occasion.

Independent clause form would be appropriate even now if in argument we were refuting some very ignorant person who declared 'Mr Callaghan is Prime Minister' by saying 'He isn't Prime Minister (Silly!) – Mrs Thatcher is!' This is an affirmative correction of a denial whose fully explicit form could have been prefaced by **That's not true**. Independent clause form is also appropriate where the knownness is acknowledged in some way:

(13) Economically, things seem to get worse by the week. **As we all know to our cost**, Mrs Thatcher is Prime Minister and is determined to carry out her plans for our economic salvation, come what may.

Here next is a similar signalling in the lead sentence of an article in which the writer comments on the then recent murder of Lord Mountbatten.

(14) I went to Ireland at the beginning of August and, **as we all know now**, so did Lord Mountbatten and his family, along with thousands of our fellow countrymen. (First sentence of article by Jill Tweedie, *Guardian*, 6 September 1979, p. 11)

There are, of course, other ways of indicating that independent clause is 'known' or 'fact', for example the use of the modal verb **should** plus **not** plus the present perfect tense in the evaluation clause **You should not have complained about her**, where the speaker is evaluating the fact that the decoder did in fact complain about her. What is new information is the evaluation of this action of complaining.

We have been considering the contrast in information status between independent clause and subordinate (adverbial) clause. This is only **one** of the six kinds of subordination in English. We next consider all six in their contextual roles in the clause. We are going to consider the claim that the clause, either independent or subordinate, is the minimum grammatical context for the word. In order to do so, we need to describe the subordinate clause in its environment of the independent clause to which it belongs grammatically.

Part Two

Subordination in English

Subordination and the Contextualisation of the Main Clause

If we take one of the functions of the clause as the representation of real-world events, we find that the subordinate clause functions as an analogue of the relevant part of the physical context of the real world for the main clause. As we saw in (12) above, subordination signals like **besides** -ing signal a compatible attribute which is already known about the subject of the main clause. In working out the ultimate boundary of independent clause (our clause in its sentence or communicative role), the recognition of subordinate clause boundary with respect to its main clause boundary is crucial to our parsing procedure. In is therefore useful at this point to give the reader a very general description of subordination, starting with finite and non-finite clauses which have subordinating conjunctions and then going on to non-finite clauses which do not have them.

There are six different kinds of subordination according to their syntactic function. The first three are adverbial clause, relative clause and noun clause. The fourth is confined only to non-finite verbs occurring in fixed predications with a predictive main verb. In the following example, the non-finite verb **racing** in the non-finite clause in bold type has been predicted by the (finite) verb **sent** and is an indivisible part of its grammar: He **sent** his three-quarter-centre **racing for a clearly certain try.** (In S V O terms, the object **his three-quarter-centre** is to be analysed both as object to the verb **sent** and subject to the non-finite clause which follows.) The fifth and sixth have in common a subordination whose semantics is like that of the relative clause but which must be contextually distinguished from it. These last two are the special operations clauses of cleft and psuedo-cleft sentence, and the interpolation adjunct.

The second theoretical consideration is that I regard the first four kinds of subordination as unmarked subordination, and the remaining fifth and sixth kinds as specially marked uses of subordination.

4.1   Finite and Non-finite Clauses which have Subordinators

In this type of clause, the subordinator is a clear signal of the start of its clause boundary, and as such it also signals that this clause boundary will end when its clause is grammatically completed. We take the grammatical completion of this clause as marking the end of its structural boundary when we parse the structure of its main clause.

There are three kinds of subordinate clause according to their syntactic and semantic function. The first is the relative clause, the second is the noun clause, and the third is the adverbial clause.

The relative clause is a clause which takes up the position of postmodifier to a noun head, for example the **who**-clause as postmodifier to the noun head **man**, as in (15):

> (15)   It was (the laugh of a man **who knows that his holiday will start tomorrow**). (Scheurweghs, 1959, p. 270)

The brackets indicate the nominal structure whose boundary begins with the definite article **the** and ends with the adverb of time **tomorrow**. This unmarked use of relative clause is contrasted with the marked use of relative clause which we call cleft clause. This is briefly discussed as one of the instances of special operations clauses in Section 10.

Noun clauses function as nominal structures within larger clauses. There are two kinds of noun clause, which are distinguished according to their subordinators. The first is the non-relative **that**-clause as nominal, for example the **that**-clause as object of the verb **knew** as in:

> (16)   He knew **that he was suffering from a mild attack of agoraphobia** (Scheurweghs, 1959, p. 246)

The boundary of the nominal structure begins with the subordinator **that** whose signalled clause ends with the noun **agoraphobia**. The **that**-item is exocentric and its clause must be taken as a whole as the nominal structure.

The second kind of noun clauses is the **wh**-clauses (what, when, where, why and how). These include the relative-like **what**-clauses which function as nominal structure, for example the **what**-clause as subject in the larger clause:

> (17)   **What is said** is addressed to a wider audience. (Scheurweghs, 1959, p. 260)

The boundary of the nominal structure begins with the subordinator **what** whose signalled clause ends with the finite verb **said**. The **what**-

item is endocentric; that is, it is both subject of its clause and head of the nominal group structure. These noun clauses are distinguished from the **what**-clauses of the pseudo-cleft sentence which are special cases of subordination in special operations clauses.

Unlike the relative clause and the noun clauses just described, the adverbial clause is not part of the basic clause structure of S O C or prepositional 'object', but functions as an adjunct in the larger clause. It may take front-, mid- or end-position in this clause. It suffices here to illustrate the parsing of mid-position in the larger clause for the adverbial **if**-clause, as in:

(18) So the best that Government officers can expect, **if they persist in summoning the poets together**, is an anxious collection of disgruntled poets. (Scheurweghs, 1959, p. 258)

Separating the subject **the best that Government officers can expect** from its main verb **is**, the structure of adverbial clause begins with the subordinator **if** whose signalled clause ends with the adverbial item **together**.

Beginning with the relative clause, we now consider the three kinds of subordinate clause according to their subordinators and syntax. We later repeat the sequence of description for non-finite clauses which have no subordinating conjunctions.

The Relative Clause

It is as well to remember that the noun head in our clause is what the clause is about. The relative clause, traditionally called the adjectival clause because it modifies a noun, is typically a postmodifier to the noun head. Relative clauses are traditionally divided into defining and non-defining relative, as in (15) above, and (19) below respectively.

The distinction between defining and non-defining relative clause is made with the help of the question criterion. When we start to parse (15) closely we see that the relative clause is part of the qualification of the noun **laugh**. The question seems to be 'What kind of laugh was it?' – a question about **laugh**, not **man**. The noun **man** here is a generalised noun. The whole point would not be lost if it were replaced by the indefinite pronoun **someone**. The answer is presented as a nominal group structure as 'object of the preposition of'. (The evaluatory nature of the nominal group **a man who**-clause can be seen in the following suggested appositional arrangement: It was the laugh of a happy man, a man who knows that his holiday will start tomorrow.

In (19) below, the non-defining relative is shown by the commas which separate it out from its nominal head **The Scilly Islander**.

(19)   The Scilly Islander, **who is reckoned to belong to one of the most prosperous communities of small farmers,** owes much of his firm position to the holiday trade. (Scheurweghs, 1959, p. 270)

In this example, the question is simply: 'What additional information can we take for granted about the Scilly Islander which is compatible with his dependence on the tourist trade?' When we come to the end of this relative clause we expect our main verb **owes**. It suffices to note that the main clause itself represents an answer to a **wh**-question like: 'To what extent does the Scilly Islander owe his firm (economic) position to the holiday trade?' In answering this question, the writer uses the non-defining relative clause to present as known or taken for granted the other source of the Scilly Islander's wealth, the fact that he is a farmer. In parsing this clause, we note the interruption by the relative clause in the syntactic slot between the subject and the main verb **owes**.

The main grammatical feature which distinguishes the parsing of the relative clause from that of other kinds of subordinate clause is the consequence of its being an endocentric clause, built around the **wh**-item which is a substitute for its noun antecedent. It is not a self-contained clause as is the exocentric **that**-clause which is in apposition to a noun head, for example **her appeals that he should rest more.** Unlike the declarative-type clause (that) **he should rest more** which is completely independent syntactically of the noun head **appeals**, the **wh**-item of the relative clause indicates the syntactic relation of its noun antecedent with the relative clause. Thus it indicates that its noun antecedent is subject, object, prepositional object, adjunct, etc. For instance, the **m** of the **wh**-item **whom** in (20) below signals that its noun head (even those) **writers** is object of the verb **have read**, so that when we come to parse the relative clause itself we take the predication **have read** as grammatically complete in respect of its object, and go on to parse its adverbial element as **most assiduously.**

(20) How little we know of even those writers **whom we have read most assiduously.** (Scheurweghs, 1959, p. 272)

Even without the **whom** signal, we would parse the pronoun **we** as new subject of new clause, and a syntactic expectation of relative relationship narrows down this new subject as a likely relative clause because we already have a finite main verb **know**. The presence of the adverbial **most assiduously** confirms that it is a relative clause because it appears where we syntactically expect the object of the verb **read**.

We could view the syntactic relation between the noun antecedent and its relative clause as unmarked focus; that is, part of its meaning of the nominal group head is the syntactic meaning of the noun antecedent in the relative clause, the (even those) **writers** as object of the relative clause. This should be contrasted with the relative-type clause of the cleft sentence, which is marked focus for a very different type of subordinate clause. Unlike the normal relative clause, this clause is not a defining clause but marks the role of its antecedent for a declarative clause. An example of this is the cleft clause of (21) below which marks the focus of its subject **their vulnerability as much as anything,** whose unmarked declarative form would be **their vulnerability as much as anything makes adults want to care for them.**

(21) The plain fact of the matter is that children **are** at a disadvantage, they can't cope, they can't run their lives; **it is** their vulnerability as much as anything **which** makes adults want to care for them. (*Observer*, 8 January 1981, p. 28)

(See 10.3.4 for further discussion.)

We now take up the very different exocentric subordinator, the item **that** in the use of **that**-clauses as noun clause.

The Noun Clause: the That-Clause and the Wh-Clause

6.1 Introduction

These are the clauses which function syntactically as nominals in the larger clause at the structures of subject, object, complement, adjective complement and 'object' of the preposition. In this kind of subordination the larger clause which contains them interprets the contextual meaning of the noun clause in some way. In Winter (1974, pp. 78–9), I called this larger clause *matrix clause* after Huddleston *et al.* (1968, p. 8). In (22) below, the verb **knew** of the larger clause **I knew X** is the matrix clause for the zero **that**-clause **I had been forgiven** which appears at X as object:

(22) Then I knew **I had been forgiven**. (Scheurweghs, 1959, p. 253)

Noun Clauses are all those subordinate clauses which by themselves can be replaced syntactically by the indefinite pronoun **something**. Taking (22), we rewrite it as (A) below:

(A) Then I knew **something** (comforting).

Here the pronoun **something** represents the noun clause **I had been forgiven** as being syntactically equivalent in function. The close relationship between the noun clause here and the indefinite pronoun **something** can be seen in the fact that we can use (A) to anticipate the lexical realisation of (22), as in (B) below:

(B) Then I knew **something** comforting; I knew **I had been forgiven**.

Here the indefinite pronoun **something** (comforting) as object is lexically realised by the noun clause **I had been forgiven** as object.
  There are two kinds of noun clause which have subordinating conjunctions. The first is the exocentric **that**-clause which we have just considered .above for (22), and the second is the endocentric

wh-clauses which are traditionally described as indirect questions. Both require some description in terms of their parsing analysis. The most striking difference between these two kinds of noun clause is that the **that**-clause cannot take the slot of prepositional 'object', whereas the **wh**-clause can take this slot and all the others as well. (See example (17) as an example of a **wh**-clause as subject.)

We take the **that**-clauses as noun clause first and then go on to **wh**-clauses as noun clause.

6.2   That-Clauses as Noun Clause

One of the minor embarrassments of teaching a parsing analysis is the similarity of some of the signalling items. There are no less than six **that**-items in English today: the use of **that** as substitute nominal or attributive to head, for example, **that man** in 'That man is dangerous'; the use of intensifier **that**, for example 'I am not **that** crazy'; the archaic use of **that** as adverbial clause subordinator, for example 'We dye **that** you may live colourfully'; the use of **that** as special subordinator in cleft clauses, for example 'It was then **that** he left'; the use of **that** as endocentric relative subordinator, for example 'This is the house **that** Jack built'; and finally the use of **that** as exocentric subordinator of noun clause, for example 'He suggested **that** I should stay'.

Although there is no mistaking each of these **that**-items in their contexts, we need to distinguish between the **that**-item which signals a noun clause and the **that**-item which signals a relative clause. Consider (23) below, where the relative **that**-item is object in its clause:

(23) Home and school gradually become separate, and many of the home problems are worked out or at any rate made easier with the new dimension **that school adds to life**. (*Observer*, 15 January 1967, p. 28)

First, we note the parsing point about the relative clause; confirmation that it is a relative clause comes when we reach the verb and preposition **adds to life**. It has no object and so we take the **that**-item as the object we are looking for. The **that**-item in turn refers back to its lexical referent, the nominal group **the new dimension**. Second, we note that, as object of the verb **adds** this nominal group answers the pushdown question: 'Adds what to life?' Thus we see that the meaning of object enters into the meaning of the nominal group.

In the noun clause signalled by **that**-conjunction, however, the clause is self-contained in that it does not enter into similar constituent relations with the noun head outside the boundary of its clause. By self-contained I mean that it has the syntax of the unmarked independent declarative clause without the grammatical status of independence. This is particularly clear where the **that**-clause is traditionally described as noun clause in apposition to noun (the nominal group **her appeals** in (24) below):

(24) He takes no notice of her appeals **that he should rest more.** (Scheurweghs, 1959, p. 250)

Notice that this nominal group structure is a nominalising paraphrase of the clause structure: She appealed to him **that he should rest more.** In the nominalisation process, the verb **appealed** becomes the noun head **appeals,** and the noun clause object **that he should rest more** becomes postmodifying clause to this head, with the **that**-clause elements remaining exactly as they were before. This shows that there is no syntactic relation of the clause between the noun head **appeals** and the elements of the noun clause.

Having clarified the difference between the relative that-clause and the noun **that**-clause in its postmodifying role, we continue with a brief examination of the three main slots in the clause which these noun clauses occupy. We note that except where the **that**-clause is presented initially in the clause, as in (25) below, we can delete or zero the **that**-conjunction.

(25) **That hen-pecked husbands were not entirely unknown** can be gathered from the pages of Punch. (Scheurweghs, 1959, p. 243)

The parsing point here is that when we come to the end of the nominal group **hen-pecked husbands** as signalled by the start of the verb **were,** we know from the plural s of **husbands** that the **that**-item is not a demonstrative pronoun but the subordinator **that** signalling noun clause. If we now delete this subordinator as in (26) below, we don't know that the noun clause is subject until we parse the next finite verb group, **can be gathered,** etc.

(26) Hen-pecked husbands were not entirely unknown can be gathered from the pages of Punch.

The parsing point is that when we reach the end of the first verb group **were not entirely unknown** we already have sufficient grammatical completeness for independent declarative clause but the presence of yet another finite verb group **can be gathered** compels us to reinterpret the first clause as its grammatical subject. It should be clear that we cannot delete the **that**-item from the noun clause if we are to avoid this comprehension difficulty.

Example (25) has the possibility of grammatical paraphrase with anticipatory **It** (G. Curme, 1947, p. 100; R. Quirk *et al.*, 1972, p. 955; and others), which I have rewritten below as (27):

(27) **It** can be gathered from the pages of Punch **that hen-pecked husbands were not entirely unknown.**

The parsing point is that if the item **It** does not refer back to a preceding clause or nominal group, then in the position of subject it signals that the real subject will be a clause of some kind, which will follow the predication and complete the grammatical boundary of its main clause. (See discussion of unmarked special operations clause at 10.3.3.)

(28) He fancied **that he was suffering from a mild attack of agoraphobia.** (Scheurweghs, 1959, p. 246)

Here the verb **fancied** interprets the **that**-clause object as hypothetical. The **that**-subordinator signals the start of the clause boundary of the noun clause object, and when we come to the end of this clause we come to the end of the boundary of the matrix clause.

(29) She really **believed she has to be unhappy to be good.** (Scheurweghs, 1959, p. 253)

Note here that we can still parse the noun clause as object in spite of its lack of **that**-subordinator item because we know from the verb **believe** that it has a clause object; this is confirmed when we parse **she** as new subject in new finite clause just at the position where we expect an object. (We can in any case put back the **that**-subordinator in making the subordination further explicit.)

6.3 Two Kinds of That-Clause Complement

So far we have discussed the noun clause as subject and object of the larger clause. What is less satisfactory is the analysis of complement, which we show as C in S V C analysis. I wish to broaden the notion of complement to include the grammar of adjective complement (Quirk *et al.*, 1972, p. 264). Thus we can have a **that**-clause as complement of the verb **is** as in (30), and a **that**-clause as adjective complement as in (31) below:

(30) The truth is **that it is not the children who have changed but their elders.** (Scheurweghs, 1959, p. 245)

(31)   She is shocked **that most people are so unfriendly.** (Scheurweghs, 1959, p. 250)

The adjective **shocked** is complement of the verb **is**, and the **that**-clause complement is part of the structural grammar of the adjective **shocked**. If we remove the adjective, the clause structure collapses: **She is that most people are so unfriendly.** This indicates that the **that**-clause is grammatically dependent on the adjective **shocked** for its meaning.

There are a number of adjectives in this pattern, such as **afraid, angry, annoyed, anxious, certain, disappointed, eager, fearful, glad, grateful, happy, keen, irritated, sad, sure,** and **worried.** These adjectives also have other predictable postmodifier-like constructions such as prepositional 'objects' and to-infinitive clauses, for example **He is worried. Worried about what? He is worried about money matters; He is very keen. Very keen to do what? He is very keen to help us.** Note that **He is afraid** can elicit the pushdown question **Afraid of what?** which can be answered either by 'He is afraid **of being arrested**' or 'He is afraid **that he will be arrested**'. Because of the close grammatical tie with postmodifier-like structures like these, I would prefer to group this kind of complement structure as complement.

Accordingly we discuss the two kinds of complement structure below.

6.3.1 **That-***Clause as Complement of the Verb* **be**

There are five contextual points to be noted of the use of **that**-clauses as sole complement of the verb **be**.

(i) The clauses are of the S **be** C pattern where the verb **be** has equative meaning, and where the item in S interprets the clause relational meaning of the **that**-clause which follows as C. (See 10.3 for the discussion of the notion of special operations clauses. See also Winter, 1977, p. 76.)

(ii) This kind of clause pattern is signalled by the presence of certain abstract nouns in S, for example: assumption, belief, conclusion, consequence, excuse, expectation, explanation, fact, feeling, idea, possibility, reason, suggestion, statement, truth, etc. (See Scheurweghs, 1959, p. 245, where he lists examples of the noun **fact, probability, reason** and **truth.** See also Winter, 1977, for the role of vocabulary-3 words.)

Parsing the clause in (32) in the normal way from front to back we note that the presence of the noun **the truth** as S signals that C will be a **that**-clause:

(32) **The truth is that it is not the children who have changed but their parents.** (Scheurweghs, 1959, p. 245)

The negative point to be noted with this pattern is that no concrete noun can fill S. This is because it is a special operations clause concerned with the clause's relation with its context and not with lexical participants.

(iii) The important contextual point with these clauses is that the presence of the non-concrete abstract nouns like **the truth** make their clause *unspecific clause* out of context, because its *specific clause* precedes it. The lexical realisation of an item like **the truth** requires at least two clauses, as we see below in (33), where the item **truth** signals that the preceding clauses are **not the truth** in addition to signalling the meaning of its **that**-clause complement:

(33) A social worker who ought to know better was complaining about a prison sentence on an elderly thief found loitering on a car park. 'Some of these magistrates never learn,' she said, 'That's exactly the sort of case that ought to go to Grendon: ordinary prison will do nothing for him.' **The truth** is that he wasn't a Grendon case: he's an old lag I have known for years and he regards all doctors and all 'treatment' with suspicion and contempt. (*New Statesman*, 6 May 1966, p. 641)

Here the item **the truth** signals for its complement clauses the semantics of denial (he wasn't a Grendon case) and *correction* (he's an old lag I have known for years). (See Winter, 1974, for denial and correction clauses.)

(iv) The contextual role of the noun subjects in these clauses can be seen in the use of the question criterion. Taking the subject in (33) above, we find that the **that**-clauses answer the following **wh**-question: 'What is the truth about the elderly thief, etc., in the statement "That's exactly the sort of case that ought to go to Grendon"?' The point to note is that the item in the question, **the truth,** has to refer to the lexical realisation of the clauses before its clause and after its clause.

(v) These clauses can be grammatically paraphrased as abstract nominal groups where the noun in subject becomes the nominal head and the **that**-clause complement becomes the postmodification clause for this nominal head, as in (34) below:

(34) There is no denying **the truth that it is not the children who have changed but their elders.** (Made up from example (32) above)

The nominal group structure is now the object of the gerundial clause verb **denying**. The linguistic significance of this nominalisation process is that it is the way in which we 'talk about' sentences like (32). The traditional term for the nominal group structure has already been noted for example (24), namely noun clause in apposition to noun.

This suffices to illustrate the use of that-clauses as complement of the special operations clause S **be** C. Next we are concerned with **that**-clauses which are postmodifier-like structures which follow adjectives which themselves are complements in basic clauses with the verb **be**. By basic clauses, I mean that the participants at S and at C are lexical participants, and not grammatical participants.

6.3.2 **That**-*Clauses Which Are Postmodifier-like Structures for the Adjective as Complement in the Clause*

We have already noted the list of adjectives and past participles which have predictable postmodifier-like structures as part of their grammatical choice. There were three kinds: postmodifying prepositional phrase, for example 'She is **afraid of going home**'; to-infinitive clause, for example 'She is **afraid to go home**'; and that-clause complementation, for example 'She is **afraid that she will have to go home**'. For convenience, the parts in bold are simply analysed as complement or grammatical domain of complement. (The claim that these adjective-plus structures are basic clause structure can be seen in the common use of them as verbless clause adjuncts, for example '**Fearful of being left out of things**, she hurried to the party'.) Of the three kinds of structure it is the **that**-clause that we are concerned with here.

Unlike the **that**-clause complement of the special operations clause S **be** C which has to have non-concrete abstract subjects, the matrix clauses for these **that**-clause complements can have any non-abstract subjects, particularly human subjects. It will be helpful at this point to remember that there are some lexical verbs which fit the verb **be** slot in these matrix clauses, two of which will suffice: **become** and **feel**. A. S. Hornby (1975, pp. 26–8) notes these verbs in the patterns as *inchoative verbs*, verbs which show changes of state, etc.

This pattern of clause has grammatical paraphrase relations with the nominal paraphrase of the adjective with its postmodification structure. For instance, there is the paraphrase relation between the adjective **indignant** in (35) and the noun head **indignation** in (36) below.

(35) They were **indignant that she should talk such nonsense**. (Made up from (36) below)

(36) There was a great deal of **indignation** that she should talk such nonsense. (Scheurweghs, 1959, p. 250)

The similarity in meaning can be seen in the pushdown questions: **Indignant about what?** and **Indignation about what?** The difference is that in (35) we have an explicit human subject: **They were indignant about what?**, and in (36), there is a covert human subject: **There was a great deal of indignation about what?**

A grammatical feature of these **that**-clause complements is that their **that**-items can be readily deleted, with the adjective itself signalling the clause pattern:

(37) She is very glad **her husband is not attracted by greyhound racing.**
(Scheurweghs, 1959, p. 253)

(38) I am afraid **Professor H has underestimated these effects.**
(Scheurweghs, 1959, p. 253)

The parsing point is quite simple: when we come to adjectives like **glad** and **afraid** in basic clause patterns like these, we know that we can predict a **that**-clause because these are the patterns that occur with **glad** and **afraid**. There is, in any case, the criterion of explicitness: we can simply insert the **that**-item in both of these cases.

6.3.3 Summary and Conclusions about **That**-*Clauses*

Summing up the discussion so far, we have seen that these noun clauses function as subject, object, complement in a larger matrix clause. Earlier we noted that the semantics of the matrix clause was contextually important in interpreting the meaning of its enclosed noun clause and hence the matrix clause in the context of adjoining sentences. In particular we noted the differences between matrix clauses with 'think' and 'know' verbs (cf. Kiparsky and Kiparsky, 1970, for a similar idea of 'non-factive' and 'factive' sentences).

The traditional term 'indirect statement' for a **that**-clause is an acknowledgement that a statement which stands alone as a direct statement (independent declarative clause) is enclosed within the grammar of another statement (independent clause). Traditional grammar is concerned largely with changes of encoder, and with how the change from independent clause to a **that**-clause is signalled in the appropriate matrix clause:

Direct speech	*Indirect speech*
I saw the boy **here** in **this** room **today**.	= **He** said that **he had** seen the boy **there** in **that** room **that day**.
(Eckersley and Eckersley, 1960, p. 364)	

What is less clearly appreciated is that these **that**-clauses in their matrix clauses are a way of 'talking about' or 'repeating' clauses, ours or other people's, either to report on them and/or to evaluate them as statements. Furthermore, the matrix clause may make explicit who the encoder is to help the decoder to assess the credibility of the source of the encoded language. In (39) below, the adjective **clear** in the matrix clause is offering the writer's comment on the information of the enclosed **that**-clause; that is, he is saying what **he** thinks of this information. This is an instance of evaluation clause.

(39) It has been **clear** for some time − except perhaps to President de Gaulle − **that the traditional nation states are too small to sustain wholly independent defence policies.** (*Observer*, 22 January 1967, p. 10)

This 'talking about' the clause should be contrasted with the contextual function of the defining relative clause. A relative clause can pick up a preceding or already known clause and use its lexical uniqueness to confer lexical uniqueness to the next mention of one of the clause participants, especially if the name of the participant is not known. This is one of the commonest uses of the relative clause in newspaper reporting. For instance, the first appearance of the clause would be declarative independent clause: **Informer lied to the court**. On the back page of the newspaper which carries the remainder of the article the story would be headed: **Informer who lied** (to court). Thus we are identifying the performer, not by name, but by his role as performer in the unique clause which we already know: **lied to the court**.

Whatever analysis we adopt in describing English, we cannot ignore the contextual function of the **that**-clause in carrying clauses for interpretation, comment or evaluation by its matrix clause.

6.4 The Wh-Clause as Noun Clause

6.4.1 Introduction

In addition to noun clauses signalled by **that** as subordinator there is a second type signalled by the elements **what, who(m), when, where, why, how, if**. Although these clauses are syntactically similar to relative clauses, their **wh**-item differs in that it is both nominal head and subordinator of its clause. For instance, the **what** of the object noun clause in **He gave me what I needed** is the endocentric head upon which the grammar of the noun clause depends. The relative clause which parallels this construction has a (generalised) noun antecedent and where the head is object of the relative clause it usually has no overt subordinator: **He gave me the things (which) I needed**. The reason why this generalised antecedent may so often be followed by a relative clause without subordinator is possibly that one basic function of generalised nouns is to allow clausal expansion in postmodifier position. Thus we find **the person** (who) **I want, the time** (when), **the place** (where), **the reason** (why). Only **the way** (in which) breaks the pattern. The pattern **Do it the way he wants it** seems unexpandable.

These items may also optionally figure in place of their whole clause. This anaphoric use can be illustrated in the co-ordinated clause pair: He has gone and I know **why**. Here the **why**-item has the syntax of nominal head as object of the verb **know**. As such it substitutes for the deleted clause **he has gone**, the non-deleted form of which is: He has gone and I know why **he has gone**. The deleted form would be the unmarked for which the non-deleted form would be the marked.

Noun clauses as *wh*-clauses have a characteristic word order. They have been traditionally described as indirect questions; they have question words but do not have the word order of direct questions. We can show this clearly by rewriting the indirect question as direct question within the structure of the larger clause. In (40) below, there are two **what**-clauses as nominals X and Y in the larger clause **X may be governed by Y**:

(40) Given that a person does decide to take drugs, the choice is wide. **Exactly what he feels when he takes the drug** may to some extent, be governed by **what he expects he will feel**. (*Observer*, 12 February 1967, Review section)

Rewriting the **what**-clauses as direct questions, we have the following:

Exactly what does he feel when he takes the drug may, to some extent, be governed by what does he expect he will feel.

The oddness of this rewriting can be seen in its parsing: by the time we come to the end of the **when**-clause in the question 'Exactly what does he feel when he takes the drug?' we have grammatically completed our question, and now find ourselves parsing the auxiliary verb **may** and being forced to reconsider the preceding question clause as a likely nominal subject for this verb. The differences in word order between direct question and indirect question are well described traditionally. The question clause **Who is he**? has the sequence of C V S? The noun clause would be **Who he is**, where the sequence C S V cues us that this is a noun clause.

Indirect questions are signalled by a **wh**-item followed by non-interrogative word order. They appear as constituent nominals in three kind of larger clauses: the first I call 'lexical clause' and the other two are special kinds of matrix clause which have the non-lexical verb **be** in its equative meaning for the purpose of using the special grammatical features of the **wh**-clause.

A lexical clause simply means a larger clause which has a lexical verb like the lexical verb **governed** of the clause **X may be governed by Y** of (40) above, where X or Y, instead of having a noun-headed construction at X and Y, have **what**-clauses. Here is an example of the verb **rejoiced**, where that **what**-clause is 'object' of the preposition **in**:

(41) They rejoiced in **what seemed to them a daring paradox**. (Scheurweghs, 1959, p. 261)

Compare this with:

They rejoiced in **a daring paradox**.

The **what**-clause expands one of the lexical clause's nominal structures; for example the **what**-clause in (41) can be seen as conveying the hypotheticality of the nominal group **a daring paradox**. Thus a lexical clause is one in which any kind of lexical choice can be made for any one of the nominal constituents in a clause which has a lexical verb, so that the choice of the **what**-clause is like any other purely nominal choice for the larger clause. The most significant linguistic point about the use of **what**-clause nominals in lexical matrix clauses is that their grammar has no bearing whatever on the main verb of the matrix clause.

6.4.2 **Wh**-*Clauses Which Are Not Noun Clauses: Two Kinds*

In contrast with lexical matrix clauses, there are two special kinds of matrix clause which have the syntactic pattern of S V C where V is the equative verb **be** and where the **wh**-clause can be either S or C. In spite of having the functions of S or C in such clauses, these **wh**-clauses are not noun clauses but require consideration as special forms of subordination structure. The two kinds of special operations clause are the pseudo-cleft sentence, for example **What we want is Watneys** and its reversed form **Watneys is what we want**, and the anaphoric/cataphoric clauses of the pattern S V C: This/that/it – **be** – C, where S = substitute nominals and where C = a range of items such as **so, the case, wh**-clauses, adverbial clause, non-finite clauses, etc.

We will take the pseudo-cleft sentence and the anaphoric/cataphoric clause in turn. As already noted, the **what**-clause in the pseudo-cleft clause, although having the constituent function of subject in its larger clause, is not strictly speaking a noun clause at all. It is a special kind of (indirect) questioning operation for the purpose of marking a constituent element of its unmarked declarative clause form. In the slot S of the framework of the non-lexical larger clause S **be** C, it anticipates the grammatical nature of what is being focused upon within the structure of C. In this respect it is like the **It** of the cleft sentence except that the **It** does not specify what its clause will be focusing upon with its C structure. It will suffice for the present to describe the pseudo-cleft sentence and let it stand in principle for the cleft sentence. In illustrating the pseudo-cleft sentence we will pay particular attention to the way in which it anticipates the nature of what is focused upon within the structure of the complement of its verb **be**. It is this syntactic operation which distinguishes it from the **what**-clauses of lexical clauses. An example now follows.

(42)   In America managing directors pride themselves on being top of the salary league; but here a kind of prudery, a fear of financial exposure, keeps salaries secret.
   What we do know, though, *is* that almost all of the people who draw salaries of more than £10,000 a year are in business or commerce. (*Observer*, 4 December 1967, Review section)

In the **what**-clause, we know from the relative-type grammar of its clause that the **what**-item is object of the verb **know** and this signals that it is the object of the very **know** that is going to be marked. Thus, although the **that**-clause is complement of the matrix clause, it is still semantically the object of the verb **know**. We can show this by rewriting the **what**-clause in its unmarked declarative clause form:

We do **know**, though, **that** almost all of the people who draw salaries of more than £10,000 a year are in business or commerce.

Notice also that the marking of the clause by the affirmative *do* is telling us that its clause is a paraphrase of the preceding clause in which keeping salaries secret means that we do not know what the exact salaries are.

Because of this anticipation of the constituent of the **what**-clause to be focused upon in the complement of the matrix clause of the pseudo-cleft sentence, we cannot regard it as a noun clause but must rather treat the relative-type grammar of the cleft and the pseudo-cleft sentences as special cases of subordination.

Next we consider briefly the anaphoric/cataphoric clause of the **this is what**-clause kind. These **what**-clauses function rather like the **what**-clauses in pseudo-cleft except that their **what**-item refers to a preceding clause via their **this/that** subject.

In (43) below, the substitute nominal **that** in its **that is what**-clause refers to the hypothetically presented information of the preceding complex sentence as that which every African and Asian will know. (The hypothetical signalling is the structure **If X, this will be because Y**).

(43) If southern Africa's white regimes are allowed to pursue an intolerable racialist course, this will be because the countries on which they depend for their trade, their financial stability and their defence — Britain and the US — have allowed them to do so. *That is what* every African and Asian will know; and that is what Mr Wilson should be telling the British and the Americans, now. (*Observer*, 18 September 1966, p. 10)

Note that the syntactic criterion of noun clause does not fit the complement slot of these clauses, for example **That is something**. This is presumably because the C slot in these clauses is reserved for grammatical interpretations of the item in S just as it is with the pseudo-cleft sentence. Unlike the **what**-item of the psuedo-cleft which refers forward to its structure, the **what**-item of (43) refers back to the preceding complex sentence as providing the lexical realisation for the object of the verb **know** in the **what**-clause. As already noted, it does this operation via the anaphoric reference of its substitute nominal subject.

The **why**-item is also not a noun clause in this pattern. In (44) below, the **this** as nominal subject and the topic of the pill in the **why**-clause itself refers back to the main clause of the preceding sentence as the *reason* why many women dislike the pill:

(44) Surely contraceptive pills, despite their obvious advantages still have the great disadvantage that they work by interfering with the delicate balance of the endocrinal system, while other contraceptive methods work as minor mechanical obstructions. *This is why* many women dislike the idea of the pill. (Letter to *New Statesman*, 10 June 1966, p. 844)

What this **this is why**-clause means is that the preceding main clause represents an answer to the question 'Why do so many women dislike the pill?' Again, the syntactic criterion for noun clause does not make sense here, for example **This is something**.

These two examples suffice to show that the **wh**-clauses as complement in anaphoric/cataphoric clauses are not noun clauses. For further discussion of 'this' and 'that' nominals, see Karlsen (1959, pp. 76–8), Winter (1974, pp. 224–33), and for the study of their contextual semantics see Jordan (1978).

Both the pseudo-cleft sentence and these anaphoric/cataphoric clauses are treated as special operations clauses. By special operations

I mean that the constituents S and C in these clauses are grammatical rather than lexical participants. We continue the discussion of these clauses in (10.3). We now turn to the lexical matrix clause as the grammatical environment for the **wh**-clause as noun clause.

6.5.1 **Wh**-*Clauses in Lexical Matrix Clauses*

Earlier in describing **that**-clauses as noun clause, we noted that these **that**-clauses were a way of 'talking about' clauses, ours and other people's. This is what the term 'indirect' in the traditional term 'indirect statement' means. It is not the statement itself but a statement which is part of the structure of a larger statement. Likewise, the term 'indirect' in 'indirect question' means that these are not questions but questions converted to nominal structures so that we can 'talk about' them as we can talk about any other noun. In an environment of lexical matrix clause, the **wh**-clause can only be a noun clause because it is behaving just like any other noun head in the clause. We accordingly speak of the noun clauses in a lexical matrix clause as lexical participants in order to distinguish them from their role as grammatical participants at S and C of the special operations clauses described above.

Noun clauses can be divided into two kinds according to whether or not they require to be lexically realised by an adjoining clause or clauses. This is not be confused with the grammatical reference operation of the pseudo-cleft clause or the anaphoric/cataphoric clauses. We now consider noun clause examples of **what**- and **why**-clause.

What-clauses as lexical participants may require lexical realisation by an adjoining clause where the lexical referent is not present in its matrix clause. Consider (45), where there is a **what**-clause object:

(45) She found **what we had lost**. (Scheurweghs, 1959, p. 261)

We can presume that the referent of the **what**-item, namely the object of the verb **lost**, can be treated as known to the writer and the readers, so that it does not require immediate lexical realisation as does (46):

(46) Come and see **what I have found**. (Scheurweghs, 1959, p. 261)

If this was a speech situation, then we could expect lexical realisation to follow the **what**-clause, for example 'Come and see what I have found – **your long lost watch**!' Notice that although the syntax of **your long lost watch** looks like apposition to the **what**-item, it is strictly speaking the object of the verb **found**. It answers the question 'What have you found?'

In matrix clauses which are don't-know replies to a **what**-question clause, the **what**-clause does not require further lexical realisation, as we see in (47) below, where the close grammatical relation between the direct and the indirect question can be seen in the relation between the headline 'What's going on?' and the noun clause **what is going on**.

What's going on?

(47) The elements of Mr Wilson's Rhodesian policies now lie buried so deep in the recesses of 10 Downing Street that even his Ministerial colleagues no longer appear to know **what is going on**. (*Observer*, 29 May 1966, p. 8)

A very important parsing feature of the **wh**-clause as noun clause is that it is often lexically realised either by a preceding clause or a following clause outside the grammatical boundary of its matrix clause. The linguistic significance of this point is that the full understanding of the information of the **wh**-clause requires its lexical realisation by adjoining clauses, often grammatically separate in terms of the Bloomfieldian sense of sentence. As an indirect question, when not lexically realised by its own clause or by its matrix clause, it demands an answer to its (indirect) question somewhere soon, preferably in the next adjoining (independent) clause. (See Winter, 1977, pp. 39–40, for discussion of the connective role of indirect questions.)

Both the point about grammatical paraphrase and lexical realisation are brought out in (48) below, where the indirect question word **why** looks both ways, backwards and forwards; that is, it is both anaphoric and cataphoric.

(48) The problems of adapting nuclear power to airships are fewer and less perplexing than those pertaining to the aeroplane. **It is perfectly plain why**: a primary consideration is weight. It has been estimated, for example, that in an aeroplane the size of the Super VC-10, of 335 000 lbs gross weight the shielding alone would exceed 250 000 lbs; obviously such an airliner would not take off, since the reactor weight exceeds its disposable lift. Increasing the size of the aircraft merely results in proportionately larger demands for power and also shielding. (*New Scientist*, 7 April 1966, p. 14)

First, the anaphoric point. The **why**-item with deleted clause can only refer back to the preceding (independent) clause here as providing the lexical realisation of its own clause. Its direct question form would be

'Why are the problems of adapting nuclear power to airships fewer and less perplexing than those pertaining to the aeroplane?' Second, the cataphoric point. The **why**-item refers forward to the very next (independent) clause as the answer to its question. Third, the point about grammatical paraphrase. The **why**-item requires lexical realisation by its own clause and by the other clause to which it refers cataphorically here. This is a requirement of its clause relation; namely, the noun clause here is grammatically paraphrasable with the next clause outside its grammatical boundary.

The clause **It is perfectly plain why** is an evaluation clause which evaluates the clause relation between the first sentence in the paragraph and the independent clause which follows it after the colon; it evaluates the enclosed clause as being **perfectly plain** in its **why**-relation with the independent clause that follows it after the colon. We can see what grammatical paraphrase means, by rewriting the two clauses in their adverbial subordinate form, using the subordinator item **since** to paraphrase the **why**-item by signalling the notion of a **basis** for the comparative evaluation of adapting power to airships versus adapting it to the aeroplane:

(48B) The problems of adapting nuclear power to airships are fewer and less perplexing that those pertaining to the aeroplane **since a primary consideration is weight**.

The clause **a primary consideration is weight** represents an answer to the more specific **why**-question 'What makes you think that the problems of adapting nuclear power to airships are fewer and less perplexing than those pertaining to the aeroplane?' As an answer, the clause **a primary consideration is weight** is a general statement: as such, its contextual grammar requires lexical realisation in respect of its lexical particulars. The next clause, signalled by the sentence connector **for example**, acknowledges this general statement and signals that its clause is providing the particulars of the *basis*. Note the evaluation clause **obviously such an airliner would not take off** with its **since**-clause providing the basis for this evaluation.

We take up the lexical realisation point again in describing two contextual categories of clause, the unspecific and the specific clause (at 11.4.3), but what we have said here suffices for the purpose of clarifying the contextual role of the **why**-clause as noun clause.

6.5.2 Summary and Conclusions about **wh**-Clauses

We have seen that **wh**-clauses as indirect questions are distinguished by two syntactic criteria from direct questions. The first is their word order, which differs from that of direct questions, for example the indirect question **Who he is**, which is C S V sequence, versus the direct question **Who is he?**, which is the sequence C V S? The sequence S V C, where the **wh**-item is S, for example **What is wrong?**, has the same sequence whether indirect question or direct question; only the syntactic position as nominal in a larger clause will signal which is which. The second criterion of indirect questions is that **wh**-clauses take the syntax of nominal structure within a larger lexical clause.

We have also seen that these two criteria while adequate for the recognition of the indirect question do not suffice for distinguishing the **wh**-clause as noun clause from the **wh**-clause which is part of the grammatical operation of specialised matrix clauses like the pseudo-cleft sentence and the anaphoric/cataphoric matrix clause **This be wh-clause**. In these two specialised matrix clauses whose main verb is **be** in its equative meaning, the **wh**-clause enters into special operations on their opposing slots in the matrix clause S **be** C. For instance, if the **wh**-clause of the pseudo-cleft clause is at subject position, it operates on the grammatical interpretation of what follows as complement, for example in **What he did was damage the car badly** the **wh**-clause **What he did** prepares us for the lexical predication of the cataphoric substitute verb **did**, so that it is within the grammar of complement that we anticipate the verb and its predicate **damage the car badly**. What specialised operation means is that this complement is not only complement in the nominal sense but, more important, it is also the lexical realisation of verb-object-adjunct for the **wh**-clause in S slot. Although the verb **damage** is presented as non-finite by this complement slot, its finiteness has already been signalled by the finiteness of the **did** in the **wh**-clause itself. (In Winter, 1974, p. 197, I note the pseudo-cleft clause as the marked replacement of the preceding clause.)

Thus, it should be clear that the slots of subject and complement in these special operations matrix clauses, while having the structural meanings of nominal, suspend the normal choices of noun head in nominal group which characterise normal lexical (basic) clauses. We could call these subject and complement slots pseudo-subjects and pseudo-complements. Any **wh**-clause in these special matrix clauses is no longer a noun clause but a special operations **wh**-clause as described above. Likewise any noun head is analysed differently in the slots of these pseudo-subjects and pseudo-complements, for example in **What we want is Watneys** the pseudo-complement **Watneys** is grammatically both object and complement, and in **Watneys is what we want**, the pseudo-subject **Watneys** is grammatically both object and subject. In parsing this second clause, we parse the subject and verb **Watneys is** as normal until we get to the **what**-item. This marks the clause and warns us that we have to reinterpret the syntax of the word **Watneys** from being subject of the clause to something else. It is only when we have parsed the verb of the **what**-clause that we reinterpret **Watneys** as being the object of the verb **want**.

Because of their grammatical marking operations in the above-mentioned specialised matrix clauses, these **wh**-clauses are not treated as normal noun clauses but as specialised uses of subordination for the purpose of marking the clause.

6.6 Summary and Conclusions about Noun Clauses

We have noted that the contextual functions of noun clauses differed according to whether they were introduced by **that**-items or by **wh**-items in the syntax of subject, object, complement and 'object' of the preposition where the matrix clause is a lexical clause. We noted that one way of characterising the contextual differences between **that**-clauses as indirect statement and **wh**-clauses as indirect questions was that the **that**-clause is a way of 'talking about' clauses as clauses while the **wh**-clause is a way of 'talking about' questions. The notion of 'talking about' includes the lexical matrix clause which evaluates the noun clauses as clauses.

We contrasted the contextual function of noun clause with that of relative clause. If the **that**-clause is a way of 'talking about' the clause and the **wh**-clause is a way of 'talking about' questions, then the relative clause is a way of 'talking about' the noun of the clause, using the lexical uniqueness of the relative clause to identify the noun head for us. For example, on the back page of the *Guardian* there is a continuation of a story on the front page, headed **Informer who lied**. The relative clause **who lied** is information already known from the front page.

The **that**-clause presents less of a theoretical problem to us than the relative clause and the **what**-clause in nominal group structure, but we need to pay careful attention to the semantics of the lexical item(s) which dominate the meaning of the matrix clause of lexical clauses. This we do in the study of the hypothetical and real relation, where the relation between different encoders or times of encoding is crucial to the grammar (see 11.6.4).

This concludes our discussion of noun clauses which have subordinating conjunctions. We take up noun clauses which do not have these signals in Section 8 below.

Adverbial Clauses with Subordinators

7.1 Introduction

We now come to a third kind of subordinate clause which is introduced by a subordinator. This is the clause which takes the role of adjunct or is adjunct-like in its main clause. By adjunct or adjunct-like in the clause, I mean that in the negative sense it is *not* subject, *not* verb, *not* predicate structure of verb plus prepositional 'object' (for example **he talks to her**), *not* complement, *not* object (direct and indirect, first and second object), and *not* object complement (for example he made her **happy**). In terms of **wh**-questions, all of these are basic clause structures which are elicited by simple **who/what**-questions. In these questions the **what**-clause asks us to complete the basic clause structure in terms of *one* missing constituent. Some examples: in the prepositional 'object' which is part of the structure of the verb **talk** in **He talks to her**, the prepositional 'object' **her** is elicited by the question: '**Who** does he talk to?'; the predication **persuaded John to leave** in **He persuaded John to leave** is elicited by the question: '**What** did he **do** to John?'; the subject in **Henry is going** is elicited by the question '**Who** is going?', etc. In contrast the adverbial adjunct is elicited by non-**what** questions such as **Where? When? Why? How? How often?** For example, **once a week** in the question 'How often does he go home? = He goes home **once a week**. Of course the description of clause structure is oversimplified, but it will suffice to illustrate the semantic difference between the constituents S, V, O, C, and prepositional object versus A. The complication in the distinction between simple **what/who** versus **when/where/why/how often**, etc., questions is that the **what**-item enters into compound meaning questions such as **What time did he leave?** for the less specific **When did he leave?** The **what**-clause question for S, V, O, C and prepositional object is presented in the role of S, V, O, C and prepositional object; for example in **Who does he talk to?**, the **Who** item is specified as prepositional object.

Taking the basic clause structures as our syntactic landmarks, an adjunct is anything that fits into the slots represented by the asterisks in each clause: * S * V *; * S * V * prepositional 'object' *; * S * V * O *; * S * V * O * prepositional 'object' *; * S * V * O C *; * S * V * C *, etc., where we ignore the restrictions on some slots for adjuncts, for example the slot between verb and object where the object is short as in 'He dismissed **coldly** the man'. We also ignore the typical premodifier slot for intensifying adverbs like **very** in the typical premodifier slot in the nominal group, for example **the very kind lady**, and in the adjective group, for example She is **very kind** to him; and the premodifying behaviour with prepositional phrases and adverbial clauses, for example 'She is **very much in the fashion**' and 'She left **largely because of him**.' Where the adverbial clause is part of complement structure in a special operations clause with the equative verb **be**, this is treated as an adverbial clause in special operations clauses, for example the clause **this is because**-clause in (49) below, where the contextual function of the complement is to *add* the postponed meaning of this **because**-clause to the immediately preceding clause. (See Winter, 1974, pp. 226–7.)

(49) . . . they stay in their cells for most of the day as well the night. **This is because** there is nowhere else for them to go, and still be under supervision. (*Daily Telegraph*, 17 June 1966, p. 18)

The **because**-clause answers the **why**-question on the preceding clause: 'Why is this?' (See Winter, 1979, p. 106 for the notion of postponed grammatical choice for the clause.)

The above sketch of the adjunct in the clause is intended as a background against which we can discuss the adverbial clause as a particular kind of adjunct in the larger clause. The discussion of the adverbial clause in English will be a discussion of how its contextual meaning differs according to where it is placed in three typical positions in the basic clause. These are (i) front-position: the position in front of the subject; (ii) mid-position: this is the position inside clause structure after the subject; and (iii) end-position: this is the position after the clause structure has been completed. These three position are illustrated below, in (50) (51) and (52), and compared with the complement slot in the special operations clause in (53):

Front-position in the clause

(50) **By pretending to be her at this critical time,** he hopes to direct the influence of evil spirits away from her and on to himself.

Mid-position in the clause

(51) The resulting loneliness, **because they feel they can't trust adults**

even when they're fast approaching the adult world, leads to boredom and then to trouble.

End-position in the clause

(52) He discovered what was wrong **by sitting in the chair himself.**

Complement position in special operations clause

(53) One way of informing these people, the station's Advisory Board believes, is **by persuading the British government to finance more scholarships for young foreign engineers** . . .

The notion of adjunct or adjunct-like clause means that in the first three examples (50-2), we can remove the adverbial clause and an independent clause remains, *grammatically complete and capable of standing alone.*

(50a) He hopes to direct the influence of evil spirits away from her and on to himself.

(51a) The resulting loneliness leads to boredom and then to trouble.

(52a) He discovered what was wrong.

But when we come to (53) we no longer find a grammatically complete clause:

(53a) One of the ways of informing these people, the station's Advisory Board believes, is ____.

What is missing from (53a) is the complement of the verb **is** which is grammatically required. The complement, the adverbial clause **by** **-ing**, is explicitly anticipated by the lexical item **way** in the subject which paraphrases its instrument meaning (see Winter, 1977, vocabulary 3). Thus we see that in this (unmarked) special operations clause the subject itself signals adverbial clause to come in its complement.

As already noted, this section will be devoted entirely to the adjunct functions of the adverbial clause and the problems of how sequence affects their contextual meanings.

Like the relative clause (with the items **who, whose, whom, which, when, where, why** and **that**) and noun clause (with items like **that** and **wh**-items such as **what, when, where, whether, why** and **how**), adverbial clauses are very easily recognised from their similarly finite, though much larger vocabulary. The well-known items are set out below:

> **after, (al)though, apart from** -ing, **as** (3), **as far as, as well as** -ing, **at the same time as, on the basis that, because, before, besides** -ing, **by the time that, by** -ing, **despite** -ing, **except that, far from** -ing, **from the moment that, given that, granted that, on the grounds that, however, if,** (as + if), (even + if), **in addition to** -ing, **in order to, in order that, in spite of** -ing, **in case, in the event that, instead of** -ing, **in as much as, no matter what/how,** etc., **now that, once, on condition that, provided that, rather than** -ing, **seeing that, short of** -ing, **since** (2), **so that** (2), **so . . . that, such that, so much so that, supposing that, unless, until, whatever, when, whenever, where, wherever, whereas, while** (2), **with the result that,** etc. (see Winter, 1977, pp. 14 – 15, and many others).

'Knowing' these subordinators, it is easy to parse them. We take the subordinator as our cue and expect to parse its clause as a self-contained structure. Its subordinator signals that its clause will do one of three things, depending upon which slot in the main clause its clause is taking. (i) In front-position, it will delay the start of its main clause structure; (ii) in mid-position, it will delay by interrupting the completion of the structure of its main clause; and (iii) in end-position, it will delay the completion of its main clause boundary.

Adjunct status for the adverbial clause means that the adverbial clause can take front-, mid- or end-position, but what is perhaps still not generally recognised even now is that the adverbial clause changes its contextual meaning according to which of these three positions it occupies in the main clause. Successful parsing must take these meanings into account. Unfortunately, there is still much work to be done on the contextual meanings of subordination, but it suffices for my present purposes to set out the 'state of the art' so far, where this knowledge will facilitate comprehension of meaning and parsing procedure. To simplify the problems of description, this is done in three stages of unequal size, with acknowledgments throughout where the limits of our present knowledge lie: (7.3) parsing front-position, (7.4) parsing end-position, and (7.5) parsing mid-position.

In Winter (1977, pp. 49–50), I noted that the meaning of adverbial clauses differs according to whether they are front- or end-position, but did not pursue the matter in any detail except to note that we could account for these differences of meaning according to whether the **wh**-question is used to elicit the adverbial clause or whether it is used to elicit the main clause. This section goes into more detail.

Front- and end-position are contrasted in respect of their contextual meaning in the same function of introducing a new (sub)topic and then seen in contrast with mid-position, which does not appear to share this function. Mid-position is interesting to us because it is seen as *interrupting* the structure of the main clause. Theoretically, the phenomenon of interrupting the clause is important as it affects the structure of the main clause. In studying the interruption of the clause, we are acutely aware of where the interruption takes place, so that we anticipate the grammatical completion of the remaining part of the main clause. Besides adverbial clauses which interrupt clause structure, there is the supra-adjunct-like function of interpolation in which the interpolating structure can interrupt the clause at any structural boundary whatever *including the usual slots for adverbial clause.* Much less is known about the whole phenomenon of interruption in the clause than is known about the simpler matter of front- and end-position. I accordingly concentrate more upon front- and end-position before tentatively taking up mid-position.

The key contextual notion in studying the relations between (independent) clauses in sequence lies in the (unbroken) relation of their topics and subtopics. Where two or more independent clauses are put together as 'belonging', they are closely related in topic and subtopic. Where a topic is being developed in a sequence of clauses, this may lead to a regular change in the subtopic. We are concerned in this study with a preliminary description of how in front- and end-position there are significant changes of contextual meaning for the topic which affect the meaning of the adverbial clause with respect to its main clause. We have already noted that one function of the adverbial clause is to indicate what is 'known' or 'given' for the audience or the reader. (See discussion of the independent clause **Mrs Thatcher is Prime Minister** and its subordinate clause form of **besides being Prime Minister** in 3.2.)

The reason for putting front- and end-position together is that they play an important role in the development of (sub)topic and its contextual meaning. To consider this we need to take the role of adverbial clause and its main clause in full contexts *where there are clauses preceding and clauses following it.* These clauses may be independent clauses or subordinated to independent clauses.

The key contextual point about the clause pair with adverbial subordination is that (a) there is a change of (sub)topic, and (b) this clause pair work together to change the contextual nature of the (sub)topic of the preceding clause(s), with the new (sub)topic being developed by the next immediate clause(s). The system appears to work from the first to the second clause irrespective of whether the first clause is adverbial or not.

If we use the symbol S for both topic and clause, subscript numbers to snow changes in (sub)topic, and brackets to show the grammatical boundary of the sentence of the clause pair, then reading from left to right, the first member concludes from or finalises the (sub)topic S_1 of the preceding clause(s), while the second member S_2 introduces the new (sub)topic, which is then developed by the next clause(s) of the next sentence(s):

$$\ldots S_1 \, S_1 \, (S_1 \longrightarrow S_2) \, S_2 \, S_2 \ldots$$

Our starting point is the observation that adverbial clause subordination means that there is a change of (sub)topic between the clause pair irrespective of the sequence between the main and the adverbial clause. However, changes of sequence for adverbial clause and its main clause means a change of contextual meaning for the development of (sub)topic. Part of this change of contextual meaning lies in the difference in contextual meaning between the grammatical status of independence and subordination. The practical significance of these changes of sequence for the members of the clause pair need to be explained. We now consider the changes of sequence from the vantage point of adverbial clause and its main clause in turn.

In front-position, the adverbial clause has a very strong tendency to refer back to the (sub)topic of the preceding clause(s), while in end-position it introduces a new (sub)topic which will then have a strong tendency to be developed by the next clause(s). In both cases the reference to (sub)topic is beyond the sentence boundary. As already noted, with this change from front- to end-position goes a change in contextual meaning for the adverbial clause. This change of meaning is shown by the change of **wh**-question: in front-position, the adverbial clause is part of the structure of the **wh**-clause which asks for the main clause information; in end-position, the main clause is part of the structure of the **wh**-clause which asks for the adverbial clause information.

Similar considerations apply to the role of the main clause. With its adverbial clause in front-position, it has a very strong tendency to refer forward to the development of its new (sub)topic in the next sentence(s). With its adverbial clause in end-position, it has a very strong tendency to refer backwards to the (sub)topic of the preceding clause(s). Again, as with the adverbial clause, there is a corresponding change of contextual meaning. In the subsections that follow, we examine the criteria used for determining the differences of contextual meaning for both adverbial clause and its main clause.

Before we can examine front-, mid- and end-position in any detail, we need to clarify the kind of descriptive apparatus we bring to the semantic description of the position of the adverbial clause.

7.2 The Descriptive Approach to the Analysis of Sequence for the Adverbial Clause, and its Limitations

7.2.1 Notions of 'Given' and 'New' Information

We have already noted that subordinate clause presents its information as in some way 'given' and that independent clause presents its information as 'new'. These two notions of information status, originating largely from the Prague School, have been much used over the past twenty years by people like M. A. K. Halliday, not merely in discussing made-up examples but in discussing where they are particularly important. Valuable as they are, something more specific is required for discussing the communicative role of adverbial clause and independent clause meanings.

These terms are used here to refer to the various states of knowledge being signalled by the clause as a whole rather than by individual items of the clause itself which we would take into account in a study of intonation. By 'states of knowledge' I mean the signalling as to what we do and what we do not know.

Taking the notion of 'given' as it applies to the adverbial clause, we note that it represents the following states of knowing something to be true: assumed known or already verbalised and hence known, and taken for granted (as true), which includes taking the very obvious for granted. Adverbial subordinators can signal 'that which is known to be an intrinsic part of the description of X'. (By this I mean that it is some distinguishing feature whereby we might identify X.) Let us take as our X teachers in their expected role as teachers (we ignore the point that professors don't profess and other such problems). We now consider the effect of reversing the sequence of the two nouns **nursemaids** and **teachers** by means of the adverbial subordinator **as well as** in (54) and (55) below.

(54) The teachers were complaining that they were expected to be **nursemaids as well as teachers**.

(55) The teachers were complaining that they were expected to be **teachers as well as nursemaids**.

In the underlined construction, one noun is subordinated to the other adverbially by **as well as**. In principle, the second noun is subordinated to the first in sequence so that the first noun presents the 'new' information and the second, subordinated, noun presents the 'known' or 'given'. If we accept that teachers by their very nature teach, then we accept the sequence in (54) but not in (55). In a context where (55) would be true, it means that teachers have changed their intrinsic roles from teaching to nursemaiding, with teaching being presented as 'new'. However, if we re-present (55) as (56) below, by using the co-ordinator **and** which paraphrases the compatibility meaning of the subordinator **as well as**, we have no problem about the intrinsic nature of X:

(56) The teachers were complaining that they were expected to be **teachers and nursemaids**.

Here we have the option of stressing 'and nursemaids' in speech to indicate its new information in the co-ordination of this particular context. This example sums up in principle the contextual difference between subordination (**as well as**) and co-ordination (**and**): in co-ordination both items are presented as being informationally equal; that is, both items are 'new' or both are 'given'. With subordination, the information status of the two items is unequal; that is, the one is 'given' and the other is 'new', with the 'given' reflecting the contextual significance of the item. This is the information model which we bring to an examination of the well-known paraphrase relation between the co-ordinator **but** and the subordinator **although** at 7.4.3.

Adverbial clause signals a conviction on the part of the encoder as to the knownness or taken-for-grantedness of the information of the clause in the particular meaning of the subordinator as it relates to the 'not hitherto assumed known' or 'not hitherto verbalised' information of the independent (main) clause. Put in simpler terms, if you use adverbial clause to signal something to be taken for granted as true, this signals your conviction about how true you take the information to be. What adverbial clause is doing is to communicate as a whole the known or hitherto verbalised for the main clause's new information.

There are complications to this notion of subordination as 'already known' or 'taken for granted as true' below, when we come to the interaction of 'known' and 'not assumed known' in the communicative function of the clause pair. One of the complications is the existence of independent clause statements on their own, aphorisms or truisms, for example 'Man is mortal.' Why are these not always presented as subordinate clauses if they are so well known? We take up this question with independent clause below.

We now take up the notion of 'new' as it applies to the description of independent clause here. 'New' represents the new information of independent clause; that is, 'not assumed known' or 'not previously verbalised in the present form of the clause'. (This is the meaning exploited in the clause connector **in other words**). Here we can treat both meanings linguistically as 'not hitherto verbalised in this unique form of the clause'.

There are two problems in this approach to the grammatical status of independent clause. The first is that independent clause has to have its own balance of 'given' and 'new' items in which the 'given' are used to communicate the 'new'. This would correspond with stress in the spoken language. (See Halliday, 1967, pp. 206–44.) 'Given' items are what have to be given with the clause regardless of its semantics, and this is the repetition of the already known participants in the action, state or description. This point is noted when we consider how we use the **wh**-question to realise the main clause; the 'given' parts of this main clause will be part of the main clause of the question; for example the participants **he** and **her** are specified for some kind of transitive verb reply for the **wh**-question '**What did** he **do to** her when he saw her?' The parts in bold show what is 'known' in the question; note the **when**-clause in particular. What is already presupposed is that some kind of directed action had taken place when he saw her, and we now wish to know what this action is.

The second problem is that if independent clause always means 'not hitherto assumed known or verbalised', how do we treat such aphorisms as 'man is mortal', the truth of which nobody disputes? The obvious answer is that we don't normally use these sentences to communicate with; they are specialised uses. We recognise from its single sentence context that it is a fossilised truth; but, more important, how would we store this truth if we did not use its independent clause form? It couldn't be subordinated because it would have to be tied to a main clause. There is, however, an important point about these sayings and this is that they often have the special role of pointing a moral or evaluating other 'not hitherto assumed known' independent clauses. That is to say, their creativity as clauses lies in the clauses which they comment upon, for example

(57) He had hoped to live beyond a 100. He died, still hale and hearty, in a car accident at 96. Alas, man is but mortal after all.

Notice that the clause is in use and thus communicates in terms of the preceding clauses. In particular note the new information of the evaluative **Alas** which emotively comments on both clauses, the clause connector **after all** signalling a taken-for-granted reason for dying, and the non-coordinator item, the limiter **but**, signalling the reaffirmation as true in actual use.

7.2.2 The Signalling Bias of Independent Clause/Subordinate Clause

We now bring together the 'assumed known' and 'not assumed known' of the adverbial clause and the independent clause and ask what they signify of the communicative role of (independent) clause. Is it enough to say that they represent the communicative principle in which we communicate the unknown of the independent clause in terms of what is known in the adverbial clause? The answer is that, crucial as this principle must be to the grammar of the clause, it is not enough to account for their joint signalling roles *as part of the larger signalling whole*. This is simple enough: taking the examples of the clause **he died last night** below, we note that unless otherwise signalled as hypothetical (as in 60) or indefinite (59) we take the signals of grammatical status for both independent clause and subordinate clause as presenting their information on trust as true in the sense of the signalling of their clauses.

To illustrate this point, we note the unmarked signalling role of independent finite clause in (58), the signalling by modal verb of (59), and the various kinds of signalling by matrix clause in (60), (61) and (62), where the lexical items **think, know** and **true** interpret the noun clause **he died last night**.

(58)   He died last night.

(59)   He **may have** died last night.

(60)   **I think** he died last night.

(61)   **I know** he died last night.

(62)   **It is true that** he died last night.

In (58), the simple past tense presents the events in its clause as an accomplished 'fact'; the implied source of the statement is the encoder. Such a clause represents an answer to a **wh**-question something like 'What do you **know** about him in last night's events?' I call the answer to such a question a 'know' clause. This distinguishes it from the 'think' clauses of (59) and (60). In (59), the modal verb **may have** signals that this is a 'think' clause. It presupposes a previous knowledge of the clause. Evidence for this would be how it arises as answer to a yes/no-question: 'Did he die last night?' The clause **he may have died last night** is not a direct answer, but presupposes the following preamble reply:' I don't know; he may have (died last night).' The first clause **I don't know** makes explicit that you can't reply **yes** or **no** because you do not have the knowledge; the second clause **he may have** could be represented as an answer to a **wh**-question: 'Well, what do you **think** happened last night?' In the examples (60), (61) and (62), the noun clause **he died last night** presupposes a previous verbalisation of the clause **he died last night**, but the interpretations of its context differs for each matrix clause.

In (60), the subject and verb of the matrix clause signal the encoder and what interpretation he puts on the noun clause: **I think**. This signals that the clause is hypothetical. This is an explicit 'think' clause. In (61), the subject and verb likewise signals 'real' or 'fact' for the noun clause. This is an explicit 'know' clause, for which (58) is its unmarked form. Finally, in (62), the matrix clause **It is true that**-clause confirms that the clause has already been verbalised as independent clause in the form of (58); it is an explicit comment on this clause as its topic. The **yes/no**-question would make this explicit: 'Is it true that he died last night? This matrix clause is the marked statement as true; that is, we are not relying on positive and affirmative clause to signal this in the unmarked form **he died last night**, but 'say so' ourselves. (See Winter, 1974, p. 288.)

7.2.3 Presupposition and Prediction

We use the term presupposition to consider the relation of the independent clause of the clause pair with the topic of the preceding clause(s). Presupposition goes with the meaning of independent clause grammar; it means 'not hitherto verbalised as a unique clause in the preceding text'. This difference of approach requires some explanation. As is well known, the term presupposition has been much used in linguistics recently to talk about a plausible context for the typical made-up sentences of transformational generative grammar linguistics, as in Keenan (1971, pp. 45–52). Such sentences, being made-up, are not merely without their all-important context of adjoining sentences, but are also without much of the normal contextual cues. For instance, the sentence connector **therefore** of the clause **They are therefore worth a passing thought** is a signal that the preceding sentence provides a basis for this conclusion.

I also use presupposition as a device of linguistic speculation, but with the following differences. I distinguish between two notions of presupposition. The first is *textual* and the second is *pragmatic*. Textual presupposition is used to speculate on the most likely preceding sentence(s) for your sentence in context. This might coincide with its real world presupposition. In pragmatic presupposition, we speculate about the real-world knowledge which we use to account for the meaning of our sentence in context, as in **Mr**

Dhladhla is refused entry into Britain. From the name Dhladhla, we presuppose that he must be an African (Zulu) because the name sounds like African names we know. In our discussions about clauses here, we are concerned with whether it has been predicted or previously verbalised in some form, in the preceding text or outside of it, or whether it is a truism in the real world, for example 'Teachers teach', 'Man is mortal', etc. Whatever way we use the notion of pre-supposition, it must be used to account for the clause in its (written) context, especially its preceding context.

Presuppositions are found by asking of each independent clause what question would elicit it. Ideally, the information in the question should match the semantic content of the preceding sentence. When we look ahead of our clause at the immediately succeeding clause(s) in its paragraph, we speak of *prediction* for what the present clause pair presupposes as the relevant development of its new topic. Thus, it will be seen that presupposition is speculating backwards and prediction is speculating forwards.

In discussing presupposition of the main clause and the backward reference of the adverbial clause, we are concerned with the notion of topic and the meaning of topic as this is expressed in the relation between the clauses. Topic must be distinguished from the notion of participant. Participants are the doers, the undergoers, the described, etc.; they are 'given' to any clause in the sense that they are obligatorily mentioned in the clause; they are also obligatory repetitions in the clause in order to maintain the connection between clause and clause. They are normally the names, the things, actions, states, etc., which are talked about as subject, object, complement and 'object' of the preposition (She talked to **the girl**). They answer the item questions '**Who** or **What** did it? **Which** one do you mean?', etc.

Topic is what the participant is doing, having done to him by others, etc.; that is, topic is what is predicated by the verb of the participant in relation to other participants or things. Topic is the answer to questions about the role of the participant(s): 'What is he doing? What is he doing about it? How does he feel about it?' We return to both topic and participant throughout this book. What I have said here suffices for the purpose of discussion.

7.2.4 *Member, Completion and Clause Relation*

In this subsection, we are concerned with the semantic relations between clauses and groups of clauses, or sentences and groups of sentences. By semantic relation, I mean the relation of the meaning of a clause as a semantic whole with that of another clause as a semantic whole. In studying clause relations, the important notion is that of *member* (Quirk, 1954, p. 6). A member is the unit of clause or group of clauses which is in a binary relation with another member. The semantics of membership is called clause relations (Winter, 1971, 1974, 1977 and 1981).

A clause relation is where we have the semantics of the one member completed by the semantics of another member. Let us consider the relation of *reason* and *result* or *consequence*, taking (49) as our example, and rewriting it so as to remove the special operations clause structure **This is because**. We start with the relation which holds between the two clauses as if they were independent clauses in (63) below:

(63) They stay in their cells for most of the day as well as the night. There is nowhere else for them to go, and still be under supervision.

We can relate the two clauses by showing that the second clause is an answer to a **wh**-question on the first: 'Why do they stay in their cells for most of the day, etc.?' This question asks for a *reason* for what is happening in the first clause. In (63), both clauses are presented as 'new' to the reader. However, if we now join the two clauses together grammatically by subordinating the second clause to the first as an answer to the **why**-question, we have (64):

(64) They stay in their cells for most of the day as well as the night **because** there is nowhere for them to go, and still be under supervision.

The linguistic point of interest to us in this book is that (64) is not the same as (63) in contextual meaning. In the first place, there is no explicit sign of *reason* in (63); the reason notion has to be inferred as part of the clause relation; that is, as to how the second clause is completing the meaning of the first clause. In the second place, the two clauses of (63) are independent clauses while the clause pair of (64) has an independent main clause and an adverbial subordinate clause. We cannot ignore the adverbial subordination of the second clause of (64). The contextual point is that the adverbial clause is part of the grammar of its main clause, so that for the purposes of production we take the main clause as given for the **why**-question 'Why do **they stay in their cells for most of the day**, etc.?' In contrast, we could regard the production of the two clauses in sequence in (63) as answers to two separated **wh**-questions in turn: '**Where** do they stay (in prison) and for **how** long each day?' followed by the next question, '**Why** do they stay there for so long?'

The relation of reason belongs to the logical sequence relation (see Winter, 1971, 1974, 1977 and 1979). This is a general term for clauses which are sequentially related by the semantics of a deductive reasoning which implies the logic of time sequence or by time sequence itself. In logical sequence the meaning of the sequence itself is crucial to identifying the relation. Thus, in (63), we have to infer an inductive reasoning relation for the second clause in the light of the meaning of the first clause. In everyday logical terms, the second clause does not follow from the sense of the first as it does when we reverse the sequence of the two clauses as in (65) below.

(65)   There is nowhere else for them to go, and still be under supervision. They stay in their cells for most of the day as well as the night.

Looking at how the second clause follows from the first clause, we can say that it is a *consequence* or a *result* of what is happening to them in the first clause. However, it is not as explicit as it is in (66), where we express this notion by means of the sentence connector **so** or **consequently**:

(66)   There is nowhere else for them to go, and still be under supervision. **Consequently**, they stay in their cells for most of the day as well as the night.

The significance of saying that sequence is crucial to the meaning of the logical sequence relation can be seen in how the sequence of the two clauses in (63) and (65) is connected. We can use the matrix of the special operations clause **This is because** X to fit the sequence of (63), but not of (65). Similarly, we can use the sentence connector **consequently** or **so** to fit the sequence of (65), but not of (63). It should be noted that each of the grammatical paraphrases of *reason* and *result* here imply different contexts.

In contrast with logical sequence, the matching relation (see Winter 1971, 1974, 1977 and 1979) does not impose a logic of sequence upon its members other than that of the logic of comparison. In the matching relation, we are concerned with a matching or comparing of people, things, attributes, actions, states, descriptions, etc. Consider the following pair of clauses of the uncoordinated clause pair in (67) below. This is a relation of matching by contrast.

(67)   Spinsters have been regarded with pity, celibates with total incomprehension.

The following linguistic features of the matching relation should be noted.

(1)   This is a comparison of the attitudes towards spinsters and

celibates. We could presuppose it as the answer to the following questioning: How does this society regard its spinsters and its celibates? Do they have the same attitude to both of them? No, they differ in their attitudes.

(2)   Notice that the second clause repeats the verbal part of the predicate but replaces the prepositional 'object' **pity** with the nominal group **total incomprehension**. This replacement is a function of the repeated clause structure X **have been regarded with** Y. (See 'Replacement' in Winter, 1974 and 1979). We can show that the repeated part of the verb predicate has been deleted by reinstating the deletions in (68) below.

(68)   Spinsters have been regarded with pity; celibates **have been regarded** with total incomprehension.

This is the marked form for which (67) is the unmarked.

If we take this clause pair, we can further show the matching relation by the criterion of questions. Taking the first clause, we ask the following **yes/no**-question: 'Have celibates been seen in the same light (as spinsters)?' **No**, they have been regarded with total incomprehension. If we reversed the clauses of (68), we still ask the same kind of question: 'Have spinsters been seen in the same light (as celibates)?' = No.

If we take the replacement of **pity** by **total incomprehension** as contrastive in the sense that pity implies some kind of understanding or comprehension, then we could subordinate whichever of the two clauses we wish to present as 'given' by means of the subordinator **whereas** as in (69) below.

(69)   **Whereas** spinsters have been regarded with pity, celibates have been regarded with total incomprehension.

This subordinator paraphrases the replacement meaning between the two clauses which is summed up by the special operations matrix clause: What is true of the attitude to spinsters is not true of the attitude to celibates. Thus we see in these clauses a matching of what is true.

In our discussion of adverbial clause placement that follows, we are concerned with the logical sequence relation and the matching relation and with the multiple relation which is composed of logical sequence and matching, traditionally called the concessive relation. The semantics of concession can be seen in the paraphrase relation between the subordinator **although** and the sentence connector **yet**. We have already noted the larger clause relations of situation and evaluation and hypothetical and real. The logical sequence and the matching relation may be components of these larger clause relations.

7.2.5   *Difficulties of Description with Front- and End-Position*

There are four closely related difficulties of describing front- and end-position. The first is the nature of the adverbial clause and its main clause as they refer back to the topic of the preceding clause(s). The key difference is the difference in contextual semantics between adverbial clause and main clause according to sequence. We cannot avoid this difficult area and must try to get to grips with it. The second difficulty is our very great ignorance of what adverbial subordinators mean contextually; the item semantics seems simple enough. There is an abysmal chasm between our passive knowledge and our active knowledge here. To pursue this matter of contextual meaning in principle, I have tried to analyse one particular subordinator in greater detail than the others; this is the **although**-clause in both front- and end-position. The third difficulty is the difficulty of eliciting certain kinds of adverbial clause by means of **wh**-questions – the **although**-clause with its sentence connector paraphrases by **yet, in spite of this, nevertheless,** etc. This is presumably related to the fact that a subordinator like **although** cannot be made the focus of a cleft sentence. Accordingly, the focus of description in end-position is on this particular subordinator, where its contextual semantics are compared with that of the co-ordinator **but** in a criticism of the traditional idea that they are in a paraphrase relation for the same clause pair. Crucial to this criticism is the notion of 'assumed known' versus 'not hitherto assumed known or verbalised' set against the attitudinal notion of *surprise.*

The fourth difficulty is working out what is presupposed by the topic of the preceding clause(s). Whether the adverbial clause is in front- or in end-position, the main clause is still presupposed by the topic of the preceding clause(s) as a development of its topic. In front-position, we use the adverbial clause as part of our question to elicit the presupposed main clause, with the main clause as the dominant meaning; in end-position, we use the presupposed main clause as part of our question to elicit the adverbial clause in reply, with the adverbial clause as the dominant meaning.

Finally, one danger of using question criteria has to be taken into account. This is that question criteria depend on how well we comprehend the meaning of both the clauses of the clause pair under discussion, and their adjoining context of clauses. In turn this depends on how well we know and understand the topic being developed, which includes our real-world knowledge and experience.

7.3 The Adverbial Clause in Front-Position

7.3.1 Introduction

The main contextual feature that distinguishes adverbial clauses in front-position is their very strong tendency to refer backwards to the topic of the immediately preceding clause(s). The nature of this reference backwards can be seen in the nature of the **wh**-question which elicits its main clause. The adverbial clause is marked as 'known because already verbalised or taken for granted'. It also marks the encoder's conviction that the relevant development of the preceding topic has reached its end for the purpose of his communication. It takes the shared information and evaluates its significance in terms of the particular adverbial subordinator used. The subsequent main clause introduces new information in the context of this evaluation.

7.3.2 Examples of Adverbial Clause in Front-Position

We now consider examples of the use of the subordinators **because, when, although, since, besides** -ing, and **if**.

In (70A) below, the **because**-clause is in front-position in sentence 4. We incorporate the information of the adverbial clause within the **wh**-question which we use to elicit the information of the main clause as our reply: 'How does the conclusion that **there appears to be no sense in the hierarchy of salaries** affect the attitudes of the (lowest paid) workers?' Notice that the given information of the main clause part of the question represents the presupposition by the preceding topic that the attitudes of the lowest paid workers is to be made known.

> (70A) (1) There is a still deeper reason for salariat resentment. (2) This is the absence of any apparent logic in the whole salary structure. (3) The man earning a salary tends to compare himself with other white-collar workers – with the result that the great yawning gaps between the lowest and the highest paid cause considerable jealousies. (4) **Because there appears to be no sense in the hierarchy of salaries**, there is a feeling of injustice. (*Observer*, Week-End Review, 4 December 1966, p. 21)

There are four points to be noted about the preceding context of three sentences for sentence 4:

(i) The information of the **because**-clause closely paraphrases and thus repeats sentence 2; that is, the phrase the **absence of apparent logic in X** exactly parallels the phrase **appears to be no sense in X**. Note in this paraphrase that **logic = sense**, and **salary structure = hierarchy of salaries**.

(ii) Notice that sentence 4 and particularly its main clause **there is a feeling of injustice** is predicted in the signalling grammar of sentence 1. Here the grammar of existential **there is**-clause signals that the next sentences will identify a still deeper reason for salariat resentment. As an unspecific clause, it requires lexical realisation by specific clause(s). Sentence 2 supplies an evaluative generalisation which is still unspecific and so the specific clause is still to come. Sentence 3 supplies the specific clause required; it answers a complex **wh**-question: 'What does absence of logic mean in this context? Explain by an example!' or 'Can you give me an example of what you mean by absence of logic in this context?'

(iii) Notice that the last sentence in this paragraph, sentence 4, is a conclusion drawn from sentence 3 as mediated by the **because**-clause. Sentence 3 is an evaluation of the problem which results when the man earning a salary compares himself with other salaried workers.

(iv) The use of **because**-clause for repeating, with slight change, the general statement of sentence 2 shows that the writer is confident that sentence 3 has fully justified sentence 2. The slightly changed generalisation of sentence 2 is presented as a confident conclusion that can be taken for granted. The change of clause-structure to **there appears to be X** confirms that the still deeper reason for salariat resentment has now been identified. The important point is that the main clause is presented as a conclusion to be drawn from the information of this **because**-clause. The essence of salariat resentment turns out to be a feeling of injustice.

If we now rewrite the above clause pair as (70B) below, using the same preceding context, the effect of changing to end-position is easier to study.

(70B)   (1) There is a still deeper reason for salariat resentment. (2) This is the absence of any apparent logic in the whole salary structure. (3) The man earning a salary tends to compare himself with other white-collar workers — with the result that the great yawning gaps between the lowest and the highest paid cause considerable jealousies. (4) There is a feeling of injustice, **because there appears to be no sense in the hierarchy of salaries**.

Following the rule about end-position, we now incorporate the main clause within our **wh**-question clause in order to elicit the information of the **because**-clause: 'Why is there a feeling of injustice (in the lowest paid)?' This is a strange question to be asking since the main clause could be concluded to follow from sentences 2 and 3; we already know *why* by the time we come to sentence 4, but this is not made explicit until we see the **because**-item of the **because**-clause which repeats the substance of sentence 2 as a new conclusion to be drawn from sentence

3. Clearly end-position will not do in this context.

So far we have considered a clause pair where the main clause is not followed by further sentences in its paragraph. We now consider a clause pair which has both the preceding and the succeeding clauses to which the clause pair refers in its paragraph. We note how the new topic of its main clause is developed by the sentences which follow, and we note how the backward reference of the **when**-clause and the forward reference of its main clause is impeded when we reverse the clause pair so that the adverbial clause is in end-position.

In (71A) below, the **when**-clause is in front-position where it introduces an example of 'other ways in which aggression is expressed' – the term 'aggressive salesmen'. Notice how we incorporate the **when**-clause into the **wh**-question clause which we use to elicit the information of its main clause. Notice how the main clause presupposes that business firms must have some kind of attitude to the kind of man they employ: 'What can we conclude about the kind of man whom the advertiser is seeking **when business firms advertise for "aggressive salesmen"**?'

(71A)   (1) The preceding paragraphs equate aggression with violence. (2) It may be argued that much 'aggression' is expressed in other ways. (3) **When a business firm advertises for 'aggressive salesmen'**, the advertiser is not, presumably, seeking men eager for unarmed combat. (4) There is, in fact, a shift of meaning here. (5) One needs to distinguish between animosity, on the one hand, and dominance (in the everyday sense) on the other . . . (*New Scientist*, 28 May 1966, p. 539)

There are five points to be noted about the backward reference of the **when**-clause and the forward reference of its main clause in their role of changing the (sub)topic.

(i) Note that the **when**-clause is playing the role of the specific clause for which the preceding clause is its unspecific clause. This firmly ties them in their topic connection.

(ii) Note that the **when**-clause is not a time adverbial here but expresses a situation. This meaning for the **when**-item can be shown in its possibility of a paraphrase which incorporates the item **situation** in it, as in **in situations where** a business firm advertises for 'aggressive salesmen', etc.

(iii) Note the deductive relation signalled by the lexical item **conclude** in the main clause of the **wh**-question and by the evaluative adverbial item **presumably** in the main clause itself.

(iv) Note how the denial in the main clause implies a shift in meaning from unarmed combat to something else. This is the change of topic.

(v) Notice how sentence 4 as the basis for the denial in the main clause of sentence 3 now picks up its implicit topic of a shift in meaning and makes it explicit. Note the presence of the adverbial adjunct **in fact** as a mark of basis or real.

If we reverse the clause pair as in (71B) below, we see that the end-position for the **when**-clause means that the main clause now impedes its backward reference to the preceding topic of the unspecific clause for which it offers specific clause, and the **when**-clause itself impedes the forward reference of the main clause to the development of its new topic 'shift of meaning' in sentence 4.

> (71B)   (1) The preceding paragraphs equate aggression with violence. (2) It may be argued that much 'aggression' is expressed in other ways. (3) The advertiser is not, presumably, seeking men eager for unarmed combat **when business firms advertise for 'agressive salesmen'**. (4) There is, in fact, a shift of meaning here. (5) One needs to distinguish between animosity, on the one hand, and dominance, on the other.

We note that the **when**-clause now in end-position appears to be elicited by the **wh**-question which incorporates as its 'given' the main clause 'In what circumstances is the advertiser presumably not seeking men eager for unarmed combat?' Clearly, this sequence does not fit the context here, nor does the meaning implied by the **wh**-question.

In the next examples from (72) to (75), we no longer reverse the clause pairs as part of our methodology of discussion since the principle of reversal seems clearly established. Readers are invited to experiment with reversing the examples for themselves. We continue a detailed study of the backwards reference of the adverbial clause, the introduction of new (sub)topic in the main clause, and the forward reference of the main clause into the next sentences.

So far we have had an easy ride with the subordinators **because** and **when**. These subordinators can have their clause as the focus of a cleft clause. However, clauses with the subordinator (al)**though** and other subordinators – **besides** -ing, **whereas**, **since** (indicating reason) – cannot be the focus of a cleft clause. It is beyond the scope of the present work to speculate why this might be. All we are interested in here is our special difficulty at this stage of our knowledge in eliciting the information of the main clause. Unlike the use of **when**-clause in our last example, we cannot use the subordinator **although** in our **wh**-question to elicit the main clause. Even greater difficulty arises when we come to the end-position for the **although**-clause. The solution to both problems is that we try to paraphrase the clause relational meaning of the **although**-item in some way.

In (72) below, we see the **although**-clause and the **since**-clause in front-position. This text is from an article about progress in the use of computers at the time of publication. The problem referred to is the problem of being able to talk to the computer in our own language.

Missing Rules

(72) Once again the problem looks much less formidable than it did a few years ago. Much of this advance is due to the work of a linguist Noam Chomsky, working at the Massachusetts Institute of Technology. Chomsky is attempting to discover a finite set of formal rules which will generate any grammatical sentence. **Although most of us are unaware of these rules**, they must be represented in our own brains. Otherwise we would be unable to speak our own language or to understand it when we heard it spoken. **Since Chomsky's rules are well defined and do not depend on intuition for understanding**, it is possible to programme a machine to act in accordance with these rules. (*Observer*, 9 April 1967, p. 21)

The **although**-clause picks up the notion of **a finite set of formal rules** and states what could have been derived from reading Chomsky, namely the 'fact' that we are not aware of these rules. The **although** clause expresses this 'fact' as a conviction whose main clause denies the following conclusion, made explicit by the clause connector **therefore**:

Most of us are **un**aware of these rules. They must **therefore not** be represented in our own brains. (See Winter, 1974, p. 170)

Next, the **since**-clause signals *the writer's conviction as true* of his own evaluation that Chomsky's rules are well defined and do not depend on intuition for understanding. Again, this conviction could be derived from Chomsky as Chomsky's own conviction of the worth of his rules. The question which the main clause seems to be answering is one of application of Chomsky's principles: 'Given the fact that Chomsky's rules are well defined and do not depend on intuition for understanding, is it possible to programme a machine to act in accordance with these rules?' The main clause represents the **yes**-answer to a **yes/no**-question. This change of subtopic from Chomsky's principles to their possible application is further developed by the next sentences of the paragraph, which is given in full below as (73).

In (73) we consider the reference backwards of the **although**-clause in front-position of a clause pair which evaluates the preceding computer programme.

(73) Several programmes have already been written that enable a computer to accept a typed input in natural language and to give appropriate answers. For example, a computer has been fed with

detailed information on baseball games played in the American League, and with a rudimentary grammar for construing simple English sentences about baseball. The computer will 'understand' and answer such questions as 'How many games did the Yankees play in July?' 'What teams played at Boston in June?' **Although the subject-matter may appear trivial**, much information about programming was gleaned from this exercise.

We could view the last sentence as answering a question for the evaluation of the computer exercise: 'Was anything useful gained from this apparently trivial exercise?' In replying to this question, the writer is forced to concede the obvious objection before countering it with the positive side of the results. The **although**-clause signals the writer's conviction that his readers could object to the apparently triviality of the subject. The clause signals that its main clause will counter this objection in some way that denies the triviality. As such, the main clause is the anticipated denial to a question something like this: 'Doesn't it follow from the apparently trivial subject matter that little information was gleaned from this exercise?' = 'No, much information, etc., was gleaned from it.' The point is that the **although**-clause signals a conviction that the subject matter was not as trivial as it appeared. The modal verb **may** is not a signal of tentativeness here, but a signal which disputes something as being considered true.

So far we have considered examples of front-position where the adverbial clause made clear reference to the preceding topic and concluded from it as well as concluding it. Another possibility is that where there is no apparent reference to a preceding topic the subordinate clause could present information which is true or known to the reader. By known, we mean that the clause could be repeating a particular clause from the larger context. Repeating a clause is synonymous with it being true in that it has prior existence as a clause. In (74) below, the **besides** -ing clause repeats what the readers of *The Times* would know from its news reporting, namely that the Russians had indeed replaced 80 to 90 per cent of Egyptian aircraft losses in the June War with Israel.

(74) It is believed that the capacity for survival of Egypt's air force is being improved by some of the following actions:

Installation of improved air defence missiles in Egypt and improved early warning radar in Egypt, Syria and Iraq.

Thousands of Soviet advisers and technicians are said to be deployed, drilling the local military on how to operate and maintain radar and other key systems. 'Before the June debacle the Egyptians were proud of how they ignored Russian advice,' said one diplomatic official. 'Now they listen attentively.'

Besides replacing 80 to 90 per cent of Egyptian aircraft losses,

the Russians earlier this month flew in 10 TU-16 twin-jet bombers for a goodwill visit. Some observers expect that the Russians, by their presence at unknown Egyptian bases, hope to inhibit an Israel strike in some future tense period for fear of hitting and involving them. (Guard against surprise air attack', *The Times*, 29 December 1967, p. 3)

There are three points to be noted about the **besides**-ing clause.

(i) There is no prior mention in the text of the Russians replacing Egyptian aircraft losses. This had already been done by the time the article was written and had been well reported so that the readers of the newspaper would know about it.

(ii) The **wh**-question incorporates this knowledge by means of the **besides**-ing clause as the given or known part of its question: 'What else have the Russians done for the Egyptians earlier this month **besides replacing 80 to 90 per cent of their aircraft losses?**'

(iii) Both the **besides**-ing clause and its main clause are compatible with the preceding paragraph as instances of Russian help, so that the front-position of the **besides** -ing points in the direction of the preceding paragraph as being a development of the topic of Russian help.

A common function of adverbial clause in front-position is to repeat the preceding clause, either lexically or by substitute clause. This preserves the carrying over of the topic status of the preceding clause. One function of repeating the preceding clause is to hypothesise about it. In (75) below, the **if**-clause substitute presents a negative hypothesis for the preceding clause, with its main clause presenting the *consequence* as a development of new topic.

(75) MINISTERS are not always unanimous in their decisions. But under the principle of Cabinet responsibility, while they may agree to differ inside No. 10 they present a united front in public. **If any one of them cannot do so**, he resigns,
    MR COUSINS had every right to be at the Conference. But his mere presence among former colleagues so fiercely opposed to present ones who govern the country surely reflects his own views. (*Daily Mail*, 1 October 1975, p. 1)

There are two points to be noted. First, the main clause answers the following **wh**-question: 'What happens **if any one of them cannot do so?**' The simple present tense of the main clause's verb **resigns** presents the clause as true in general. Secondly, we cannot reverse the clause pair if only because of the pronoun **he** whose reference is to **one of them** in the preceding **if**-clause.

7.3.3 *Summary and Conclusions about Front-Position*

In discussing front-position, we were largely concerned with the semantics of back reference of the adverbial clause and the role it played in providing the logical basis for the question which elicited its presupposed main clause. In all cases, we had to look for what presupposed the elements of the main clause in the **wh**-question itself as this had to indicate the nature of the information to be made known by the main clause in conjunction with the adverbial clause element. It was the adverbial clause which determined the nature of the answer in the main clause by concluding from the preceding topic.

Some of the presuppositions which the adverbial clause determined for the main clause are sketched as follows: that salaried workers have a particular (hostile) attitude to salary hierarchies, in (70A); that business firms have a particular attitude to the men they employ, in (71A); that computer programmes are expected to yield useful information, in (73); the **besides** -ing clause presupposes that the change in topic will be another instance of Russian help in the form of aircraft support, in (74); the response expected from a minister as this is determined by a negative hypothesis of the preceding topic, in (75). Readers could probably develop this description of presuppositions further.

We noted that the backward reference of the adverbial clause worked by the following means:

(i) By directly repeating a preceding clause in various ways, as in (70A) by lexical paraphrase repetition, and in (75) by substitute clause. By repeating the clauses, we were re-using their unique verbalisations as 'knowns' to communicate the new information of their new clauses.

(ii) By presenting as 'known' something which is related to the preceding topic but not directly mentioned in the text, for example the Russian help in replacing Egyptian aircraft losses in (74).

(iii) By hypothesising about a preceding clause, as in (75) where the **if**-clause repeats the preceding clause as a negative hypothesis whose consequence is stated in the main clause.

(iv) By conceding as a conviction as true from a text outside the present extract, for example the **although**-clause which refers to writings by Chomsky in (72), and by presenting as a conviction the basis for a conclusion in its main clause, for example the **since**-clause in (72).

(v) By conceding an obvious or taken-for-granted objection by the reader as part of an evaluation of a preceding experiment, for example the **although**-clause of (73). This is outside the preceding text and represents the encoder's anticipation of an obvious objection.

The point of interest about adverbial clause in front-position is in its contextual meaning as clause. We have noted that it represents a conviction about what is already known or verbalised in the text or outside it, but the obvious question which we have so far ignored is this: what new information does the adverbial clause give if we insist that every clause has to have its own balance of given and new information, however low-level it may be? What new information is given with adverbial clause in front-position?

There are two kinds of new information which go with subordination. The first is the particular contextual meaning for the clause – **because, if, since**, etc. The second is the information which we have been describing as a conviction about the preceding topic. The new information is the evaluation by subordinate clause of the preceding topic. It is an evaluation of the stage of development of the preceding topic in that it represents a decision as to how to end or to conclude on it. We have noted that the adverbial clause in front-position mediates between its main clause, which is to introduce the change of topic for the topic of the preceding clause(s). What we are saying is that this 'mediation' is an evaluation of the relevance of the preceding topic in subordination terms. As evaluation, it represents the new information of subordination.

The semantic dominance of the main clause in end-position is a function of its introducing a change of the topic which it offers for development by the next immediate clause(s). We noted in (71A), (72) and (74) that the changes of topic in the main clause were continued by the next clause(s) of the paragraph. The point that needs to be made strongly is that end-position for the main clause does not mean that its new topic has to be developed; only that its new topic is the most likely topic to be developed if the paragraph is to be continued.

Finally, we noted in (70) and (71) in particular that if we reversed the clause pairs they could no longer fit the context. The same is true for the remaining examples.

We next consider end-position, which in principle will be the same as front-position. Both front- and end-position are brought together in the subsection 7.4.3.2, 'Paraphrases and change of sequence' where we look at how changes of subordination and sequence for the same clause pair affects their contextual meanings.

7.4 The Adverbial Clause in End-Position

7.4.1 Introduction

When an adverbial clause occurs after the main clause itself has been grammatically completed, the initiating subordinator of the adverbial clause warns us of two things: (i) that the final boundary of the sentence will be delayed by the structure of its clause, and (ii) that when the structure of its clause is complete, its particular clause meaning will complete the contextual unit meaning of its main clause with the other main clauses in the context. With the adverbial clause in end-position, we lose the grammatical anticipation of the main clause because it is now the main clause which leads the clause pair. We also lose the evaluation of the preceding topic; instead, we gain anticipation of the next sentence's topic, where the topic is continued.

The loss of grammatical anticipation by subordinator is to some extent compensated for by semantic anticipation of the next clause relation. The main clause now in front-position may have semantic features whose items may predict the particular relation for its adverbial clause in end-position *if that relation has not already preceded the main clause* (see Winter, 1974, pp. 525–8). For instance, the lexical verb **discover** predicts the instrument question **how?** in (76); the modal verb **could** in its possibility meaning in the special operations clause **This could happen** predicts the question **Under what condition(s)?** in (77); the modal verb **could** in its ability meaning in the clause **X could do a great deal to make Y easier** predicts the instrument question **how?** in (78). A parsing which anticipates the adverbial clause needs to know about this kind of anticipatory semantics in the main clause.

In end-position, the reference and the topic roles of the clause pair are reversed from what they were in front-position. Now it is the main clause which refers back to the topic of the preceding clause(s), while it is the adverbial clause which introduces a change of topic and has a strong tendency to refer forwards to the next clause(s) of the paragraph for further development as new information. The important feature of this sequence is that the change of topic now has the grammatical status of adverbial clause. This means that it presents *as new information* its conviction of its clause as 'already known' or 'taken for granted as true'. The main clause still presents its clause as 'not hitherto known or verbalised', but it is now concluding upon or concluding the topic of the preceding clause(s). It is still presupposed by the topic of its preceding clause(s), but now has to be reconciled with its adverbial clause which in end-position may still be referring backwards in spite of signalling forwards. Here the adverbial clause is elicited by a **wh**-question which incorporates the main clause as the 'hitherto assumed known' information for which it is to be the *'already known' or 'taken for granted as true' information.*

The item (al)**though** is theoretically interesting because it is one of the subordinators which is traditionally paraphrased by the co-ordinator **but** as the 'approximate equivalent'. It certainly has semantic features in common with this co-ordinator, but the whole point of this study is to show where they are contextually different, the most important part of this difference being the difference between subordinate clause and independent clause status. To consider the paraphrase 'equivalence', we need to have examined both front- and end-position first. Accordingly, we leave the **although**-item to the last. As it represents the core of our problems with the sequence of the adverbial clause, this item will be treated in greater depth than any other subordinator.

The strategy of describing end-position is to work out the presupposition of the main clause upon which the questioning for adverbial clause will depend. We begin by considering the effect of reversing the sequence from end-position to front-position. Bearing in mind the adverbial clause as the logical basis required for the main clause, we note the backward reference of the main clause and in particular how the topic of the preceding clause(s) may presuppose it. Next we note how the adverbial clause changes the topic, and how the next clause(s) of the paragraph may develop this new topic. As with front-position, substitute clauses are introduced as a stock way of repeating the preceding clause(s), this time by the main clause as independent clause repetition, for example **This could happen** with the modal verb **could** as an important signal of 'possibility', and **this they did**, with the modal verb **did** signalling a contrast by finiteness for a preceding non-finite clause.

As with our discussion of front-position, we consider the direction of reference for main clause and subordinate clause in the context of adjoining clauses. In end-position we are concerned with the backward reference of the main clause and the forward reference of the adverbial clause. The points of connective reference to the topics of adjoining clauses are clearly shown. Up to example (79), we are concerned with subordinators other than the subordinator **although**; thereafter we concentrate on this subordinator in some depth.

7.4.2 *Examples of Adverbial Clause in End-Position*

The description of example (76) below concentrates on explaining how the sequence of main clause followed by adverbial clause fits into their context of adjoining clauses. As with the discussion of the reversal of the clause pair in front-position, we note the clash between the references backwards and forwards and the meaning of the subordinator when we reverse the clause pair. The adverbial clause has its reference forwards impeded by its main clause, and its main clause has its reference backwards impeded by its adverbial clause.

In (76A) below, the **by** -ing clause answers a question on its main clause: 'How did he discover what was wrong with (sitting in) the chair?', and the last sentence lexically realises the anaphoric/cataphoric **wh**-noun clause **what was wrong**.

(76A)   A DENTIST WAS ONCE taken aback by his patients showing a new
and exceptional nervousness as soon as they sat in his chair. He
discovered what was wrong **by sitting in the chair himself**. For he
then noticed that on a wall immediately opposite there had
appeared a poster bearing this message: 'Prepare to meet thy God'.
(Supplement on Advertising VIII, *The Times*, 4 May 1966)

Before discussing the presupposition of the main clause, we need to
clarify the introductory description of the prediction of the
subordinate clause and the prediction of the nature of the next
sentence. First, the **by** -ing clause is predicted by the verb **discovered**
whose past tense implies success. It is this notion of success which
would raise the **how**-question. Second, note the anaphoric/cataphoric
role of the **wh**-noun clause **what was wrong**. Its anaphoric reference
can be shown by reinstating the deleted prepositional phrase
postmodifier **with (sitting in) the chair**. Its cataphoric reference means
that the next sentence can be seen as an answer to the direct **wh**-
question 'What was wrong with (sitting in) the chair?' There is the
slight complication in this analysis that the sentence connector **for** also
signals that its clause is the *basis* or *reason* for discovering what was
wrong. This is an instance of the common phenomenon of multiple
signalling of the clause relation.

How might we regard the main clause **he discovered what was
wrong** as being presupposed by the preceding context when we have
only one sentence? We have already noted the anaphoric reference of
the object of the verb **discovered**, and we have the same leading
participant, the dentist himself. The **wh**-noun clause object implies
that it is asking the direct question of the first sentence: 'What is wrong
with (sitting in) the chair?' This question implies that the dentist sees it
as a problem for his patients. The **by** -ing clause picks up the preceding
topic of 'patients sitting in the chair' and changes it to 'dentist sitting in
the chair'. The next sentence develops the new topic. The **by** -ing
clause is the new information of the second sentence; it is the
interesting part of the second sentence: the dentist discovers what the
problem is by putting himself in the patient's place. In the third
sentence, he identifies the nature of the problem for himself, as this
clause relational paraphrase of the sentence connector **for** and the
time adjunct **then** shows: *Because when he sat in the chair himself* he
noticed that on a wall immediately opposite . . . "Prepare to meet thy
God".' Summing up the rhetoric of this passage, it is the means of
making the discovery (the **by** -ing clause) which enables the dentist to
specify the nature of the problem. These are the highlights of the
story.

In (76B) below, we experiment with changing the sequence of the
adverbial clause from end- to front-position, using the same context as

before. There is no prediction of means/manner by the verb **discovered** as this kind of clause has already preceded it. The front-position of the **by**-ing clause signals that its achievement will follow in the main clause.

> (76B) A DENTIST WAS ONCE taken aback by his patients showing a new and exceptional nervousness as soon as they sat in his chair. **By sitting in the chair himself** he discovered what was wrong. For he then noticed that on a wall immediately opposite there had appeared a poster bearing this message: 'Prepare to meet thy God'.

Notice that the domination by the **by**-ing clause in (76A) has changed to the domination by the achievement meaning of the main clause; that is, the information of interest is now on discovering what was wrong and not on the means of discovering this. This is shown by the question which elicits the main clause: 'What did he achieve by sitting in the chair himself?' The awkward anaphoric point is that the adverbial item **then** in the last sentence refers back to the lexical realisation of the **by**-ing clause, which ideally should be its immediately preceding clause as it is in (76A). Instead, the main clause impedes its reference backwards. Clearly the sequence of front-position will not fit the rhetoric described for (76A).

This example suffices for illustrating the experimental reversals of sequence. The readers are invited to experiment for themselves with the remaining examples. It should be noted that it is difficult to discuss such reversals, if only because this was not how they were written, so we can only speculate with varying degrees of conviction on the changes to the context that these reversals produce. We return to a discussion of reversal of sequence in (81) below, when we discuss **although**-clause.

In the next three examples (77), (78) and (79), we consider three straightforward examples of end-position.

In (77) the main clause repeats the topics of the preceding co-ordinated **if**-clauses as a hypothetical possibility; this is signalled by the use of the modal verb **could** in a substitute paraphrase clause **This could happen**, where the substitute item **this** as subject and the lexical paraphrase verb **happen** repeat the co-ordinated **if**-clauses.

> (77) It would certainly be a serious matter for Britain if all Middle East oil supplies were to be banned — and especially if, in addition, physical damage were done to pipelines and other installations. This could happen **if Israel puts her enemies to total rout, and the Arab governments become unable to keep their outraged populace in check.** Present circumstances have not reached this point: if it were. reached, private motorists would have to be rationed, and some

restraint might even have to be imposed on industry and commerce.
('Oil and the War', *The Times*, 7 June 1967, p. 11)

There are five points to be noted.

(i) The main clause repeats the lexical realisation of the preceding
co-ordinated **if**-clauses, thus preserving their two topics, the banning
of Middle East oil supplies and the physical damage being done to
pipelines, etc. What we have here is a replacement of the grammatical
status of the **if**-clause subordination by the independent clause status
of the main clause. (See discussion of replacement of grammatical
status for the same clause on pp. 22–3.)

(ii) Notice that the main clause is hypothesising about the realities of
the war as represented in the two **if**-clauses. It represents a complex
answer to a preamble **yes/no**-question 'Could it (actually) happen?'
The presupposed **yes**-reply raises the **wh**-question 'Under what
conditions that we know about?' As a **yes**-reply, it becomes the
hypothetical member for which its own **if**-clause in end-position
provides a speculative condition.

(iii) The co-ordinated **if**-clauses in end-position introduce a change
in the topic of the Arab–Israeli conflict from the double topic of the
'banning of Middle East oil supplies' and 'physical damage being to
pipelines, etc.' to the double topic of 'Israel putting her enemies to
rout' and 'Arab governments being unable to check their populations'.

(iv) The first clause of the last sentence develops this double topic by
referring to them anaphorically and by paraphrase in the clause
Present circumstances have not reached this point. This is the first of
the two evaluation clauses connected by colon in this last sentence.

(v) Of these two clauses, the first evaluates the circumstances of the
two topics as *not* having been reached, and the second is an evaluation
of what would happen if it were reached. Note the clause pair here
with its **if**-clause in front-position.

In (78) below, the **by**-clause in end-position answers a **wh**-question
on the main clause: 'How can parents do a great deal to make the first
going to school easier for the child?'

(78) I remember my own early childhood days as a 'blooming buzzing
confusion' until repetition and custom brought some sort of sense and
order to the days.

Not too rosy

Parents can do a great deal to make the first going to school easier **by
answering the child's question – which may be spoken outright,
or shown less directly – 'What will it be like?'** It is a mistake to
paint too rosy a picture or to over-reassure the child that he will like
school. I have found the best way to help him over his natural
apprehension about this unknown experience is to make it a real and

manageable experience in his mind. (Mary Miles, 'Live and Learn', *The Times Educational Supplement*, 15 January 1967)

There are four points to be noted.

(i) The main clause is connected to the topic of the preceding sentence, namely the problem of the child's confusion when first going to school. It presupposes that parents do have control over their child and hence the solution. It answers the general **wh**-question which might be something like this: 'In your knowledge of parents and children, what can parents do to make the first going to school easier for the child?'

(ii) The new information in the main clause is the evaluation as **a great deal** and the information of the **by** -ing clause. The focus of the reply is on this clause.

(iii) The **by** -ing clause offers the change in topic from problem to solution: answering the child's questions about school.

(iv) The next two sentences develop the new topic of answering the child's questions about school. The first of the two sentences evaluates the wrong way to answer the child's questions; the second cites a finding of how best to answer them.

The final example before we get to the problem of how to treat **although**-clause in end-position is the example of the subordinator **whereas** in (79) below. Like the subordinator **although,** this subordinator cannot be the focus of a cleft sentence.

In (79) below, the subordinator **whereas** and its main clause are answering the **wh**-question 'How does the time scale for assessing the sales campaign compare with what you (as writer) assume your reader agrees with you as "known" about the time scale for assessing research progress?'

(79) It is not possible to calculate the rate of return from a given investment in research because the very nature of innovation is the emergence of something new, which cannot be predicted. Indeed, as Sir Solly Zuckermann has pointed out, attempts to plan and predict research progress can stifle its creativity.

The time scale for assessing the success of a sales campaign is fairly short, usually weeks or months, sometimes days, **whereas research often takes years to mature**. The time lag between a really fundamental discovery in science and its widespread application is rarely less than 20 years. Hence a company which invests too little in research can fall years behind, or whole industries can decay. Some remedy is available in the purchase of know-how and the placing of sponsored research contracts, but a company which purchases too much of its knowledge from outside finds itself always behind in the race. (*New Scientist*, 8 December 1966, p. 586)

There are five points to be noted.

(i) Notice how the question for our clause pair is presupposed by the topic of the preceding paragraph, namely that there must be a rate of return from a given investment in research and this has a time scale.

(ii) Notice that the main clause offers information not assumed known to the reader while the **whereas**-clause in end-position offers what is *assumed known in general*.

(iii) The **whereas**-clause introduces a change of topic from one member of the comparison to the other: from the time scale for assessing the success of a sales campaign to the time scale of assessing the application of research.

(iv) The next sentence develops the new topic of the time scale for assessing research. It assumes that the implications of the generality are not known to the reader in any detail; this is what the independent clause status means.

(v) It will be noticed that we had the lexical item **compare** in the **wh**-question to elicit the **whereas**-clause. This is part of the clause relation of matching whose semantics is *contrast*; that is, what is true of assessing the time scale for success of a sales campaign is not true of assessing the time scale for research.

Finally, we now proceed to a discussion of the subordinator **although** in end-position. The main problem of analysing end-position is the complex nature of the questions used to elicit it by taking account of what is already known. In asking for the adverbial clause in end-position we are asking for what is (already) assumed known, what is given or what can be taken for granted. The above example of the **whereas**-clause in (79) was simpler in this respect than the **although**-clause which now follows in that we can get everything we need into one complex question for eliciting both the main clause and its **whereas**-clause: 'How does the time scale for assessing the success of a sales campaign compare with what is already assumed known about the time scale for assessing research (programmes)?' Unfortunately with the **although**-clause in end-position, it does not seem possible to get everything required into one complex question. We appear to need at least two questions to account for its complex semantics.

In (80) below, we have an **although**-clause in end-position in a sentence taken from a newspaper extract reporting on the rapid advance of Israeli armoured columns against the Egyptian forces in the Sinai campaign of 1967 as compared with that of 1956.

Road ends

(80) As we stand, trying desperately to shield our eyes and noses from endless swirling dust, there is a steady banging of heavy artillery in the distance. We are unable to go farther forward because the road,

which is not exactly the M1, peters out altogether as far as the eye can see, and reporters take second place. According to the officer in charge of this section, Egyptians fell back here with heavy losses in captives and equipment. The speed of advance up to now has been comparable with the Sinai compaign of 1956, **although the Egyptian equipment is considerably better**. The Israelis faced Russian T54 tanks, specially developed for this type of rough going. They also had Russian SU 100 self-propelling guns and ZIL trucks. (*Guardian*, 7 June 1967, p. 1)

The **although**-clause in end-position is semantically very complex so that it is necessary to begin with the simplest points first. There are five points.

(i) The main clause refers to the preceding progress of the Israeli army as its topic and compares the campaign then with that of 1956.

(ii) The **although**-clause changes this topic to the related question of equipment used in the fighting. The next two sentences which end the paragraph develop this topic in detail in answer to the question 'How much better is Egyptian equipment: give me some examples of the superior (Russian) equipment in the fighting?' (There appears to be some error in the printing of the last sentence: to be compatible with the signalling by the adverbial adjunct **also**, the pronoun **they** requires the verb structure to be expanded from **had** to **had to face** – if they refers to **the Israelis** of the preceding sentence. Failing this correction, the pronoun **they** could be replaced by **the Egyptians** as users of the Russian SU 100 self-propelling guns.)

(iii) Notice in particular two features of the semantics of the underlying clause pair (that is, the clause without the subordinator **although** to connect them). First, each clause contains a comparison: the first clause is a comparison of equality, and the second is a comparison of inequality. Second, their juxtaposition does not make sense to us because the second clause contradicts the first: we cannot simultaneously have equality and inequality for the same thing:

The speed of the advance up to now has been comparable with the Sinai campaign of 1956; the Egyptian equipment is considerably better.

What we require is some explicit connection to make sense of the clause pair for us. This is a feature of the concessive relation which I noted in Winter, 1977, p. 44. We take this matter up after this example at 7.4.3, where we discuss how Quirk *et al.* (1972) treat the concessive clause.

(iv) The main clause evaluates the comparison between the campaign in 1956 and the Sinai campaign (now) as being equal. From the main clause we could drawn the conclusion that the equality means that the latest advance in the campaign does not represent an improvement of the Israeli battle position over 1956. However, the **although**-item prevents us from drawing this conclusion. It warns us that its clause will deny such a conclusion. In the light of its taken-for-granted knowledge we reinterpret the equality as a significant achievement by the Israelis after all. We can paraphrase the relation by using the adverbial adjunct **in spite of the fact that X**:

> The speed of the advance up to now has been comparable with the Sinai campaign of 1956 **in spite of the fact that** the Egyptian equipment is considerably better.

What the writer is saying is that we can take it for granted that the equality in speed of the two advances does not logically follow from the inequality of military equipment in Egypt's favour. There is contradiction plus logical meaning here.

(v) It is difficult at this stage of our knowledge to be sure about what questions would elicit **although**-clauses in end-position. All I can suggest is the following. We have to take into account what we already know and what we think the reader already knows when we try to use questions to recreate the clause pair under examination. In a comparison between adversaries in a modern war using mechanised and electronic equipment, we expect to take these means of conflict into account. The above clause pair assumes this knowledge in its **although**-clause in end-position. The question criterion we use must account for both the **although**-clause and its main clause. We do so in a composite of two sequenced questions, in which the second depends upon the reply of the first: 'How does the present campaign in the Sinai compare with the one in 1956 in the light of what is known of Egyptian military equipment?' and then 'Does the comparison follow logically from what is known of this Egyptian military equipment?' The answer to the first question gives us the main clause: the speed of the advance up to now has been comparable with the Sinai campaign of 1956. The immediately following subordination by the **although**-item is an acknowledgement that we cannot stop here because we still have to indicate whether it is progress in the light of what is already known, or not; we still have to answer the second related question. I suggest that the **although**-clause as a reply to this second question can be paraphrased as follows: 'No, it does not follow logically from what I know of Egyptian military equipment – theirs is considerably better (than the Israeli equipment).' The end-position for the **although**-clause puts the emphasis on this 'known' information. The implication is that it is denying the conclusion that the superior military equipment of the Egyptians should have slowed down the Israeli advance compared with that of 1956.

The above **although**-clause was sufficiently complex for us to ignore the traditional paraphrasing of **although** by the co-ordinator **but** as approximately equivalent in meaning. They are equivalent inasmuch as they both *deny* something, but we cannot ignore the fact that the **although**-item is a subordinator and the **but**-item is a co-ordinator, with corresponding differences of contextual meaning due to the different grammatical status of their clauses. It suffices here to note that if we used the co-ordinator **but** here instead of the subordinator **although – but the Egyptian equipment is considerably better** – it would have implied the surprise of new 'facts' to the reader. It would assume the information is 'not known', or at least 'not known' or understood in this particular connection. It is this notion of 'assumed known' versus 'not assumed known' that has been ignored, but to appreciate this point we need to consider in some detail the arguments about the paraphrase between the subordinator **although** and the co-ordinator **but**. This now follows in two parts.

7.4.3 *The Traditional Idea of a Paraphrase Relation between Concessive Clause and the Co-ordinator 'But'*

7.4.3.1 Introduction. The whole matter of the traditional paraphrasing of the subordinator **although** by the co-ordinator **but** is illustrated in the most recent restatement of it in Quirk *et al.* (1972, pp. 745–6) in a section entitled 'Clauses of Condition and Concession', from which I quote the following extract:

Overlap of condition and concession
Two classes of adverbial clause between which there is considerable overlap are those of condition and concession. Whereas conditional clauses state the dependence of one circumstance or set of circumstances on another:

If you treat her kindly, she'll do anything for you

concessive clauses imply a contrast between two circumstances; i.e. that in the light of circumstances in the dependent clause, that in the main clause is surprising:

Although he hadn't eaten for days, he looked strong and healthy

From this we see that **although** as a subordinator is the approximate equivalent of **but** as a coordinator (9.54):
He hadn't eaten for days, **but** he looked strong and healthy

There are four points we might consider about the relevance of this extract to the discussion of front- and end-position, especially in view of our previous exercises in changing front-position to end-position and vice versa. We have noted repeatedly that there is a contextual and semantic difference between these two positions in the clause. How does this square with the traditional paraphrasing of the subordinator **although** and the co-ordinator **but**? What we have got to get clear is the difference between the 'given' and 'new' relations between subordination represented by the subordinator **although** and co-ordination represented by the co-ordinator **but**. For 'new', we take the clause as presenting its information as 'not assumed known' or 'not taken for granted'; and for 'given' we take the clause as presenting its information as 'assumed known' or taken for granted (as true).

(i) Notice the definition of concession as 'concessive clauses imply a contrast between two circumstances; i.e. in the light of the circumstances in the dependent clause, that in the main clause is surprising'. I have already noted that the surprise meaning belongs to the co-ordinator **but** in that it can be paraphrased lexically as 'not expected'. (See Winter, 1974, pp. 166–9). Jespersen (1940, Part V, pp. 360–1) also uses the surprise meaning for the concessive but does not paraphrase (al)**though** by the co-ordinator **but**.

(ii) The suggestion that the subordinator **although** is the approximate equivalent of the co-ordinator **but** ignores the all-important fact that, as first member of the clause pair, **although**-clause is subordinate clause. Elsewhere, Quirk *et al.* (1972, p. 795) speak of a preference in spoken English for co-ordination over subordination structures: 'It is notable that in spoken English, where immediate ease of syntactic composition is at a premium, co-ordinate structures are often preferred to equivalent structures of subordination:

SUBORD: **Although** it was fine, we decided to stay at home
COORD: It was fine, **but** we decided to stay at home.

Further, spoken English, though less complex in structure of subordination, is more inclined than written English to provide the kind of link that can be made by co-ordination.'

This misses the point. We cannot just turn subordination and co-ordination on and off in order to be comprehended more easily. If there is a statistical disproportion between co-ordination and subordination within spoken as over written English, then we ought to look for the differences in face-to-face exchanging of information in terms of 'given' and 'new'.

Paradoxically, what a disproportion between co-ordination and subordination might mean is that there are fewer clauses where we signal our conviction that something is already known or taken for granted as true. Could it be that when we speak face to face with people who share our convictions and our experience of the world we don't bother to give these friends the information of these clauses because we share this knowing, so that there is less of it in our exchanges? It is impossible to answer this question without statistical evidence; in any case, any research must look closely at the subject matter of the exchanges, whether these are trivial largely phatic exchanges of daily news or more serious less phatic exchanges in which we argue whether something is true or not. Whatever the results of this research, the difference between subordinate clause and independent clause is not to be ignored.

This ignoring of the significance of the information status of the clause is characteristic of both traditional grammar and modern linguistics. As might have been noticed in the discussion of adverbial clauses so far, it is one of the principal tools we use to describe the contextual differences between the meanings of subordinate clause and independent clause.

(iii) Notice particularly that when Quirk *et al.* talk here about the paraphrase of **although** and **but**, the **although**-clause is in front-position, and that their definition seems to fit this sequence with the emphasis of the relation coming on the main clause in end-position: 'that in the light of the circumstances of the dependent clause, that in the main clause is surprising'. If **although** and **but** really paraphrase each other, then there is the problem of end-position for **although**-clause in (81) and (82) below. Is it still the main clause which is 'surprising'? To attempt to answer this question, we need to re-examine the nature of the grammatical choices for subordination and co-ordination, using the **although**-clause as our model.

(iv) It is not practicable to discuss the paraphrasing of the made-up examples which Quirk *et al.* cite because we need a context in which to examine the semantics and grammar of the clause pair, and to note how changes of sequence and of explicit connection affect its fitting the context.

We now consider another example of **although**-clause in its context in two stages. The first is a straightforward analysis of the kind we have been doing so far; the second is an examination of how the various paraphrases fit the context.

In (81) below, we have an **although**-clause in end-position of a co-ordinated clause pair in sentence 3 of a paragraph about the Mbuti people (in Africa) who obliged the film-makers by allowing the film-makers to coach them to make spectacularly dangerous river crossings by 'pigmy' bridge and by swinging on vines from one side to the other. It is important to note that sentence 1 is an evaluation clause which evaluates the achievement of the Mbuti people as described in the next three sentences.

(81) (1) They were undoubtedly an obliging people. (2) The famous

photograph of the pygmy 'bridge' and the spectacular technique of crossing a river by swinging on a vine from one side to another was taught to the Mbuti 'not without difficulty' by an enterprising movie-maker. (3) The group were able to keep it up for some years and obligingly repeated the act for 'documentary' film units **although they preferred to cross the river by wading or by walking over a tree trunk**. (4) It was far safer. (*New Scientist*, 11 August 1966, p. 333)

The co-ordinated clause pair of sentence 3, whose second clause has the subordination by **although**-clause, concludes the topic of crossing the river by swinging on a vine, etc., with the **although**-clause changing the topic to their preference for crossing the river by other means. Sentence 4 continues the new topic by answering the **wh**-question 'Why did they prefer to cross the river by wading?' Let us consider the presuppositions which underlie the main clause and what could be regarded as assumed known or taken for granted by the adverbial clause.

We begin by sketching out the general outline of the semantic structure of this paragraph. Sentence 1 is affirming a previous evaluation of the Mbuti people and is marking it as certain with the adverbial adjunct **undoubtedly**. This last item strengthens our prediction of an explanatory *basis*. If we think of premodifier **obliging** as meaning that the Mbuti people willingly do what they are asked to do, then we see sentences 2 and 3 as two separate instances of willingly doing what they were asked to do. These sentences provide the basis of the evaluation in sentence 1 by answering the **wh**-question 'What did they do that makes you think they are so undoubtedly obliging?' In sentence 2, they are taught dangerous feats with difficulty by movie-makers; in sentence 3 they keep up these dangerous feats for years for the movie-makers in spite of their preference for other ways of crossing the river. Sentence 4 is the reason for their preference. It is sentence 3 that justifies the evaluation of the Mbuti as an undoubtedly obliging people, because in the light of the preceding dangers of sentence 2, made further explicit by the **although**-clause in end-position, they must have been very obliging indeed.

To explain the choice of the adverbial **although**-clause, we need to go into more precise detail about the relation between sentence 3 and the preceding sentence 2 as separate answers to the above mentioned question on sentence 1: 'What did they do that makes you think they are so undoubtedly obliging a people?'

If the writer had stopped writing at sentence 2, this would not constitute an adequate reply as this assumption shows: 'You say that the famous photograph of the pygmy "bridge" and the films of spectacular ways of crossing rivers by swinging on a vine from one side to the other was taught "not without difficulty" by enterprising movie-makers. This was obliging of the Mbuti, but it was just a start. You do say that they **are** undoubtedly obliging and presumably mean that they obliged by doing what they had been taught to do. What have they done since then that you think is so undoubtedly obliging of them, **given the difficulty of teaching them these dangerous techniques?** Are you implying that they kept it up after that?'

Taking the first of these two sequenced questions, the **wh**-question, we note that its main clause elicits the co-ordinated main clauses as a **yes**-reply to the second question, the **yes/no**-question; its adverbial clause elicits the new information of the **although**-clause: their preference for safer ways of crossing the river. We already know that the movie-makers had difficulty in teaching the Mbuti these dangerous feats; now we learn from the adverbial clause something we could easily have guessed, that they were scared and naturally preferred their usual ways of crossing rivers. Paraphrasing the **although**-item, we have: 'As you can see from the difficulty of teaching them these dangerous feats, it does **not** follow from their obligingly repeating them for some years that they did not prefer crossing the river by wading, etc.' What the **although**-clause means is that there can be no question of this preference for more traditional means of crossing rivers, etc.

7.4.3.2 Paraphrases and change of sequence. We now examine the various paraphrases and changes of sequence for the clause pair of (81) with a view to establishing whether these changes mean that the clause can no longer fit the context.

Taking the sequence of **although**-clause first, as already noted above Quirk *et al.* always use front-position when speaking of its paraphrase with the co-ordinator **but.** We observe that the present clause pair is fixed in some way that what is subordinate and what is independent cannot be interchanged:

(82) **Although** the group were able to keep it up for some years and obligingly repeated the act for 'documentary' film units, they preferred to cross the river by wading or by walking over a tree trunk. it was far safer.

This sequence now makes a nonsense of the context. What is new information is now given or known, and what is given or known is now presented as new information. Worse, the surprise is on the main clause as new information when we know full well that the writer signalled his conviction that because their preference for safety could be taken for granted there could be no surprise in it. This second objection to the independence of the second clause would apply equally to the co-ordination by **but**, making both clauses of this sequence independent:

> (83) The group were able to keep it up for some years and obligingly repeated the act for 'documentary' film units, **but** they preferred to cross the river by wading or by walking over a tree trunk. It was far safer.

Here we are using the co-ordinator **but** in the same grammatical slot and sequence as the subordinator **although**. In this position, the co-ordinator **but** is emphasising the surprise of the preference. This clashes with the subordinator **although** in (81) which makes it clear that there can be no surprise at this preference.

The front-position for the **although**-clause of (81) preserves the taken for granted or known versus the not hitherto known of the main clause, but the emphasis of the relation is now on how obligingly the Mbuti kept up this dangerous act for some years, etc., and not on their taken for granted preference for safer ways of crossing the river which end-position emphasises in (81):

> (84) **Although** the group preferred to cross the river by wading or by walking over a tree trunk, they were able to keep it up for some years and obligingly repeated the act for 'documentary' film units. It was far safer.

There are three points to be noted about the theoretical significance of the reversal of the **although**-clause to front-position for the description of both front- and end-position so far.

(i) Ignoring the question of whether (82) or (83) can fit the context of (81), we note yet again the reversal of the adverbial clause sequence from the end-position of (81) to the front-position in (84) above will not do, (i) for the reasons of emphasis described above for (81), and (ii) because each member of the clause pair now obstructs the reference to adjoining clauses. The main clause now obstructs the last sentence **It was far safer** in its reason relation with the adverbial clause as well as its anaphoric relation with the pronoun **it** = crossing by wading, etc. The adverbial clause now obstructs the anaphoric relation of the pronoun **it** in the main clause – keep **it** up and **swinging on a vine**, etc., in sentence 2. This is another way of talking about the obstruction of topic reference. It sums up the reversals of both front- and end-position in principle.

(ii) An important theoretical question is raised by the switched-around subordination of (82). Why can't we switch around the adverbial clause subordination of clause pairs? The answer is that adverbial clause subordination preserves the sequence of 'basis' and 'deduction' or synonymously 'grounds' and 'conclusion', with the adverbial clause presenting the 'basis' and the main clause presenting the 'deduction', *irrespective of the sequence of main clause and adverbial clause*. What this means is that with front-position adverbial clause we have the sequence of 'basis' and 'deduction', and with end-position we have the sequence of 'deduction' and 'basis'. In philosophy this has long been recognised as *deductive* and *inductive* sequence respectively. The role of the adverbial clause in end-position is to signal that there is *inductive sequence* in which 'basis' is given.

The **although**-clause has multiple clause relation elements of deductive reasoning (logical sequence) and of denial (matching). We can show what the **although**-item is denying by rewriting the front-position here as **because**-clause as in (85) below. The example is simplified.

(85) **Because** the group preferred to cross the river by wading, etc., they were **not** able to keep up their dangerous act of swinging on a vine, etc.

Notice that the **although**-clause version in (84) is denying the concluding of negation for the main clause in (85). (This relation between clause and concession was noted by Quirk (1954, p. 8) when he noted a similar relation between the sentence connector **yet** and **therefore**.)

If we now switch the subordination roles around, as in (86) below, we have a logical nonsense:

(86) The group preferred to cross the river by wading, etc., **because** they were **not** able to keep up their dangerous act.

Like the switching around of the **although**-clause in (82), this clause pair is violating the deductive sequencing role of the adverbial clause subordinator; that is to say it is **not** presenting the 'basis' for which its main clause should be the 'deduction' *as this relation is understood for the original context in (81)*. The clause pair of (86) might do for a very different situation, where perhaps the Mbuti might actually want to keep up their act, etc.

We come to the crucial question: how do we know which of the two clauses of the clause pair is the 'basis' and which is the 'deduction'? We have already noted that the logical sequence relation has implications of a time logic. The 'basis' member must be preferring safety since it existed in time before the event of doing dangerous acts took place.

(iii) The reversal of the **although**-clause from the end-position of the original (81) to front-position in (84) raises theoretical problems with Quirk's definition of the concessive relation in which he uses

although-clause in front-position as his paraphrase of the co-ordination of the same sequence of clauses by the co-ordinator **but**. The first problem is whether the paraphrase by the co-ordinator **but** applies only to the front-position sequence of the adverbial clause. The second problem is that contrast by definition should necessarily be surprising. For instance, if we expect dissimilar things to happen, then the actual occurrence of similarity will be surprising. The third problem is the definition of the concessive subordinate clause, according to which, as we have noted, the surprise comes in the main clause. The question is, does this apply to end-position as well as front-position, and, if so, how might it work?

We conclude this subsection with an attempt to answer this question by examining the notion of surprise and concession in turn. The way to look at the surprise notion is to remove the **although**-clause from (81) and see what effect it has on the comprehension of the main clause with the context of its preceding sentences, as in (87) below.

> (87) (3) The group were able to keep it up for some years and obligingly repeated the act for 'documentary' film units.

Unqualified by the **although**-clause which qualifies it in (81), the main clause seems surprising in the light of the implied dangers of the method of crossing the river and the understated difficulties of teaching the Mbuti tribe their acrobatics. Acting against this surprise is our anticipation from sentence 1 that the Mbuti are going to do this anyway because they are so undoubtedly obliging; note the repetition of the premodified adjective **obliging** by the adverbial of manner **obligingly** in sentence 3. The **although**-clause would also act as a check against the surprise by presenting what was not surprising, and placing the emphasis of the relation on it. At this point, it is worth noting that, if we remove the subordinator **although** and juxtapose the two clauses, the clause pair has the same concessive illogicality which we observed of the equivalent clause pair in (80), as in (88) below:

> (88) The group were able to keep it up for some years and obligingly repeated the act for 'documentary' film unit; they preferred to cross the river by wading or by walking over a tree trunk. It was far safer.

There are two points about the juxtaposition of independent clauses connected by semicolon. First, some acknowledgement is required of the implicit negative induction relation between the two clauses. This is supplied by the **although**-subordinator in the original example. Second, independent clause status signals that the clause is assumed *not* taken for granted as true: we are being told something we did *not* know about the human preference for safety first, despite strong hints of this in sentence 2. As something which we take for granted as true, the clause requires acknowledgement by the appropriate (concessive) subordination.

If we now put back the **although**-subordinator into (88) to signal this denied 'basis' for the conclusion of the main clause, we can reconsider the problem of what has happened to Quirk's surprise in the main clause. With front-position there is a coinciding of both surprise and the emphasis of the clause relation on the main clause. However, with end-position, these two are separated out, with the surprise on the main clause in front and the emphasis of the clause relation on the adverbial clause's meaning. The question which arises now is, can we have both surprise and emphasis on the opposite of surprise in the same clause pair? Like much else in subordination grammar, this matter requires further investigation.

7.4.4 Summary and Conclusions about End-Position

Part of the difficulty in working out what the adverbial clause is doing is that, in end-position, I am assuming that it signals forward to the next immediate clause(s) of the likely development of new topic as information 'not assumed known'. In working out the knownness or taken-for-grantedness of the information of the adverbial clause, we had to try to relate the linguistic signals of shared knowledge between writer and reader from a decoding point of view to our knowledge of the world, and of the subject matter of the text. We can divide the sources of information for the adverbial clause into roughly three kinds:

(i) The information as already known outside the text by the readers. Examples are (77) the fact that Israel was then at war with the Arabs which is hypothesised by the **if**-clause, and (80) the fact that Russia had already supplied to the Egyptians much of their military equipment before 1967 and this was well commented upon before then.

(ii) What is taken for granted as true (including general knowledge). Examples are (76) the obvious sense in sitting in a chair to find out what was wrong with it; (78) the assumption that parents should answer their child's questions; (79) the general knowledge that research takes years to mature; and (81) the very obvious idea that human beings prefer safety first.

(iii) Information which is traced back to a preceding topic. Examples are (76) the notion of sitting down in the chair; (76) the preceding sentence saying what school was like for the writer; (79) the notion of research maturing referring to the idea of calculating the return of a given investment in research; and (81) the idea of preferring safer ways of crossing rivers, etc., is implied by the preceding topic 'not without difficulty' in the teaching.

The important point about the above kinds of knownness is not that we want a new philosophy of knowledge to use as semantic categories, but rather that we need to study the linguistic cueing of these states of knowledge, so that one day we might be able to reconstruct the writer or speaker's knowledge of the world or subject matter from linguistic cueing alone.

As with front-position, we noted the connection between the change of topic in the clause pair and how these topics connected with the topics of their adjoining clauses. This time we noted how the semantics of the subordinate clause dominated the clause pair. As with front-position, too, we noted that in no case could we reverse the clause pair in their contexts, but the important point of all this is that discussion of the significance of changing the sequence of the clause pairs could not take place out of context.

In the subsection 'Paraphrases and change of sequence', we noted that the fundamental contextual function of adverbial subordination was to signal to us which of the two members of the clause pair was the basis or grounds, and which was the deduction or conclusion to be drawn from this basis or grounds. In Winter, 1974, pp. 454–7, I noted that the choice of sentence connectors such as **therefore** or **then** depended upon their clause pairs being in 'normal time sequence'. This simply means that the event in the clause presented first had to happen before the event in the clause presented second. In Winter, 1977, pp. 6–7, I speak of both deductive reasoning and a time logic. In deductive reasoning, we reason from a basis that happens before the event we use for our conclusion happens. The explanation of the difference between front-position and end-position lies in the fact that the function of adverbial clause is to present the basis for the deduction or conclusion in the main clause, *so that, no matter what the sequence of the adverbial clause is, it still signals basis for which the main clause is deduction.*

We can sum up the difference between front- and end-position of the adverbial clause in terms of *deductive sequence* and *inductive sequence*. With front-position, the emphasis is on deductive reasoning; with end-position the emphasis is on inductive reasoning. With mid-position, the emphasis seems to be neutralised. Deductive sequence is the unmarked sequence for independent clauses in sequence; it is the environment signalled by such sentence connectors as **then, thereafter, therefore, thus, hence, so** (see Winter, 1968, p. 584 and Winter, 1977, pp. 47–52).

The question which now arises is, where do the concepts of 'given' and 'new' fit into the above description of the fundamental cueing function of adverbial clause? The answer should not be surprising: 'given' corresponds with the 'basis' member and 'new' corresponds with the 'deduction' member. What is interesting about this correspondence in sequence is its implication of time logic, both of real time and of the presentation of earlier clauses in the text or its context.

Next, we briefly consider mid-position in the clause as being in contrast with front- and end-position in that its new topic does not seem to be further developed outside its main clause.

7.5 The Adverbial Clause in Mid-Position

7.5.1 Introduction

The mid-position placement of the adverbial clause is only perfunctorily treated after the detailed examination of front- and end-position. The reason I gave earlier was that both front- and end-position can clearly be shown to share a change of topic while this does not appear to be the case with mid-position. I cannot say this with any certainty because I do not have sufficient examples of mid-position to go by. Here we confine ourselves to what seems to distinguish mid-position from front- and end-position.

Mid-position is the position in the middle of the main clause. The key notion here is of the interruption of the main clause structure itself. The adverbial clause interrupts the structure of the main clause *after the subject* (in its normal position), and may appear anywhere within the structure of the clause between subject and predicate, verb and object, verb and complement, etc. These slots are illustrated below.

There are two important signalling features of the interruption of clause structure by adverbial clause.

(i) By interrupting clause structure, a strong anticipation is set up for the grammatical completion of the main clause structure by its structural elements still to come. For instance, if you interrupt the clause after S V, where V is a transitive verb, you set up a strong anticipation for grammatical completion by the O element, and so on.

(ii) By interrupting the clause structures, the adverbial clause sets off the part of the main clause which precedes its point of entry from the part which follows it and completes its clause structure. In principle it is just like the focus by mid-position adjuncts described for sentence connectors such as **however** in Winter, 1968, p. 590, and simultaneously in Greenbaum, 1969, pp. 24–5. This is illustrated by (89) below, where the adverbial **however** focuses on the time adverb

now which immediately precedes it in the clause. Notice how it focuses on the adverb **now** as being in contrast with the preceding adverbial **as recently as 15 years ago**.

(89)   As recently as 15 years ago some physiologists held that transmission at the synapse was predominantly, if not exclusively, an electrical phenomenon. **Now, however,** there is abundant evidence that transmission is effectuated by the release of specific chemical substances that trigger a regeneration of the impulse. (Osti Programme No. 33063)

It is also like the interruption of the clause by *interpolating* structures, from phrases, subordinate clauses of all kinds, and verbless clauses to independent clauses, all of which can interrupt the grammar of the clause at any kind of syntactic boundary whatever. This is a freedom of 'intrusion' which is not open to the normal adverbial clause. As interrupting structure, interpolation acts as an evaluating postmodifier of the meaning of the preceding part of the clause structure at the point of entry into the clause. This is illustrated by (90) below, where the bracketed independent denial clause interrupts the syntactic relation between the premodified noun head **The familiar political argument** and its postmodifying prepositional phrase **against such a course**.

(90)   First, the Government should announce a time-table for the withdrawal of our East of Suez forces. The familiar political argument **(there aren't any economic ones)** against such a course is that the result would be to create a vacuum. But an announcement now of a withdrawal in two or three years' time would compel others – whether the United Nations or alliances – to prepare to take over our responsibilities. (*Observer*, 29 January 1967, p. 1)

Note that the denial, that there aren't any economic arguments, modifies the meaning of the premodified noun head to something like this: **the familiar solely political argument against such a course.** We take this matter up again when we come to apposition, interpolation and evaluation. We return to the interruption of the clause by adverbial clause and how this focuses attention on the preceding clause structure at the point of entry and anticipates the grammatical completion of the clause.

Two examples of mid-position will suffice.

In (91) below, the **because**-clause interrupts the slot between the subject and the predication **leads to boredom and then to trouble,** with the focus upon the abstract subject **The resulting loneliness,** for which we anticipate its independent clause predicate.

(91) Mr Abernathy insists that leaders don't have to be soft. 'These kids don't mind being jumped on when it's warranted but one must never be unjust. Children have an inbuilt sense of justice and if this is shaken they're inclined to see the adult world's hypocrisy more strongly. The resulting loneliness, **because they feel they can't trust adults even when they're fast approaching the adult world**, leads to boredom and then to trouble.' (*Guardian*, 14 September 1966, p. 6)

The parsing point here is interesting in the way it reflects the semantic nature of the interrupting **because**-clause in its clause relation with the subject itself. When we reach the end of the abstract nominal group **the resulting loneliness** and expect the main verb answering the pushdown question 'Does what?' or 'Is what?', we find instead a **because**-clause which answers the **wh**-question 'What precisely is causing this loneliness in children?' It implies that the speaker anticipates that his listener will not readily understand what is meant by the subject **the resulting loneliness** in its clause relation with the preceding sentence. The nominal group **the resulting loneliness** is the nominalised and hence unmarked form of the clause **This results in loneliness (for them)**, a clause which answers the **wh**-question 'What does this result in for them?' Having parsed the **because**-clause we anticipate the predication which answers the delayed pushdown question 'The resulting loneliness does what to them?'

In (92) below, the cataphoric **though**-clause interrupts the slot between the predication of the passive verbal group of the anticipatory **It**-clause and its real subject, the noun clause.

(92) But this autobiography is given both shape and tension by the fact that Nicolette Macnamara married into an extremely respectable family of dignified and dutiful City merchants. It is true that her husband was himself a painter, but he was never a bohemian. Indeed it was generally considered — **though she does not mention this** — that his paintings were too respectable by half. (*Observer*, 16 October 1966, p. 27)

There are four points to be noted about this example.
(i) Note the paraphrase environment of the interrupting **though**-clause, in which the sentence connector **indeed** echoes the meaning of the item **true** in the preceding sentence: 'It is even truer to say that his paintings were too respectable by half.'
(ii) Notice that the subordinator **though** focuses on the preceding part of its main clause **It was generally considered**, especially upon the verb (generally) **considered**. At this point when we come to the

though-item, we have already had the structural signal of anticipatory **It** that its real subject will be a noun clause which will follow the predication and with it the as-yet-unanswered question 'What was generally considered about him as a painter that was compatible with his being no bohemian?' Along with such a question would go the stock question of the autobiographer: 'Did she mention it?'

(iii) The unspecific **though**-clause answers this stock question before it answers the main question, so that when it is eventually answered by the specific **that**-clause it will have been anticipated in two ways: grammatically as the completion of the grammar of its main clause, and cataphorically as the necessary lexical realisation of the substitute nominal **this** which points forward from the **though**-clause.

(iv) By using subordination with **though**-clause, the writer indicates that he is taking for granted his own conclusion that the wife would not mention a general view of this kind; if he had used the parenthetical independent clause form '– she did not mention this –', then he would simply be nothing the fact that she did not mention it and marking it by parenthesis. The **though**-clause betrays what the reviewer takes for granted as true about the wife as an autobiographer of her husband.

7.5.2   *Summary and Conclusions about Mid-Position*

Of necessity, the summary and conclusions for mid-position must be much more tentative than for front- and end-position with which it is being contrasted, but the following three points seem to be fairly well established.

(i) The interrupting adverbial clause splits up the main clause with two kinds of emphasis by structural meaning. First, there is the focus upon the preceding main clause structure at the point of entry, for example the focus upon the abstract subject **the resulting loneliness** in (91), or the preceding subject and verb predicate **It was generally considered** in (92). Second, there is the powerful anticipation of grammatical completion by the remainder of the main clause structure after the point of entry, for example, the predication **leads to loneliness,** etc., of (91) and the **that**-clause as real subject of (92).

(ii) It seems reasonable to say that the meanings of the grammatical structures before and after the point of entry play an important part in the semantics of the clause as determined by its topic development.

(iii) We have noted the similarity of the intrusion between the adverbial clauses described here and the independent clause interpolation in (90) by the denial clause **There aren't any economic ones.** In both kinds of intrusion, the principle seems to be the same: to interrupt but not to change the topic of the main clause in its relation with its succeeding clause(s). It is here that mid-position differs from front- and end-position, quite apart from the intrusion of its grammatical structure.

Non-Finite Clauses Which Have No Subordinators

8.1 Introducing the Non-Finite Clause

Some readers might find the word 'clause' unfamiliar for these non-finites. The idea of calling them clauses is fairly recent. In Huddleston *et al.* (1968), we applied this term to all uses of non-finite 'phrases' except the premodifying use, for example 'a **rotating** drum'. A. S. Hornby (1954, revised 1975) refers to them as 'phrases', and G. C. Scheurweghs (1959) calls them by their traditional names, present participles, past participles, gerunds and infinitives (with or without the **to** element) and does not use the term 'clause', though he does speak of them as verbs that have passive constructions, perfect present participles, objects, etc. Sinclair (1972, pp. 44–7) calls them P-bound clauses. Following Huddleston *et al.* (1968, pp. 134–61) we call them non-finite clauses.

Unlike the relative clauses, noun clauses and adverbial clauses so far described, non-finite clauses are used without subordinating conjunctions to guide us to their meaning. Instead, their signalling relies on the semantics of their morphology and on their syntactic positions in the main clause. Non-finite clauses are very important in English syntax and deserve the kind of treatment which is given to the adverbial clause. For the purpose of this work, it suffices, however, to briefly consider the salient points of non-finite clause in its role as subordinate clause.

Taking morphology first, there are four kinds of non-finite clause according to the morphology of their verbs: the **ing**-verb (present participle and gerund), the **ed**-verb (past participle), the **to**-infinitive, and the bare infinitive (only occurring in fixed constructions). For instance, the morphology of **to** signals the non-finiteness of the verb **to admit** and with it the subordination of its clause in the structure of **to admit a television camera into the House for the first time**. We know from the **to** that we have started our clause boundary, and we wait for the completion of this clause structure as the final boundary of the clause. Our cue here is the prepositional phrase **for the first time**; the last word **time** completes the grammar of the prepositional phrase and hence of adjunct for this non-finite clause. With this adjunct completed, we end our non-finite clause.

Taking syntactic position next, we make a distinction between two groups of non-finite clause uses according to their syntactic positions. The first group consists of those non-finite clauses which are (a) noun clauses (including 'objects' of preposition), (b) relative clauses, and (c) adverbial clauses. This group differs grammatically and semantically from group 2, whose non-finite clauses occur in fixed positions of the clause and do not have relative clause, noun clause or adverbial clause meanings but are a predictable part of the meaning of a preceding verb or adjective pattern of the clause. Of the two groups, group 2 is more important from a parsing point of view since its grammar is predicted and is an indivisible part of the structural meaning of the main clause.

8.2 Group 1: Non-Finite Clause as Relative, Noun and Adverbial Clause

These uses are like the subordinator subordination of relative clause, noun clause and adverbial clause described so far. Although these non-finite clauses are equally deserving of the treatment given to the subordinator clause forms, particularly the adverbial clause, they are simply noted here for the purpose of contrasting them with group 2 that follows.

8.2.1 *Postmodifier Clauses (Relative Clauses)*

In (93) below, we have the use of the past participle clause:

(93) The language **used by McCritty** authorised Denis punishing him on the spot. (Scheurweghs, 1959, p. 193)

Here we parse the clause whose first cue on its point of entry into the main clause is the **ed** ending of its verb, and with the completion of the preposition **by** by the nominal **McCritty**, our clause has come to an end. The same kind of treatment can be given to (94) and (95) below.

In (94) and (95) we have the use of the to-infinitive clause and the present participle respectively:

(94) The great evils **to be fought** were those of bad housing and unsatisfactory sanitary conditions. (Scheurweghs, 1959, p. 216)

(95) They sent a reply **deprecating detailed records of such discussions being published**. (Scheurweghs, 1959, p. 194)

Notice that the postmodifier analysis of (95) means that it is answering the pushdown question 'They sent **what kind of reply?**'

8.2.2 *Noun Clause*

Noun clause function is where the non-finites (all except past particle clause) function as nominal elements in subject, object, complement and 'object' of the preposition.

In (96), the to-infinitive clause functions as nominal in two places, in subject and in complement of an equative *be* clause:

(96) **To write the life of Marlborough** is **to write the history of the reign of Queen Anne** (Scheurweghs, 1959, p. 202)

Notice that the complement is being identified as the same thing as the subject.

In (97), the gerundial clause is object of the verb **love**:

(97) She loves **buying clothes and jewelry**. (Scheurweghs, 1959, p. 187)

Notice that the non-finite clause as object of verbs like **love** can have two meanings out of context according to the stress of new information. If it is on **buying**, the question which is being answered is: 'What does she love?' If, however, it is on **loves**, then the question is different: 'How does she feel about buying clothes and jewelry?'

Gerundial clauses as 'object' of prepositions are common in English; we parse the gerundial clause in the same way as we parse the nominal structure as 'object' of the preposition **in** as follows:

(98) The party believes in **hastening slowly**. (Scheurweghs, 1959, p. 182)

The noun clause can be seen as the answer to the question 'What does the party believe in?' This should elicit a noun or a gerundial reply, but we could have a gerundial question: 'What does the party believe in doing?' The kind of preposition plus gerundial clause is not to be confused with the subordinator-type preposition plus present participle clause such as the **by** -ing instrument clause of (99) below.

(99) Man can imitate the majesty of space and time **by thinking nobly**. (Scheurweghs, 1959, p. 182)

Here the clause **thinking nobly** can be shown to be an adverbial clause by the question which could elicit it: '**How** can man imitate the majesty of space and time?' The main clause elicits the adverbial clause in end-position. The reader is reminded here that **ing**-clauses are traditionally called gerunds when they function as noun clauses as in (97) and (98), and present participles when they function as adjuncts as in (99) above and in (101) below.

8.2.3 Adverbial Clause Use

We recognise adverbial clause function from the position of these non-finite clauses in the slots of the main clause as we did for the subordinator adverbials. We look for front-, mid- and end-position as before. Instead of the particular adverbial meanings of subordinators such as **because, if, since,** etc., we have the abstract semantics of the morphology of the non-finite verbs, with the affix **ed/en** signalling passive meaning, the affix **ing** signalling progressive meaning, and the more complex **to** having various meanings such as purpose or result with the notion of a future action which they can both imply.

In (100) below, we have a co-ordinated past participle clause in front-position, as adjunct of circumstance of use.

(100) **Spun as a stable fibre, and mixed with wool**, rayon can produce a wide variety of clothes. (Scheurweghs, 1959, p. 161)

Notice the similarity of the questioning as with front-position in 7.3.2: 'What can be done with rayon (in circumstances where it is) spun as a stable fibre and mixed with wool?'

In (101) below, we have a present participle clause in mid-position, interrupting the slot between the subject and the verb of the main clause:

(101) One of these dogs, **being mistaken for a wolf by a man he was digging out of the snow**, was shot dead. (Scheurweghs, 1959, p. 161)

Scheurweghs shows his awareness of the focus on the subject by these clauses by noting: 'The adjunct sometimes follows the subject, and has almost the character of a quasi-predicative adjunct.' Notice that it is not a postmodifier of **dog** as the question for the main clause shows: 'What happened to one of these dogs (on) **being mistaken for a wolf, etc.**?' This is a question for *consequence*, with the adjunct clause providing the *cause*.

In end-position, we have both purpose and result with the to-infinitive clauses in (102) and (103) respectively.

(102) Young people entered the monasteries **to be trained as novices**. (Scheurweghs, 1959, p. 219)

(103)   They urged the inspection of public schools, **to be met with the reply that this would degrade them.** (Scheurweghs, 1959, p. 219)

We can distinguish between purpose and result by means of the purpose subordinator **in order (to)**; it can be used to connect (102) but not (103), which is 'result'. Similarly we can distinguish between these **to**-infinitive clauses according to the questions that elicit them: 'For what purpose did young people enter the monasteries?' for (102), and 'With what result did they urge the inspection of public schools?' for (103). This last relation of resultative has long been recognised as paraphrasable by co-ordination in a manner which (102) is not: 'They urged the inspection of public school **and were** met with the reply that this would degrade them.' The relation of expectation is imposed by the co-ordinator **and** on the two events both presented as 'not hitherto known' following one another in normal time sequence. We have now lost the conviction of the resultative subordination by the non-finite clause.

This brief discussion suffices to show the similarity of these non-finite clauses to the subordinator adverbial clauses in end-position in 7.4.

So far, the description of non-finite clauses has paralleled the three kinds of subordinate clause by function for the subordinating conjunctions, namely relative clause, noun clause and adverbial clause. To these three kinds of subordination by function, we now add a fourth kind, which is unusual in that it exists only in non-finite clause form. These are the non-finite clauses which are structurally part of the predication of the preceding verb in their clause structure. These are taken up as group 2 below.

8.3   Group 2   Structurally Predicted Non-Finite Clauses

8.3.1   *Introduction*

The object of this description is to develop in the reader a notion of what constitutes a basic clause structure where there are at least two verbs in the structure, one of which is subordinated to the other. By basic clause structure I mean that you cannot have the one verb as clause without the other. Both Hornby and Scheurweghs have given a thorough description of verb patterns where there are two verbs in a larger clause: a first verb, usually but not necessarily finite, predicts a second non-finite clause *which grammatically completes its structure as clause*. An example of this from Hornby (1975, p. 63) is 'Do you **wish** me **to stay**?', where the choice of the verb **wish** predicts the non-finite clause (me) **to stay** as the grammatical completion of its predicate structure. We cannot reduce this clause to *Do you wish me?*, without destroying the meaning originally intended. Thus we see that the non-finite clause **to stay** is part of the basic clause.

It is necessary to contrast the non-finite clauses of group 2 with those of group 1. As already noted, the grammatical function of group 2 non-finites differs from that of group 1. Unlike group 1, group 2 non-finite clauses are not relative clauses (postmodifiers), not noun clauses, and not adverbial clauses; they are non-finites which are tied to a subject (usually the object of the preceding verb) and behave like any other independent clause except that they are non-finite and are tied grammatically and semantically to the preceding verb. For instance, the present participle clause **racing for a clearly certain try** in (104) below, is a non-finite clause whose subject is **his centre-three-quarter** which in turn is the object of the verb **sent** in the independent clause **He sent his centre-three-quarter racing for a clearly certain try**.

All four kinds of non-finite clause appear in these larger basic two-verb clauses. They are set out below in their various patterns, together with a list of some of the verbs which predict their structures to come. Of these four kinds of non-finite clause, the one which has received the most attention in linguistics is the **to**-infinitive clause, and two of its predictor verbs **expect** and **persuade**. Accordingly, we examine the to-infinitive clauses in more detail.

8.3.2 Present Participle Clause after the Object

These non-finite clauses are predicted by verbs like **get, catch, keep, leave, send, set, start, take**, etc. (See Scheurweghs, 1959, pp. 168–9.) Here is an example of the verb **sent** in (104) below:

(104) He **sent** his centre-three-quarter **racing for a clearly certain try**.
(Scheurweghs, 1959, p. 169)

Notice that we cannot remove the non-finite clause. This means that the meaning of the non-finite clause is in some way tied directly to the meaning of the verb **sends** in front of it. The same is true of all the remaining kinds of non-finite clause here.

8.3.3 Past Participle Clause after the Object

These non-finite clauses are predicted by a restricted range of verbs like **find, get, have, make** and **want**. (See Scheurweghs, 1959, pp. 167–9.) Here is an example of **want**:

(105) I do not **want** any other woman **substituted for Sarah**.
(Scheurweghs, 1959, p. 169)

8.3.4   Bare Infinitive Clause after the Object

These are the infinitive clauses whose verb does not have the *to* which
we observe in the **rather than**-clause, for example '**Rather than starve,**
he surrendered.' In this pattern, they are predicted by a more restricted
range of verbs than the **to**-infinitive clauses in 8.3.5 below. The verbs
are **feel, have, hear, help, listen to, see** and **watch**. (See Scheurweghs,
1959, pp. 239–40.) Here is an example of **feel**:

(106)   She **felt** her whole body **relax into the sweetest kind** of **peace**.
(Scheurweghs, 1959, p. 239)

8.3.5   To-infinitive Clause after the Object

Of the four kinds of non-finite clause described here, this pattern has
the widest range of verbs which predict it. According to Scheurweghs
(1959, pp. 227–9), there are at least 42 verbs in this pattern. here is his
list for the active infinitive clauses: **allow, ask, bear, beg, bring, cause,
challenge, compel, dare, direct, empower, enable, encourage, entitle,
expect, forbid, force, get, hate, help, intend, invite, lead, leave, like,
order, persuade, pledge, prefer, press, prompt, provoke, request,
require, summon, teach, tell, urge, want, warn,** and **wish.**

The significance of saying that these non-finite clauses are *not*
postmodifier, *not* noun clause and *not* adverbial clause can be seen in
the following three points about not postmodifier and not adverbial
clause. First, compare the postmodifier **to**-infinitive clause **to resume
work** of **we took the decision to resume work at that meeting**. We can
remove the clause **to resume work** without the collapse of the
grammar – **We took the decision at that meeting** – but we have lost the
pushdown information 'What decision?' Second, there is the negative
point that none of the patterns here can be *purpose adjuncts* or
resultative adjuncts which commonly take end-position. An example
is **Paulinus was sent from Kent** (in order) **to convert Edwin of
Northumbria and his people.** Like the postmodifier **to resume work**,
this adverbial adjunct can be removed without the collapse of the
grammar of the main clause.

Third, a curious thing about this verb pattern in transformational
generative grammar linguistics is the long and enduring popularity in
the literature of the two verbs **expect** and **persuade**. What is largely
ignored in the discussions of the grammar of these two verbs is the
meaning of their basic two-clause clause. This is the meaning of the

superordinate verbs in the **wh**-questions which steer the selection of lexical choice for both verbs. These are the verbs **do** (factive) and **think** (non-factive) which underlie the semantics of many verbs.

For the purpose of argument, let us take these two simple verbs and apply them to the verbs **persuade** and **expect** in turn. The **do**-question which we deal with here is the **do-to**-question, where the subject of the clause affects somebody else or something else. This question accounts for most of the verbs in this pattern. We begin by taking the verb **persuade** as an answer to a **do-to**-question:

(107) I had to **persuade** him **to desist from repainting an early work**. (Scheurweghs, 1959, p. 228)

Notice that the question which elicits this clause pattern must specify the participants to the reply: 'What did you have to do to him (about his treatment of an early work)?' Notice that this kind of question cannot be applied to (108) below:

(108) The Russian have always **expected** their novelists **to produce the political message of their time**. (Scheurweghs, ibid.)

Notice that there is no 'doing to' on the part of the Russians towards their novelists in the question 'What have the Russians always **thought** their novelists would/**should do** (in their novels)?' This question elicits both the first verb **expected** as an aspect of 'think', and the second verb **to produce**, etc. Otherwise, the question could be: 'What have the Russians always expected their novelists to do?' Such a question elicits only the **to**-finitive clause **to produce**, etc.

I hope it is plain from the above discussion that there is much work still to be done on the semantics of the above pattern as with the other three patterns. By presenting only the S V O types where O is taken as S of the non-finite clause, I have oversimplified the patterns of English verb which have predictable non-finite clauses ending their predicates. For example, I have conveniently ignored examples like the **to**-infinitive clause in (109) below, where the clause is superficially like that of the two-clause basic clause patterns of (107) and (108):

(109) He **had** many scathing remarks **to make about the matters discussed**. (Scheurweghs, 1959, p. 216)

The difference here is that the **to**-infinitive clause is a predictable postmodifier of the noun head **remarks** which is itself a predictable part of the grammatical structuring of the verb **have**. This pattern clearly does not belong to the **to**-infinitive clauses of 8.3.5 above because it is a postmodifying clause of the nominal structure **many**

scathing remarks. In (110) below, we have a present participle clause directly following the main verb **came**.

(110)   The child came **shouting his name**. (Scheurweghs, 1959, p. 159)

Here the non-finite clause is a predictable part of the semantics of the verb **came**; that is, the set notion that somebody comes doing something as they come. We have the problem of deciding to what extent the verb **came** requires grammatical completion by the non-finite clause. One solution is to regard the non-finite clause as part of its fixed structure, as we do for the non-finite clauses of 8.3.5.

Notwithstanding these important omissions, what I have said of the obligatory nature of the grammatical completion of the pattern by these non-finites shows their main clauses to be basic clause structures which are grammatically and semantically indivisible.

8.4   Summary and Conclusions about Group 1 and 2 Non-Finite Clauses

My purpose in describing the non-finite clauses was to distinguish between group 1 and group 2. Group 1 were those non-finite clauses which could be added to basic clause structure such as postmodifiers, noun clauses and adverbial clauses. These are the non-finite clauses over which we have grammatical choice according to what additional meaning we require in our basic clause. They contrast with group 2, where we have no such grammatical choice. We noted that the non-finite clauses which complete the grammar of the first verb of their two-verb clauses form a fourth category of subordinate clause according to function.

Although these non-finite clauses were defined negatively as *not* meaning postmodifier, noun clause or adverbial clause, it is clear that they do have a unique functional meaning of their own according to the kind of non-finite verb of their 'trapped' clause. What distinguishes this subordination from any other kind of subordination is that given the choice of the first verb of the pattern, the choice of the second non-finite clause is an obligatory part of the grammar of the structure which parallels **that**-clause subordination after verbs of saying and thinking. All we have been saying is what has long been known: that there are grammatical patterns in English which are fixed in both grammar and meaning. However, we saw that the same pattern could have at least two very different underlying meanings, for example in the **to**-infinitive clause pattern of group 2, where we had the verbs **persuade** and **expect** elicited by questions having the superordinate verbs 'do-to' and 'think' respectively.

Postmodifying Structures Other Than Relative and Adverbial Clause: Apposition and Interpolation

9.1 Introduction to Apposition and Interpolation

So far we have considered the various subordinate clauses which can modify the clause and its parts in various ways. If we ignore the premodifiers of all kinds, there are two other important ways of modifying the clause and its parts, both of which behave sequentially and syntactically like postmodifiers; that is, they refer back to and thus postmodify the meaning of the clause structure that immediately precedes them in much the same way as the postmodifiers of noun heads except that they are grammatically and semantically very different things. These two ways are apposition and interpolation (parenthesis). We can think of them as a kind of subordination *if only on the grounds that they are included physically within the boundary of a main clause*, as in (111) and (112) below. Any structure, including independent clause, must be regarded as in some way subordinate if it is enclosed within the boundary of a main clause.

Apposition can be defined as a special compatibility relation between two like structures of the clause in which the second structure may narrow down the meaning of the first. This compatibility meaning may be achieved by means of a repetition of the like, though more precise, structure in the clause. For instance, in (111) below, there is the repetition of the adverbial **if**-clause structure in front-position of its main clause, where the apposition is signalled by the structural connector **that is**.

(111) **If** we now add the force on all the particles, **that is if** we take the sum of all the Fi's for all the different indexes, we get the total force, F. (Osti Programme M. P. 1 Text)

Note that the presence of the connector **that is** prevents us from taking the two **if**-clauses as being co-ordinated, and that there is not merely the repetition of the semantics of **if**-clause but also a more precise meaning in the second **if**-clause. The first **if**-clause is the unspecific for which the second **if**-clause is the specific clause. Note, too, that the second **if**-clause interrupts the boundary between the first **if**-clause and the start of its main clause structure **we get the total force, F**, and in presenting the specific clause for the unspecific of the first **if**-clause it is postmodifying the meaning of this first **if**-clause.

Contrast this similarity of structure in apposition with the interpolation in (112) below, where we have a dissimilarity of structure in which a simple nominal group **The theory** is followed by an independent clause **and it is only a theory**, which is evaluating it.

(112)   The theory – **and it is only a theory** – is that these early frogs fed on smaller animals along the shores and banks of ponds and streams, and the shortest cut to safety when attacked was to leap into the water. (*New Scientist*, 23 June 1966, p. 763)

Note the independent clause signalled as interpolating by the co-ordinator **and** in its non-coordinate role. Note in particular the interruption of the subject **The theory** and its verb **is that**-clause. This interrupting clause is *evaluating* the significance of the word **theory** as a word in this context.

The difference between apposition and interpolation can be summed up as follows. Apposition may repeat a preceding structure of the clause, narrowing down its meaning, and in doing so delay the completion of the structural boundary of the first structure in its clause. Interpolation may interrupt the completion of clause structure at any point with an evaluation of what it is interrupting. A more precise description of the difference between apposition and interpolation now follows.

It is necessary to distinguish in more detail between the apposition of (111) and the interpolation (evaluation) of (112). Of the two, the less problematical is apposition because more is known about it than about interpolation. Interpolation is almost entirely ignored as part of regular grammar. Part of the problem is defining its exact grammatical status along with other more easily definable structures. In (112) we have an independent clause, admittedly indicated as interpolating, which interrupts the structure of its main clause in mid-position just like the mid-position interruptions of the adverbial clause already described. The semantics of interpolation is that of an *internal evaluation* of the clause or clause structure which has preceded it. What internal evaluation means will become clear below. The semantics of apposition, as we have noted, is that of a more precise definition of the first element by the second.

9.2.1   Introduction to Apposition

Apposition syntactically resembles co-ordination in that we nearly always have *a conjoining of like grammatical structures*. The big difference is the meaning of the conjoining of structure. With co-ordination, we can have like with like (What else?) or a change in time/space meaning (What follows next?), as in (113) and (114) respectively.

> (113)   He was himself a great public character **and a figure in local civil life.** (Scheurweghs, 1959, p. 312)

Here we have the co-ordination of the nominals **a great public character** with **a figure in local civil life,** in which the second nominal structure answers a question on the first: 'What else (is he)?' We don't take the second nominal as a narrowing down of the first nominal but merely as something else which is compatible with it as a description of him.

In (114) below, we have co-ordination between two independent clauses.

> (114)   Shortly afterwards England beat Australia, **and** the Ashes were said to have been brought back. (Scheurweghs, 1959, p. 312)

Here we have the second clause answering the question on the first, 'And what happened to the Ashes after that?' This is a question for a main clause. These two co-ordination examples suffice to show what apposition is not.

Apposition uses the power of structural conjoining to enforce a synonymy in which there is a narrowing down or a redefining of the meaning of the first structure by the second. There can be a repetition of structure that enforces some kind of synonymy by the power of its structural similarity. The second, similar, structure replaces the meaning of the first so that both meanings enter into a composite sum total while remaining distinctly separate contributions. This narrowing down of meaning can be seen in its explicit signals, starting with its typical questions: 'What is X?' and 'What do you mean by X/by that?'

The question **What is X?** is a very basic question for the identity of X throughout sequenced utterance. In appositional function, it can be either a pushdown question or a question for a clause reply. If the apposition is within clause structure, the question is a pushdown question; that is, we question the preceding structure only as part of the larger clause which we are not questioning. If, however, the apposition is between two independent clauses, the question is not pushdown but a question for a clause as reply; that is, it is not concerned with part of the structure as a structure within its main clause but rather with the relation between two independent clauses, for example 'What is X?', etc. Note that the question could equally well mean: 'What do you **intend to mean by X in this particular context?**' (The corresponding question for interpolation is 'What do you **think of X within the context of this clause?**')

There are various kinds of explicit connector for apposition. The (clause) connectors that follow require to be sorted out, but for the present purpose of this book they suffice: **more specifically, to be precise, namely, notably, in particular, that is, that is to say, or at least/rather, if not** (the dual semantics of these last three items are taken up below in 9.2.3). Included in apposition are two special operations clauses – **this is that**-clause, and **this is like saying that**-clause – which function as independent clauses where the **that**-clause complement contains the appositional element and the nominal **this** as subject refers back to the preceding clause.

9.2.2 Examples of Apposition

In the following examples, note how some of the writers show their awareness of the need for apposition by their uses of inverted commas around the particular words or phrases. The apposition is printed in bold.

In (115) below, the appositional structure of nominal groups function as 'object' of the prepositional phrase complement of the verb **sold**. The relation is made explicit by the connector **that is**. Notice how the interpolation **and a big one at that** interrupts the position between S and V of the relative clause of the second nominal head.

(115) It will be sold primarily as **a 'machining centre'; that is, a single automatic machine tool at which an entire component** – and a big one at that – **can be machined at one setting.** (*New Scientist*, 12 May 1966, p. 361)

The apposition here answers in pushdown form the question: 'What do you (intend to) mean by a "machining centre"?'

In (116) below, the apposition is between two independent clauses and revolves around the complement of the first clause **strongly piezoelectric**.

(116) According to J. N. Maycock and D. E. Grabenstain, many explosives are **strongly piezoelectric** – **they respond to pressure by the appearance of considerable electric voltages.** (*New Scientist*, 5 May 1966, p. 314)

The apposition here is presented as being between two independent clauses. It answers in clause form the question 'What do they mean by saying that many explosives are strongly piezoelectric? What has electricity got to do with their being strongly piezoelectric?'

In (117) below, the apposition is again between two independent clauses and is made explicit by the connector **that is**:

(117) These devices are at present only of the 'open-loop' type; **that is, they draw little or no information from the organ that they assist**, and thus involve very little control theory. (*New Scientist*, 30 June, 1966, p. 831)

Here the apposition appears to be answering in clause form the question 'What do you mean by saying that these devices are at present only of the "open-loop" type; what exactly do you mean by "open-loop"?'

So far we have considered the 'explaining' of certain words in the preceding clause or in the same clause, but sometimes the narrowing down is made explicit by certain words in both members of the apposition relation. In (118) below, the words **narrow scope** in the first clause of the second sentence and the limiter **only** in the second clause of the second sentence are printed in bold type; these words signal the redefinition of the meaning between the two clauses.

(118) The Government's Bill to appoint a Parliamentary Commissioner — the title chosen for Britain's Ombudsman — is all the more welcome since the whole project had appeared to be threatened with political euthanasia. Indeed, the suspicion felt by civil servants and the jealousy felt by M.P.s are still reflected in the **narrow scope** allowed to the Ombudsman: he can inquire **only** into complaints referred to him by M.P.s about the conduct of Government departments.

    This leaves a good deal outside the Ombudsman's brief: notably complaints against local Government. (*Observer*, 20 June 1966, p. 10)

The apposition relation between the clauses is between the nominal group **the narrow scope allowed to the Ombudsman** and the second clause which provides a clause reply to a pushdown question: 'What do you mean by the narrow scope allowed to the Ombudsman: how narrowly are his activities circumscribed?' Notice how the meaning of **narrow scope** is picked up by the limiter *only*. It is, perhaps, in this example that we can see the difference in meaning between connective adjuncts like **to be more precise** and **that is**. The adjunct **that is** is more appropriate here than the adjunct **to be more precise** as there is a close definition of **narrow scope**. The adjunct **to be more precise** is what it says it is: the concern is with greater precision as such rather than with definition as such. The linguistic point is that neither adjunct is used here because there are sufficient semantic features to signal the relation.

We might note the two examples of nominal apposition which occur in (118). First, there is the very common kind of *name* or *title* apposition in the first sentence; here the appositional structure is the object of the verb **appoint** which itself is part of the postmodifying clause of the main nominal head **The Government's Bill**: a Parliamentary Commissioner – **the title chosen for Britain's Ombudsman**. This could be the pushdown answer to the question 'What's that a title for?' Second, there is the apposition signalled by the adjunct **notably** in the last sentence; here the appositional structure is the object of the verb **leaves**. The appositional member is the lexical realisation of the items **a good deal**, as we see in the pushdown question 'A good deal of what?' The first nominal apposition structure delays the completion of the subject and hence the onset of the verb **is**; the second nominal apposition delays the completion of the object and hence of its main clause structure.

Finally, in (119) below, we have an example of special operations clause, the anaphoric **this is that**-clause, where the **that**-clause carries the appositional clause whose first member is referred to by the nominal **this** as subject.

(119) (1) There seems a good case, therefore, for Professor Lees's argument that the professions should be registered – and looked at – under the Restrictive Practices Act.

    (2) But it might be worth considering another approach, too. (3) **This is that the public should be represented on the governing bodies of the professions and associations.** (4) In the case of the Press Council (although journalism is a trade or art, not a profession) this kind of mixed set-up has worked well. (*Observer*, 6 February 1966, p. 10)

First, notice that sentence (2) here evaluatively mediates between the two arguments, the one in sentence (1) and the one in sentence (3), by signalling that the second argument is to be the next topic. Second, notice the question which elicits the apposition: 'What is this other approach that might be worth considering too?' In particular, notice the role of the modal verb **should** as part of the reply which matches it with the first argument in the first sentence here.

9.2.3 Problems: Where the Semantics of Apposition and Interpolation Meet

What we have so far ignored is the problem of the dual semantic relations which are inherent in the syntax of apposition structuring. By dual semantic relations I mean that there can be a dual relation consisting of apposition which is superimposed upon by interpolation. (It will be recalled that I call interpolation an internal evaluation of the clause as clause).

There are three reasons why apposition and interpolation have been put together for comparison and contrast. First, both apposition and interpolation postmodify their structures. Second, in their syntax both apposition and interpolation, especially in mid-positions of their clause, delay the completion of the syntactic boundaries of the structures which they are postmodifying. The significance of the notion of delay will be made clearer in the description of interpolation below. Third, their semantics differ sharply: apposition answers **What is X?** questions while interpolation answers **What do you think about X?** questions.

The clause connectors **or rather** and **or at least** impose dual relations of apposition by similarity of structure and of evaluation by the change in choice of lexical item being apposed. This point is illustrated by the use of the verbs in (120) and (121) below. In both of these appositional structures, the writer appears to be anticipating the reader's objection to the full meaning of the first verbs of the constructions.

In (120) below, we have the clause connector **or rather** signalling the apposition between the **to**-infinitive clauses of the **for-to**-infinitive clause subject, the break being shown by the full stop separating the two elements in bold type.

(120)   No wonder the gnomes snigger in the Prime Minister's face when he tells them there is a squeeze on. It is all well and good for Mr Wilson **to stop rich people from going abroad. Or rather to make rich people go abroad as if they were poor people with only £50 walking around money.** (*Guardian*, 14 June 1966, p. 7)

The writer's apposition here anticipates the reader's objection: 'Surely you don't really mean that Mr Wilson actually stops rich people from going abroad, do you?' The writer offers his reformulation of the meaning of the verb **to stop, etc.**, by the second verb predicate.

In (121) below, we have the clause connector **or at least** signalling the apposition between the passive verbs of the predication, reformulating the verb **shared** as **sympathised with**.

(121)   It [The Royal Shakespeare Company] wants the theatre to be democratic, to cease to be the playground of the comfortable middle sections of the community. I believe this ideal is **shared — or at least sympathised with** — by nearly everyone whom one admires in the theatre. (*Sunday Times*, 14 August 1966, p. 28)

The writer's apposition here anticipates the reader's objection: 'Surely you don't really mean that this ideal is shared by everyone, do you?' = No, but they do at least sympathise with it. The writer offers his reformulation of a reduced scope of meaning for the verb **shared** as **sympathised with**.

The theoretical question which now arises is this, why didn't the writer simply use the second verbs, the apposed verbs, **make**, etc., in (120) and **sympathised with**, etc., in (121) above, and cut down his message to what he really meant to say in the first place? I suggest that in these cases the writer intends to retain some of the meaning of the first verb, so that its meaning is extended in its range by the meaning of the second, apposed, verb. More simply, the writer intends to use both meanings.

9.2.4   *Summary and Conclusions on Apposition*

We have briefly considered the appositional structuring between nominals, clauses and independent clauses, noting the various appositional meanings by means of the **wh**-questions used to elicit the appositive element. We noted that that appositional structure between nominals were pushdown answers to questions such as 'What machining centre? What do you (intend to) mean by a machining centre?' (115), and that the appositional structuring between independent clauses were **wh**-questions which focused on certain nominal or adjectival elements of the preceding clause, for example 'What do you mean by saying that many explosives are **strongly piezoelectric**?' (116), (117), (118) and (119).

We also noted the problem of dual semantic relations of apposition and interpolation in the reformulated verbs of (120) and (121). We have ignored other similarly interruptive uses of adverbial subordination of elements which were used to reinterpret or reformulate a first lexical element by its subordinated reformulation within the same grammatical structure, for example the use of the **if-not** intrusion in (122) below, where the first adjective, **cynical**, is emphasised as new information by its given adjective head **hostile**:

> (122)   In Great Britain, the whole pervading tone of television, whether BBC or Independent, is unmistakeably Leftish in politics, permissive in morals, cynical **if not actually hostile** in its attitude to established religion and all traditional (though not progressive) forms of authority. (*Daily Telegraph*, 28 September 1966, p. 16)

Somewhere in the studies of English grammar all these reinterpretations have to be brought together.

Although we noted the postmodifying behaviour of apposition, we did not go into any detail about its potentially interruptive nature, apart from comparing it with the interpolation example of (112) above. This deficiency is partly made good in 9.3 below, where we discuss in more detail the interruptive nature of interpolation. The process is the same in principle.

Our theoretical problem in analysing apposition is the relation between independent clauses where we note that the actual apposition seems to be between a semantically significant nominal element in the first clause and its apposition in fully independent clause form. Since the second clause is independent, there is no way in which we could call it subordinate to the first clause, though we could note that in spite this independence, we must take the clause pairs in (116), (117), (118) and (119) as single semantic units, that is, as semantically indivisible linguistic units. This is particularly noticeable with special operations clauses like the **This is that**-clause of (119), which if taken out of context becomes meaningless as a construction. We have already noted the linguistic significance of unspecific versus specific clause on page 10, and in 2.3 and 2.4, where specific clause is the necessary lexical realisation of unspecific clause.

9.3 Interpolation as an Internal Evaluation of the Clause: the Super-Adjunct

9.3.1 Introduction

Theoretically, I see the clause in its executive function of independence as a potential vehicle for representing what we know and how we think about what we know. The unmarked state in communication is *know* and the marked state is *think*, though telling people what we know about something betrays what we think by what we have selected for our lexical realisation. The basic function of independence is to 'tell people something they don't know in terms of something which they do know', with the adverbial clause carrying what the encoder is presenting as known or given. The relation between 'think' and 'know' is brought out clearly in the impatient demand we might make of an opinionated person: 'Please don't tell us what you think; tell us what you *know*!' Interpolations are the encoder's anticipated answers to both 'think' and 'know' questions which we make in the middle of our clause, or at the end of the clause before we start our next independent clause structure. (Note that 'know' questions in interpolation are requests for significant facts, facts which are assessed as significant at the point of intrusion.)

9.3.2 *The Present Approach towards Interpolation*

I see both interjection and interpolation as belonging to the logical category of evaluation whose superordinate verb in **wh**-questions is 'think'. Interjection expresses our emotions on how we feel about the clause; needless to add, this is the slot for swearing. Interpolation expresses what we 'think' or 'know' to be significant to the clause which we are encoding. The linguistically important feature of interpolation is that it works in two ways: it signals what we as encoders think or know about the clause, and at the same time it signals what we might want our decoders to think or to know.

The notion of evaluation needs some explanation at this point in view of my title 'Interpolation as an Internal Evaluation of the Clause', and the point I have just made that evaluation is at the heart of the semantics of both interjection and interpolation. First we note that evaluation as a 'think' category covers a range of subjective ways of thinking or looking at things. Consider the following verbs as superordinate selective items of **wh**-questions: **assess, comment upon, compare, evaluate, judge, express an opinion**, etc. Second, we must distinguish between an evaluation (includes comment) clause from interpolation clauses which evaluate.

An evaluation clause is where the whole clause is devoted to an (independent) clause answer to an evaluation question. In (123) below, the last sentence typically evaluates or comments upon the preceding three sentences of its paragraph.

> (123) Mr Johnson decided that there was a great deal to be said for saying nothing. He made no public statement and no private comment intended to find its way to the public. He permitted none by his aides. **It was a wise policy.** (*Daily Telegraph*, 17 April 1967, p. 14)

Note the question: 'What do you think of Mr Johnson's policy (towards the Kennedy Affair) as it is reflected in his decisions and their implementation by himself and his staff?' It is important to notice that the comment of the last sentence is not treating the preceding sentences as *reasons* but rather as its topic for which it is the comment. What this means is that if there is going to be a further sentence it is most likely to be 'Why was it a wise policy?'

By contrast with the comment clause of (123) above, an interpolation clause evaluates an already existing host clause, as in (124) below, where an independent clause interrupts the slot between the indirect object and the direct object of the verb **tell** of the host clause.

> (124) However, the authorities tell me — **and I think now that I believe**

them – that there isn't any real need to lose any sleep over him. (*Observer*, 28 August 1966, p. 13)

Notice that, as with the comment clause, the independent clause expresses the answer to a think-question: 'What do you think of what the authorities tell you here?' In particular, note the verbs **think** and **believe** in the interpolating clause. Note also that it is an anticipatory evaluation of the direct object of the verb **tell**.

9.3.3 A Redefinition of Interpolation

In the light of the foregoing discussion of interpolation, I would like to redefine it for the purpose of examining the examples which follow. I see interpolation as one of the theoretical problem areas in the description of English grammar not so much because it is inherently difficult but rather because it has been largely neglected. As already noted, I see interpolation as the same grammatical category as interjection except that interpolation is less emotional and more informative in having clauses rather than emotive nouns, adjectives, etc. We now note that interpolation differs syntactically from interjection in that it cannot take front-position and only comes into play once its host clause has been started. (Note that end-position is interruptive in that it delays the finalisation of its host clause's sentence boundary.)

Except for front-position, it can interrupt almost any structural boundary whatever including all the other slots open to adverbial clause, for example A * S * Vi * Vii * O * etc. A key feature of its signalling is that it has a separate tone group or special intonation to mark off its intrusion into clause structure, a feature which is reflected in written English by the use of two commas, two dash signs, one dash sign, or a pair of brackets.

The most important thing we can say linguistically about interpolation is that it represents the encoder's conscious awareness and control over the production of his clause; its ubiquitous powers of intrusion suggest that it is at the heart of our control. We can best explain its textual function by adopting the old terms 'Topic' and Comment', but with necessary changes. We ignore the old confusion of topic and comment with theme (given) and rheme (new), proposing the following scheme for topic and comment instead. We assume that the communicative function of independence for the clause is to present a topic or develop a topic. As we noted earlier, my notion of topic is not theme but participants plus the semantics of the predication and this includes both given and new.

R. H. Robins (1967, p. 53) noted that Priscian treated interjection as a separate word class instead of treating it as a subclass of the adverb as Thrax and Apollonius had done before Priscian. I incline strongly to the analysis of Thrax and Apollonius, and take interjection and interpolation as a class of adverb or adjunct. Where I differ from this analysis is that I see interpolation as a super-adjunct in a class of its own. My reason for calling it a super-adjunct is that it has infinitely greater powers of intrusion into the clause than the adverbial clause as well as having its own kind of meaning. Perhaps we could call it an evaluation adjunct.

Taking each clause as presenting its topic, the clause structure becomes the minimum *linguistic* situation that expresses the topic. Its unmarked state is topic only; the marked state is where comment is included by interpolation. This is what I mean by saying that interpolation is the internal evaluation of the clause. In short, the clause is the linguistic situation (topic), and the interpolation is its comment. As an evaluation adjunct, it evaluates the clause or the contextually significant parts of the clause.

One of the theoretical problems to resolve in interpolation is the question of how marked interpolation is. Obviously we could not interpolate in every sentence we utter if only because the constant momentary suspension of its production would be intolerable to our decoders. There seems to be good reason to believe that interpolation by independent clause is the most marked kind of interpolation. In our discussion of interpolation, we consider only interpolation by clause.

9.4   Some Problems in Analysing Interpolation

9.3.1   Introduction

Before examining examples of interpolation by clause we need to consider two kinds of syntactic problem: interruptive co-ordination and apposition-like interpolation. These are separate areas of modification for the clause which have to be taken into account. We take interruptive co-ordination first.

9.4.2   Interruptive Co-ordination of the Clause

R. A. Hudson (1968, p. 369) has described in some detail textual examples of interruptive co-ordination under the concept of *extended domain*. This is the syntactic notion of two or more clauses sharing grammatical constituents when they are being co-ordinated. The particular kind of extended domain we are considering here is represented by the example 'He likes, **but does not drink**, coffee.' Here the second clause **but does not drink** shares both the subject **he** and the object **coffee**, interrupting the constituent relation between the verb of the first clause **He likes** and its object **coffee**. Notice that the participants in the clause pair are lexical, and not elements of special operations clauses like the **it** of the cleft clause. The criterion for recognising this kind of interruption is whether we can rewrite the clauses as a normally sequenced clause pair – **He likes coffee but (he) does not drink it** – where we represent the object **coffee** by the pronoun **it**. What is not generally understood is that in doing this the meaning of the co-ordination is changed. Two textual examples will suffice.

In (125) below we have the second clause of the co-ordination interrupting the syntactic relation between the **to**-element of the **to**-infinitive clause whose lexical verb and predicate it shares:

(125) The question is, do we want to – **and can we afford to** – invest the money to provide the gas and electricity capacity to meet the demand in a few days of the year when the weather conditions are exceptional? (*Observer*, 21 November 1965, p. 10)

We could rewrite this example by removing the interrupting co-ordinate clause and placing it after the first question clause as a second question: '**And can we afford to** (invest the money for this purpose)?' The length of the predication of the first question militates against this change, but we move from a combined question and the difference of emphasis inherent in having two questions; we separate out **wanting to** from **affording to invest**. See Quirk *et al.* (1972, pp. 592–3) and R. A. Hudson (1969, p. 3) on this matter of difference in co-ordinating questions.

Next, in (126) below, we have the interruption of S and V structure by the replacement of the subject whose clause value and its clause-relational meaning is signalled by the clause connector **therefore**. This kind of interruption is the unmarked form where there is a repetition of the predication.

(126) The reasons for this are complex: it seems that while society feels that death is a tragedy, divorce remains something of a permissible crime; someone, somewhere, must be to blame. So divorcees, **and therefore their children**, are still ostracised. For it is impossible to penalise the parents without also punishing their children. We cannot, as yet, show our children that divorce is a symptom of emotional change and not battle, or failure. (*Guardian*, 10 August 1966, p. 6)

There are three points to be noted about this co-ordination. First, in the original text the clause connector **therefore** is italicised, thus emphasising its particular meaning as we would with stress. Second, notice that the sentence which follows it is an evaluation of it as the situation in which divorcees and therefore their children find themselves. Third, we can rewrite the clause pair in the sequence signalled by **therefore**: So divorcees are still ostracised **and therefore their children** are still ostracised. We now have a very highly marked second member which has lost the confidence by givenness of the interruptive form of the original. (We call this significant lexical repetition.)

In both of these examples there is a sharing of the clause structure which has lexical participants. This sharing could be rewritten as normal non-interruptive co-ordination, but with changes of meaning. It is clear that there is no confusing this with interpolation by independent clause.

9.4.3 *Apposition-Like Interpolation of the Clause: the Verbless Clause*

The kind of verbless clause we are talking about here is where we have a nominal group which evaluates the preceding clause(s) as its situation. In end-position, such verbless nominal clauses resemble the postmodifying behaviour of nominal apposition. Like the independent verbless clause (126) above, this kind of verbless clause presupposes a deletion of their (special operations) clause structure grammatically analogous to the deletion of anticipatory *It* and its verb **be** in the change from the formal **It is a pity he left** to the informal **Pity he left**. This particular kind of special operations clause has a special subject in which there appear the substitute nominals **this, that** or **it** in a clause whose verb is the equative use of **be** and whose complement in turn contains an evaluated nominal group. The substitute items in the subject of this clause refer back to the preceding clause(s) which are evaluated by its complement. R. A. Hudson (1968, p. 510) noted this feature of certain verbless clauses in end-position. He did not speak of deletion of **this** as subject and its verb **be**, but of a 'covert subject whose referent was the situation specified by the whole of the preceding main clause, with the nominal functioning as an attributive'. For a detailed textual description of the semantics of these important substitute nominals, see M. P. Jordan, 1978, pp. 101–206.

A single example of one of these verbless clauses in its context will suffice to illustrate this kind of interpolation. In (127) below, we have a verbless clause separated from its preceding lexical referent clause by a full stop. It interpolates the writer's point of view of the preceding clause pair which are connected by a dash sign.

(127) These phrases may seem glib, but they are easily understood; they epitomise the situation in words that the man in the street understands. in this election, the Conservatives failed to do this — they went over the heads of the people. **A fatal mistake.** (Letter, *Observer*, 10 April 1966, p. 24)

There are four points to be noted. First, taking the immediately preceding clause, the idiomatic **they went over the heads of the people,** as the correction for which its preceding clause is the denial, we note that the verbless clause **A fatal mistake** could be an answer to the question 'What do you think of the fact that they went over the heads of the people like that?' = (It was) **a fatal mistake** (on their part). Second, we note that the lexical item **mistake** has clause reference; that is, it is referring to the meaning relation between the two clauses of the preceding clause pair. (See Winter, 1977, pp. 18–21.) Third, the fully explicit form **It was a mistake (on their part)** for this context loses the clause the confidence which its givenness by verbless grammar confers upon it. Fourth, the position of the verbless clause as a structure that refers to its immediately preceding clause forces us to take it as a clause of some kind in the absence of other grammatical structure.

9.4.4 *Summary and Conclusions*

We have noted that these verbless clauses are apposition-like because they are clauses realised by nominal structure in end-position, and that they are evaluations for which their host clauses are their situations. The controversial point about these clauses is the claim that they are lexically and grammatically dependent on their preceding clauses by an inclusion within them which becomes non-grammatically dependent when we paraphrase them in their fully grammatical forms. What the psycholinguists might well test is my claim here that the structural inclusion within the sentence boundary of the host clause imparts the confidence by givenness which characterises adverbial clause. As will be seen, we return to this matter of confidence by grammatical inclusion in all the instances of independent clause interpolation.

9.5 General Description of Interpolation by Clause

9.5.1 *Introduction*

There are three main problems in describing interpolation by clause. The first is how to classify it according to what it is modifying; that is, what it is referring back to. The second is meaning. The third is emphasis.

The examples are arbitrarily divided into two main kinds of (post) modification: modification of a significant noun in the host clause, especially subject or object (9.5.2), and modification of clause, especially subordinate clause (9.5.3). We are ignoring the vast range of interruptions of the host clause structure other than subject or object position such as the interruption of one of its premodifier structures, for example 'His big – **and I mean big** – problem is his manners.' Such a discussion would require a more detailed discussion of the grammar of the clause, which is beyond the scope of the present work. Of the two kinds of modification here, modification of a significant noun of the host clause is very like the unmarked postmodification of the noun head and the postmodifying relation of apposition. We need to show what the difference is between postmodification by interpolation and the stock postmodification of the noun head.

The second problem, the problem of meaning, concerns the instances of affirmation and denial clause which characterise interpolation by independent clause. How can we analyse these clauses as evaluation along with the independent clauses which appear to directly answer think-questions? I consider affirmation and denial as answers to know-questions when they are independent clauses in their own right, so why analyse them by meaning as evaluations?

In considering these questions, it is important to remember *where* they are being asked – inside the confines of a host clause boundary. First, the think-question: 'What do I think of X **that matters here?**' Next, the know-question: 'What do I know of X **that matters here?**' Both questions presuppose that these clauses have not already been said in the context of the communication for the encoder and the intended decoder. Note the bold part of these questions, **that matters here.** With the know-question, it is asking for an evaluated 'know' and by this I mean a knowledge which the encoder thinks is relevant to the purpose of the message of the clause. It is this assessing of knowledge as relevant that makes me analyse it as evaluation meaning.

The third problem is emphasis. The general point of principle about deliberate interruptions or delays in clause grammar is that any internal grammar of the clause which is strongly set off by punctuation or by intonation is potentially interpolative because its grammar choice is being emphasised. It is important to note that any marking of the clause structure signals an awareness of how it affects the contextual meaning of the clause, for example the cleft clause, etc., has in common with the interpolative process that they are both evaluative. (See discussion of the delayed adjunct for the clause on p. 152.)

9.5.2 *Interpolation of Nouns by Clause*

Interpolation of nouns by clause means that the interpolating clause refers back to the immediately preceding noun or nominal group of the structure of the host clause which it is interrupting. One of the problems in recognising the postmodifying semantics of interpolation is its resemblance physically and semantically to certain kinds of non-restrictive relative of the kind which is easily made up, for example 'George, **who had been forewarned,** evaded the police'. There is a clear causal relation between his being forewarned and his evading the police: because he had been forewarned, he evaded the police. This causal relation is also seen in the restrictive relative clause whose antecedent is an indefinite pronoun, for example. '**Anyone who had been forewarned** evaded the police.'

Interpolation of nouns by clause focuses upon the meaning of the noun as it is presented in the context of its own clause, the clause structure which immediately precedes the interpolating clause, reinterpreting its significance as a noun in that context. This is something which normal postmodifiers cannot do; they are already syntactically part of the meaning of the noun in its clause in the fixed meanings of postmodifiers which may further specify the meaning of the noun head but not evaluate it or its meaning.

Nouns may be interpolated by subordinate clauses or by independent clauses. A common kind of subordinate clause interpolation is by **if**-clause which signals a hypotheticality for the meaning of the noun and hence a doubt for it. A very common place to find these interpolations is where the noun is subject, so that the host clause is interrupted between noun and verb. However, it needs to be said that the host clause can be interpolated almost anywhere.

Interpolation by independent clause can be signalled by interpolating **And**, or it can be an ordinary independent clause otherwise unsignalled.

We begin with interpolation of nouns by subordinate clause and then follow this with interpolation of nouns by independent clause. In each case, we note how the interpolation affects the meaning of the noun. Notice how the punctuation by double commas, double dash-signs and by brackets closely reflects the separate tone group we would give these interpolations in speech. Where the interpolation ends the clause boundary, it is usually shown by a single dash sign, as it is in (128) below.

In (128) the writer converts the word **halt** as it is in its context of **called a halt** from the 'real' to the 'hypothetical'. He is expressing doubt about the nature of the **halt** in this context. Note the marked structure of C S V in which the fronted C focuses upon the word **halt**.

The interpolation ends the clause boundary.

(128)   It is still being argued that Mao Tse-tung knew all along exactly what he was doing, and that it is he who decided to call a **halt** – **if a halt it is**. (*Guardian*, 3 March 1967, p. 11)

In (129) below, with the **if**-clause focusing on the meaning of the word **movement** in S, the writer implies some disbelief about the significance of the word **movement**, quite apart from hypothesising the main clause.

(129)   In a period when the Conservatives must have hoped to recover some of the ground lost during the long parliamentary recess, **the movement – if this poll is to be believed** – has actually been sharply the other way. What does it mean?
        Surely not that the Conservatives would be ground into an early oblivion if there were an early election. (*Guardian*, 20 November 1965, p.8)

In (130) below, we have the reason conjunction **for** reaffirming the truth of the word in subject, **slaughter**, interrupting the slot between S and V. Note the marked structure of C S V in this clause which focuses on the word **slaughter**:

(130)   Sometimes the seals are trapped in nets close to shore and held under water until they drown (in Britain, I believe, it is illegal to drown a dog). This slaughter – **for slaughter it is** – is watched by the parent seals, who are driven into the water. This sickening cruelty is a high price to pay for a coat. (*New Statesman*, 29 April 1967, p. 613)

In the above interpolations, the evaluation is as follows. In (128) and (129), the expression of doubt is an evaluation of the truth of the word in the context; in (130), there is an expression of strong certainty as to the truth in the context in which the writer is 'spelling out' the meaning of the word **slaughter**. Notice that the subject **This slaughter** is itself a retrospective evaluation of the action of the preceding clause, drowning seals, etc.

In independent clause interpolation we look for other cues. We look especially for cues of evaluation or cues of affirmation or denial in the clause itself. Except for the use of interpolating **and**, there is the parsing cue of its intrusion into structure: the sudden change of structure is obvious enough. In written English, there is generally the signal of punctuation to show the sudden break.

In (131) below, we have the interruption of the simple nominal subject **the policy** and its verb **applies** by an independent clause evaluation of its meaning:

(131) So the policy (**attitude is perhaps a better description**) applies only in Africa, where the United States and France are predominant but where there is no immediate East – West struggle or contiguous military frontiers permitting the enforcement of explicit and positive alignments. (*New Statesman*, 28 August 1966, p. 294)

The evaluation is explicit in the comparison as **better** and the noun **description**. We can show the evaluation meaning by means of the presupposed questioning: 'Surely you wouldn't describe what is going on as **policy**, would you: do you really mean there **is** a policy?' = No, attitude is perhaps a better description.

In (132) below, the independent clause in brackets **and they are many** interrupts the simple nominal subject **the others** and its verb predicate **have to reply**, etc.

(132) Some captains, whose aircraft have doppler or inertial aids, have no difficulty in maintaining true courses along their alloted [*sic*] tracks. The others (**and they are many**) have to rely on radio aids to navigation.
      These aids are good enough when there are no atmospheric disturbances although they are not available to liners following the more southerly course. (*New Scientist*, 16 June 1966, p. 693)

The evaluation here is a reaffirmation of the significance of the plurality of the indefinite anaphoric pronoun **others** by showing that it is not a vague small **others** but has significance in its (large) numbers. This is to be compared with the reaffirmation of meaning of the word **theory** in (112): 'The theory – **and it is only a theory** – is that . . .' Here the writer is ensuring that the word **theory** is taken only for what it means and no more. Notice the difference in punctuation between the brackets of the above example and the double dashes of (112). There is often no predicting which of these kinds of punctuation the writer might use.

Finally, we conclude the examples of interpolation of nouns by independent clause to show the 'anywhereness' of intrusion by the clause. In (133) below, the independent clause interrupts the nominal co-ordination late in clause structure, and by this I mean that it appears just before the co-ordinator where there is one.

In (133) below, the nominal group **the colony's needs** is interpolated by independent clause, thus interrupting the co-ordination between it and the second nominal group **and the output of the largest desalinisation unit**, etc.

(133) An extensive review of the colony's remaining water resources is now at hand, but there is no sign yet that Hong Kong is ready to buy

desalinated water. For one thing, there is an immense disparity between the colony's needs — **the record is 138 million gallons one day last August** — and the output of the largest desalinisation unit now at work — 1·4 million gallons a day. (*New Scientist*, 2 June 1966, p. 595)

Here we have a 'know' interpolation which answers the evaluative 'know' question 'What do you know about the colony's needs that matters here?' The evaluation is explicit in the lexical item **record** and the figure cited is particularly significant as a contrast with that of the desalination unit. This positive clause is an affirmation clause; it affirms as significant 'fact' that the record is 138 million gallons one day last August.

9.5.3 *Interpolation of Clause by Clause*

One of the reasons for calling interpolation the super-adjunct is that it can be adjunct to our stock unmarked adjunct, the adverbial clause. As with the interpolation of nouns, we have interpolation of adverbial clause by subordinate clause and by independent clause, with corresponding differences of contextual meaning because of their differences of grammatical status. A common subordinate clause which interpolates the adverbial clause in front-position is the so-called non-restrictive relative clause. In these examples, the interpolating clause refers back to the whole of the adverbial clause *as adverbial clause in the context of its main clause*.

In (134) below, the subordinator item **which** refers back to the **When**-clause in front-position, adding the adverbial notion of **frequency** as a given evaluation of the action of its clause. The evaluation is explicit in the lexical item (not) **infrequently**, offering a judgement of the situation.

(134) When an Italian wants to wash his hands of everything (**which is not infrequently, because life in Italy is complicated**) he goes to Positano. Positano is completely Italian. It is difficult to live in, yet you are more alive when you live there. (*Observer*, 16 January 1966, p. 28)

In (135) below, the subordinator item **which** refers back to the **Once**-clause in front-position, evaluating the likelihood of becoming accustomed to finding their way around the redesigned paper. The evaluation is explicit in the verb **believe** and in the judgement of doing something **quickly**.

(135) 'Change', said Richard Hooker, 'is not made without inconvenience,

even from worse to better.' We hope that any inconvenience the unfamiliar look of today's issue of The Times will cause old readers will be short-lived, and that once they have become accustomed to finding their way around the redesigned paper – **which we believe they will do quickly** – they will agree (Leading article, *The Times*, 3 May 1966)

The confidence 'by taking something for granted as true' is a feature of these interpolations by non-restrictive relative clause. The reader can readily appreciate the taken-for-grantedness of these subordinate clauses by rewriting the relative **which** as the substitute nominal **this**, thus converting the subordinate clause to independence, for example **This we believe they will do quickly** in (135) above. With independent clause, we have lost the confidence of subordination and are now presenting the clause as new.

In (136) below, we have a very familiar kind of interpolation by independent clause, characteristically with the verb **should** or **ought to know**. The interpolating clause is offering affirmation with basis (Thurston, five times an escapee) of what is hypothesised as true (**If that is true**). The interpolation is evaluating the 'knowing' of the first sentence, 'A man on the run', etc.

(136)   A man on the run, said experienced jailbreaker Stanley Thurston, is a creature of darkness, afraid of daylight.
    If that is true – **and Thurston, five times an escapee, should know** – it is 100 times more so for Harry Roberts.
    For Thurston, despite his reputation as 'the man no jail could hold', had one thing in his favour: he was not wanted for questioning about the murder of a policeman. (*Observer*, 21 August 1966, p. 1)

So far we have considered those interpolations which interrupt the structure of their host clause in some way comparable to the mid-position interruption of adverbial clause. What requires some explanation is the claim that interpolating clauses in end-position are interrupting the completion of their host clause's grammatical boundary. As last structure in end-position it stands between its host clause and the next (independent) clause or sentence, delaying the relation between the two clauses. The significance of this 'delaying action' is best understood by examining examples of co-ordination where the interpolating clause appears just before we expect a co-ordinator like **and** or **but,** or just before we expect the onset of the grammatical boundary of the next (independent) clause.

It is important to point out here that, as with mid-position adjuncts, any obvious delaying of adjunct structures in end-position is potentially interpolative; by delaying the adjunct, we emphasise its syntactic **and** semantic meaning as adjunct, as in (137) below, where we have an adverbial clause of condition in end-position.

> (137)   If, on the other hand, these patients were merely submitted to haemodialysis as a preliminary to transplantation, and then put back on to the artificial kidney if and when the transplanted kidney was rejected by the recipient, this would involve around 2,000 transplantations a year – **always provided this number of suitable kidneys could be found**. (*The Times*, 7 December 1966, p. 13)

We conclude with three examples of 'know' interpolation. They are not intended to imply that 'know' interpolation is necessarily a characteristic of end-position; consider the example of 'think' interpolation in (127): **A fatal mistake**, where the adjective **fatal** signals the evaluation of the noun **mistake** which in turn is signalling the meaning of the preceding clause pair. It is because 'know' interpolation is more controversial than 'think' interpolation that I have chosen 'know' examples to illustrate interpolation of clause by independent clause.

In (138) below, the interpolating independent clause pair interrupts the co-ordination of the adverbial adjunct of purpose in end-position of the main clause. It does so by taking end-position in the first **to**-infinitive clause **to replace them X**. In this position, it interrupts the co-ordination at X of the correlative paired conjunctions **not so much** 1 – X – **but** 2, where 1 is the first clause and 2 is the second clause of the co-ordination.

> (138)   The whole shift of the Welfare State puts charities in a new light. It is bearing down on voluntary agencies, not so much to replace them – **on the whole it couldn't if it wanted to, and it doesn't** – but to modify their activities. There are whole areas where private and public bodies are being forced into a *de facto* merger. (*Observer*, 16 January 1966, p. 21)

Here the writer is anticipating a 'know' question from the reader for which he stops the production of the co-ordination of the adverbial adjunct: 'Can it really replace them? What do you know about it that matters here?' Notice the elements of evaluation in the clause pair: the generalisation **on the whole** and the modal verb **couldn't** hypothesised by the **if**-clause, and the denial as true in the second clause – **it doesn't** (replace them). In any case, the correlative pair **not so much . . . but** is putting the emphasis on **modifying activities**.

In (139) below, the bracketed interpolating clause is in end-position to the second independent clause of the three non-coordinated independent clauses connected by semicolons. In this position, it interrupts the boundary between its main clause and the next independent clause. Very often this is what the layman means when he talks about parenthesis.

> (139)   The social expenditure we want, the increased standard of living, the reforms of education, require rapid growth: more rapid growth requires that the capital investment targets of the Plan be broadly met (**they are not at the moment**); more investment now requires less consumption now. (*New Statesman*, 29 April 1966, p. 1)

Again we have a denial clause interpolation. The writer is anticipating the predicted 'know' question which a hypothetical clause raises; as a **that**-clause, it is signalled as hypothetical by the matrix clause verb **requires**. It raises the question 'What do you know about this: Are they being broadly met?' = No, **they are not** (being broadly met) **at the moment**.

9.6   Speculating about Interpolation

First we noted that interpolation was an internal evaluation or comment on the clause as clause. This description clearly covers mid-position, but does not appear to cover end-position unless we think of end-position as interruptive. Interpolation is self-evaluation of the clause, focusing on part or whole of the clause. Interpolation of nouns by clause (or any other part of speech, for example the subordinator **if** as in '**If** – and a very big "if" it is, too' –) is an example of internal evaluation, and interpolation of clause by clause in end-position is whole clause evaluation.

We also noted that I considered the host clause as topic (using 'topic' in two senses of the term) and interpolation as its comment. The difficulty in explaining this role of interpolation lay in its semantics and in the fact that we have an evaluation clause with the same semantics (evaluation clause is an independent clause which is non-interruptive and which is devoted entirely to evaluation or comment, for example **It was a wise policy** in (123), which answers the question 'What do you think of this policy, etc?'). Once this difference between evaluation clause and interpolation clause is clear, the reader should have no difficulty in recognising interpolation by clause.

In introducing the notion of interpolation, I hypothesised that the communicative role of (independent) clause was to tell the decoder something he did not know in terms of something he did know, and that the unmarked state of information was *know* information while the marked state of information was *think* information (for example

'It was a wise policy'). It seems that with interpolation this relation of unmarked/marked is reversed: in interpolation clause, 'think' information is the unmarked while 'know' information is the marked, though it was pointed out that the 'know' information was evaluative information.

If we have started our clause and have second thoughts about the meaning of the clause at any point, and wish to say something to our decoder about the significance of the clause at that point in the clause *without leaving the clause*, what do we do as encoders? We simply suspend operations on the clause at that point, say what we want to say about it, and, when we have said it, finish the clause. For the decoder, however, we have stopped the production of our clause and kept him waiting while we tell him something about it. Similarly, with end-position, we keep him waiting for us to start the next sentence while we arbitrarily delay completing the sentence boundary of our clause with an interpolation.

The key feature of interpolation that emerges here is that it is necessarily an *ad hoc* adjunct which can interrupt our clause according to our impression about the effect the meaning is having on our decoder. It is outside the normal choice of grammar and as such it is purely *optional* in the sense that adverbial clauses for all their vaunted mobility are not. In communicating everyday things, we do need the stock of clause relational meanings of comparison, contrast, consequence, condition, effect, cause, hypothetical, instrument, place, purpose, reason, real, time, etc., but we do not absolutely need interpolation, so why have it at all?

There are at least two reasons. The first is that it does what the adverbial adjuncts do not do: it evaluates or comments upon the clause itself. We could quite happily call it an evaluation adjunct just as we speak of purpose adjuncts, for example 'He worked in a factory **to avoid the discomfort of poverty**.' The second reason is that it enables us to exert the ultimate control over any meaning in the clause. Ignoring the role of modal verbs and their lexical paraphrases, for example **may** with **possible**, adverbial adjuncts including intensifiers enable us to exert a stock control over the meaning of the clause and its parts, but interpolation can go beyond this in the various ways described above. The important theoretical point is this: if we want to think of an infinite modulation of meaning for the clause, then this is only possible through the organised interference with the construction and completion of the clause by the interpolative function.

9.7   Why Interpolation Should Be Seen as a Super-Adverbial Adjunct

We have noted that interpolation, like interjection, is to be regarded as an adjunct but, unlike interjection, it is to be regarded as a super-adjunct. The implication of this 'naming' is that interpolation is in some way a superordinate choice to the choice of adverbial adjunct or any other kind of grammar. The problem is, what kind of adjunct are we to classify interpolation as? With adverbial clause, for instance, we have the structural signal of its subordinate clause status over independence, but with interpolation, except for the use of the co-ordinator **and** where there is no other sign of co-ordinate structure, we have no special signal of interpolation other than its interruption of the 'normal' grammatical operations of the clause.

We can conclude from this that it is a special function of control over the clause in which we evaluatively modulate the meaning at any strategic syntactic boundary, even within the co-ordination of premodifying adjectives, as in 'all traditional (though not progressive) forms of authority' in (122), where there is an interpolative use of the **though**-clause to modify the meaning of the adjective **traditional** in its context. We can speak of this control over the clause as the interpolative function.

There remains the paradox of having an adverbial clause which can be independent, with all that independence means. We now consider two examples of this kind of interpolation to examine the differences in grammatical choice between interpolation and the normal presentation of independent clause outside the host clause.

In (140A) below, we have a 'know' interpolation by independent clause, **and it has**, which is embedded inside an **if**-clause which in turn is embedded inside an **although**-clause: 'What do you know about such occasions: do they ever arise?'

> (140A)   Finally, if you can't stop your baby screaming or being sick, then the airhostess can't, either, although she can, if the occasion arises – **and it has** – save its life. (*Observer*, 30 June 1967, p. 23)

Here, the adverbial clause of hypotheticality is semantically upgraded by being affirmed as true or real. An alternative, postponing the adverbial clause until after its host clause, would be:

> (140B)   Finally, if you can't stop your baby screaming or being sick, then the airhostess can't, either, although she can, if the occasion arises, save its life. And in fact **such occasions have arisen**.

The forms (A) and (B) differ in a crucial respect. (A) carries the sense that the point of offering the hypothesis is that such occasions have arisen and are to be talked about. The interpolation lexicalises, in clause form, the presupposition carried by the **if**-clause within the context of the **although**-clause. No such presupposition holds in (B). The last clause is not presented on the assumption of being presupposed by the preceding **if**-clause, and there is no sense that it expresses something already known to, or just previously accepted as a presupposition by, the reader. In short, we have lost the confidence that comes from the grammatical inclusion within the host structure of (A). It will be noted that this is the same kind of confidence as has been described for the information of the adverbial clause, the confidence of 'givenness' or 'taken-for-granted-as-true'.

Similar considerations apply to the interpolating clause in (141A) and (141B) below, when we shift the interpolating clause from with the structure of its host clause so that it follows. In (141A), we have a 'think' interpolation by independent clause which interrupts the relation between indirect and direct object of the verb **tell**, representing an anticipatory evaluation of this direct object:

> (141A) However, the authorities tell me − **and I think now that I believe them** − that there isn't really any need to lose sleep over him.

To show the effect of the shift, the whole of the original paragraph is given.

> (141B) The problem of Guy, the huge male gorilla . . . His captivity, you feel, is somehow shameful. However, the authorities tell me that there isn't really any need to lose sleep over him. **(And) I think now that I believe them.** Guy is intensely conservative, nervous, very easily put out. The other day they introduced a new toy into his cage − a ladder − and he refused to play. They don't know what to do with him when the new Primate House is built. They daren't trust him with a mate. (*Observer*, 28 August 1966, p. 13)

Here we note that in addition to losing the attention-getting interruption of the original host clause, we are now directly interrupting the development of the topic of the clauses which precede and the clauses which follow the host clause: the description of Guy the gorilla. The sense of interruption comes from the frustration of our expectation that the topic of 'believing them' will be developed by the next (independent) clause; instead, we are back to the topic of Guy the gorilla. Interpolation as in (A) prevents the development of the topic of 'believing them'.

The whole question of how being trapped with the grammar of a host clause affects the contextual meaning of independent clause will have to be further investigated, along with the kind of interruptive co-ordination we saw in (126): 'So divorcees **and therefore their children, are still ostracised.**'

9.8   Summing Up the Case for the Super-Adjunct

We can sum up the case for calling interpolation the super-adjunct in the following six points:

(i) Interpolation is an optional interruptive process rather than a grammatical structure in its own right like the stock adverbial clause with its subordinators. it is an *ad hoc* exploitation of the grammatical organisation of the host clause in sequenced utterance.

(ii) It represents a self-evaluation of the clause, whether part of the clause or the whole of it. As such, it is the *evaluation* for which the host clause is its immediate linguistic *situation*. This distinguishes it from the *evaluation clause* (as in example 123) where the clause is an independent clause in its own right, playing its part in the normal topic development between 'sentences'.

(iii) It enables us to interrupt the construction of the clause or the completion of this clause's boundary with the next (independent) clause. It can interrupt almost any kind of structure at its boundary, including the relation of adverbial clause with main clause as in (134), (135) and (136) above.

(iv) It postmodifies as well as anticipates the meaning of parts of the clause or the whole clause according to what we think or know to be relevant to this meaning in the context of the clause itself. We can thus reinterpret the meanings of words, parts of the clause or the whole clause while still within its (sentence) boundary.

(v) Interpolation by independent clause takes the clause out of the normal topic development, as we saw with the topic of Guy the gorilla in (141); that is, as interpolated clause it cannot start up its own train of topic development. Theoretically more important, the interpolation of the independent clause semantically subordinates it to its host clause; that is, it has the same confidence of 'givenness' of the adverbial clause but still presents its information as 'not hitherto assumed known'.

(vi) Its evaluation semantics of 'think' and 'know' distinguishes it sharply from the stock semantics of adverbial clause: consequence, place, purpose, time, etc. It was noted that the 'know' information is not just 'fact', but *'fact' which is evaluated as relevant*.

If all the above six points are true, then we are justified in calling interpolation the super-adverbial clause. We could do worse than call it the adverbial adjunct of interpretation, where interpretation is understood to be self-interpretation of the clause. As super-adjunct, we would expect it to be more marked than the well-known adverbial clauses. Adverbial clauses as such, unless marked by cleft clause or by intonation signalling it as being interpolated in the clause, are the unmarked choice. As an optional choice which interferes with the grammatical organisation of the host clause, we take interpolation as being a marked choice, with interpolation by independent clause as the most marked of all. We have already noted the grounds for saying that interpolation is marked: that a regular interruption of the clause would be intolerable to the decoder.

There will of course be the inevitable objection that we can say almost anything we please in a parenthetical clause, and so we can, but the systematic trapping of this clause within the grammatical boundary of the host clause forces the decoder to try interpreting it as being in some way thought relevant to the host clause, no matter how inexplicable the parenthetical clause might otherwise be.

In discussing the written examples of interpolation, I have taken it for granted that interpolations or interruptions of the clause would have their own separate tone groups. More important, while interpolation might have the role of super-adjunct in the structuring of the clause, it is intonation that reigns supreme in spoken language. More specifically, it is intonation that exerts the ultimate control over the meaning of the structuring of the clause in the production of sentence. None of this is new. Perhaps the simplest description of its fundamentals can be found in Bolinger (1968, pp. 30–4).

Part Three

Attempting a Definition of 'Sentence'

Summing Up the Clause as a Preliminary to Defining 'Sentence'

Before we can consider the composite definition of 'sentence', we need to review how the clause has been described so far with a view to supplementing what is lacking from the description. We have concentrated on the description of subordinate clause because it is seen as essential to the definition of a 'sentence', which is very often composed of subordinate clause and an independent clause. After summarising the approach to clause instead of 'sentence', and the notion of independence versus subordination as this manifests itself in the use of subordinate clause examples, we consider briefly those aspects of clause other than subordinate clause which we might require for our definition.

10.1 A Summary of Clause and the Problems of Subordination

We began this study by considering the nature of sentence and clause, fixing upon the notion of clause as the proper object of study. This was because the clause is seen as a workable generalisation of the unit of grammar which all the functions of clause have in common – independent clause, question clause, exclamatory clause, imperative clause, indirect questions, relative clause, noun clause, adverbial clauses, non-finite clauses, verbless clauses, etc.

The central point made about the clause is its representational nature; that is, how it represents in code form the very much larger whole of the real world from which the encoder selects its lexical words. To the encoder, the clause is thus a tip of a very larger iceberg of lexical choices which he uses to describe or relate to the real world he knows. To the decoder, there is the additional context which he brings to the decoding of this clause: his knowledge of the world and his experience in it which the encoder takes into account when telling him something he doesn't know in terms of something which he does know. In this act of communication between them, the clause is seen as meaning something much more than the mere sum of its words. Simplifying this act, we have the selection of words for the clause by the encoder with the decoder 'filling in' with his knowledge of the world to gain a fuller understanding of the clause, quite apart from building upon what clauses have already been presented in the message.

As a coding device representing a larger linguistic whole, the clause is seen as a set of systematic signals of (i) the meanings of its words with respect to each other as determined by their syntactic relationships, and (ii) the relations of this clause to its adjoining clause. To examine the clause, we adapt a traditional parsing approach upon the slot and frame approach of C. C. Fries (1951) which incorporates semantics along with syntax and morphology. The clause, however, is not seen as a self-contained unit of meaning but as essentially part of the meaning of its adjoining clauses, whether connected by grammar or simply by sequence as an independent clause. In short, each clause has as its 'given' the clauses which precede it.

Having considered the abstract notion of clause, the next thing to do was to consider its most basic contextual functions of subordination versus independence, adapting the rank notion of Halliday (1961, p. 253). This is the notion that a 'sentence' consists of one or more clauses, and that where there is more than one clause one of them must be independent. (This of course ignores the minor sentence of Bloomfield and others). Accordingly, we considered the idea of clause in clause as a necessary part of the study of clause in 'sentence' as a preliminary to attempting to define 'sentence'. The main theme of this study, then, is subordination as the clause within the clause.

Following the signalling approach, we considered subordination as a way of contextualising one clause within the other. The priority was to consider the various kinds of subordinate clause as cues of context for both their clause and the main clause to which they belonged.

Having noted subordination and independence as basic contextual cues for their clause, we then considered in varying detail the parsing cues for five different kinds of subordinate clause and their contextual functions. These were (i) relative clause, (ii) noun clause, (iii) adverbial clause, (iv) non-finite clause and (v) the controversial idea of an independent clause as semantically subordinate: the interpolated clause. They are summed up below.

(i) *Relative Clause*   Relative clause was seen as a way of 'talking about' a noun, using the lexical uniqueness of the clause in which it is a constituent to identify the noun, as in (142) below:

(142)   He knew four young dons **each of whom had reached the top of the King's Chapel.** (Scheurweghs, 1959, p. 273)

Here the unique clause is '(Some) young dons had reached the top of King's Chapel.' This is unmarked focus of subject.

(ii) *Noun Clause*   There were two kinds of noun clause. One was contained within a matrix clause as a way of talking about a clause, as in (143) below:

(143)   It is a pity **she is so stupid.** (Scheurweghs, 1959, p. 253)

Here the matrix clause **It is a pity** (that)-clause is 'talking about' the zero noun clause **she is so stupid,** characterising it lexically as a 'pity'. This is the kind of clause we use to report or repeat other people's clauses. (See 'Hypothetical and Real Relation,' Winter, 1974, pp. 288–91). The other kind of noun clause is the indirect question where we 'talk about' questions, as in (144) below:

(144)   The Act is often blamed for the rise in wages. **What little effect it had** has been indirect. (Scheurweghs, 1959, p. 262)

Here we are 'talking about' the answer to the question 'What effect did it have?' The significance of this noun clause is that its matrix clause is evaluating the 'effect' of the first sentence. The linguistic point about both kinds of noun clause is that its grammar enables the clause itself to become a lexical participant in a lexical clause, for example at X in the matrix clause **X has been indirect**, where X is subject and the evaluation signalled by the adjective complement **indirect.**

(iii) *Adverbial Clause*   As adverbial clause has been the main focus of this study, it will have to be summarised in more detail than the preceding kinds of subordinate clause. Its primary contextual function is to mediate between its main clause and the adjoining context of (independent) clause(s) in *a change of topic which is most likely to be developed further by the next immediate (independent) clause(s).* In front-position, the adverbial clause picks up the topic of the preceding clause(s) while its main clause introduces the change of topic. Here the adverbial clause concludes the preceding topic. In end-position, the main clause now picks up and concludes the topic of the preceding clause(s) while its adverbial clause introduces the change of topic. Here the adverbial clause initiates the new topic. In mid-position, the assumption I made was that here the adverbial clause did not affect the topic development of its main clause, and likened it to the interpolative role by independent clause.

In analysing the difference in contextual meaning between adverbial clause and its main clause, we had to consider the contrast in their information in the well-known terms of 'given' and 'new'. The term 'given' was applied to adverbial clause and refined as 'assumed known' or 'previously verbalised' or 'taken for granted as true'. The term 'new' was applied to independent clause and refined as 'not hitherto assumed known' or 'not assumed to be previously verbalised'. In discussing the problems of analysing adverbial clauses like the concessive **although**-clause in 7.4 we noted that the basic signalling semantics of the subordinator items of the logical sequence relation like the item **although** was to signal that its clause was the *basis* or *grounds* for which the main clause was its *conclusion* or *deduction*. What this appears to mean is that the notion of 'given' in the adverbial clause coincides with the notion of basis or grounds, and the notion of 'new' in the main clause coincides with the notion of conclusion or deduction.

We can now reformulate the primary contextual function of the adverbial clause as follows. It presents its clause as 'assumed previously verbalised', 'assumed known' or 'taken for granted as true' in the meaning of its subordinator as the logical *basis* for what is presented as 'not hitherto assumed known' in its main clause, thus providing a mediating link between the main clause and its adjoining context of (independent) clauses. In addition, it signals its clause as 'assumed known', etc., if the topic referent for this clause is not already in the foregoing text.

The main point of the exercise of reversing the sequence from front- to end-position, etc., was (a) that there was a demonstrable change in meaning from the subordinate clause in these positions besides crossing wires in the change of topic, and (b) that these differences could not be demonstrated conclusively with the clause pair out of their context because then we could not trace the topic development which is necessary to explain the meanings. The significant point about the changes of sequence was that with the adverbial clause in front-position the emphasis of the relation is on the 'not hitherto assumed known' aspect of the main clause, while in end-position it is on the 'assumed known', etc., of the adverbial clause. Both changes of sequence are accompanied by changes of meaning for the adverbial clause.

In analysing the role of adverbial clause in its text, the problem was establishing the basis for its confidence of 'known', 'given' or 'taken for granted'. This was done by establishing what clause(s) in the preceding text provided the 'known' or the 'given', etc., for the adverbial clause to pick up by repeating its unique semantics as clause in some way, for example by lexical paraphrase, by lexical repetition, or by substitution of the clause(s) which immediately precede the adverbial clause in front-position. Once a clause becomes lexically realised either as independent or subordinate clause, it becomes the 'known' or 'given' for the clauses that follow it. So in working out the sources of information for our adverbial clause we first look backwards in the text. We noted that we could view the adverbial clause in front-position as a stock evaluation of the significance of the preceding text to its main clause, stock evaluation in terms of the meanings of its subordinating item.

It proved easier to establish what was 'given' or 'known' for adverbial clauses in front-position than in end-position, because in front-position they tend to pick up the topic of the preceding clause(s). It was pointed out that even if the referent of the adverbial clause in end-position is not in the preceding text, its clause signals that it is confidently to be assumed known or taken for granted as true in the real-world situation outside the text which is shared by the encoder and the decoder.

In analysing the role of the main clause in its text, the problem was establishing what in the preceding clause(s) *presupposed* the 'given' information of its clause for which 'new' information was to be supplied. This meant looking backwards. Taking the preceding clause(s) and looking ahead of them in the text, we looked for cues in those clauses which *predict* the nature of the next (independent) clause(s). As with adverbial clause, our main analysis employed questions which had to be based on (a) what was 'given' or 'known' and (b) on what was presupposed by the preceding clause(s). Unlike the sources for adverbial clause, a presupposition does not exist until it is lexically realised in the main clause.

Whatever descriptive inadequacies there are in the present study, there is no doubt that the primary contextual function of the adverbial clause is to provide the 'known' for which its main clause is the 'new', and that the immediately preceding clause(s) provide the 'given' or 'known' for this adverbial clause. We are going to need this notion for our definition of 'sentence.'

(iv) *Non-finite Clause*   As any superficial reading of English texts will show, these non-finite clauses are both ubiquitous and numerous. The non-finite clause has been treated separately from a parsing point of view: instead of depending on subordinators as signals, we depend on the meaning of the verb morphology, together with its syntactic position in the main clause. The important point to emerge here is that the non-finite clause group contained a fourth kind of subordinate clause by function: *not* relative, *not* noun clause and *not* adverbial clause, but the second (non-finite) verb of a basic two-clause clause structure, like that recalled in (145) below:

(145)   This amendment would **enable** many children **to attend these schools** (Scheurweghs, 1959, p. 228)

What distinguishes this kind of non-finite clause from any other kind of subordinate clause so far described is that it is part of the choice of the first verb of the structure (the verb *would* **enable**), so that *we have no choice whatever in using or not using this subordinate clause if we are not to alter considerably the meaning of the sentence as a whole.* This constitutes a definition of basic clause structure according to the use of the main verb. The remaining non-finite clauses have the three functions of relative noun and adverbial clause and need no further comment here.

(v) *Postmodifying Structures Other Than (i) (ii) (iii) and (iv)*   Up to this point we were safely concerned with stock subordinate clauses in (i) (ii) (iii) and (iv) above. By describing apposition and interpolation as postmodification, we entered into controversial waters. Because of their resemblances to postmodifiers by position, they had to be compared and contrasted. What they both had in common, apart from certain structural similarities, is that they both take up space within the boundary of the clause, either by interrupting the next internal structural boundary of the clause or by interrupting the next external boundary of the clause with the next (independent) clause in sequence. They differ sharply in their meanings but can meet as a multiple meaning in evaluative apposition as in (146) below, where there is an interruption of the comparison grammar of the adjective **strong** by the structure **or rather as weak**.

(146)   In many provinces their practical claim to public schools in their own language would be as strong, **or rather as weak**, as the French except that the French are more insistent. (*Guardian*, 26 July 1967, p. 8)

Apposition by repeating the structure which is being postmodified enforces a synonymy upon the apposing structure in which the meaning is narrowed down or made more specific. Such narrowing down is signalled by connectors such as **that is, namely, that is to say,** etc.

Interpolation is the much more controversial of the two kinds of postmodifier. It is, as I have noted, a self-evaluative interruptive process acting on the normal grammatical boundaries of the clause, a process which I see as marked. The main controversy is about the role of interpolation by independent clause, which I have treated as the most marked of interpolations. Here we have an independent clause presenting its clause as 'not hitherto assumed known or verbalised' but having the semantics of subordinate clause; that is, the confidence by 'givenness' *which inclusion within the host clause's boundary confers upon it.* This confidence was shown to vanish when we removed the independent clause interpolation and tried to put in somewhere else outside the host clause's boundary as a normal declarative independent clause (examples 140 and 141). I have discussed interpolation as the super-adjunct because it can interrupt the construction or the completion of the host clause's boundary with the next clause in order to reinterpret its meaning in some way, and this to me argues some kind of ultimate control over the meaning of the clause in execution.

10.2   Conclusions about Subordination in the Clause

It should be clear that, without that which it is subordinated to, subordinate clause is by definition grammatically incomplete. Thus we say that subordinate clause, whatever kind it is, including interpolation as its special case, should be regarded as a grammatical function of its main clause and that, for the subordinate clause to have any grammatical hence communicative significance as clause, its main clause must be independent, or part of a still larger clause that itself must be independent. Taking adverbial clause as an instance of subordinate clause, we say that adverbial clause is a function of its main clause. This description meets the grammatical definition of the sentence by Meillet, Bloomfield and Jespersen, but, as C. C. Fries pointed out long ago, it ignores the semantics and grammar of the larger utterance in which it occurs.

In analysing adverbial clause, we noted how the semantics of the topic development of the preceding independent clauses affected the semantics of the clause pair itself according to the sequence of the adverbial clause in it, and how the clause in turn affected the topic development of the independent clause(s) which followed it. This study of topic development semantics could have been supplemented by a study of clause relations, for example making specific the particular relations between the independent clauses in their sentence roles and the paraphrases by the clause connectors **as a result, besides, consequently, despite this, hence, however, in addition, so, therefore, thus, yet,** etc. (See Winter, 1971, 1974, 1977 and 1979.) However, the use of the question criterion sufficed fo us to examine some of the important semantic relations which connect the topics between the clauses in sequence. Future studies should combine a study of topic development with the clause relations of their clauses.

The point which follows from this is that any independent clause (including its subordinate clauses) in sequence depends very closely upon the semantics and grammar of how the topic is handled in the preceding independent clauses of its utterance. We can thus say that the meaning of this clause is a function of its adjoining clauses, so that the larger utterances to which it belongs constitutes a semantically indivisible larger whole in which the contextual meaning of each clause is a function of the rest.

10.3   Some Remaining Problems other than Subordination

10.3.1   Introduction

We now have sufficient evidence about subordination and independence in context upon which to base a composite definition of the sentence, but there are certain parsing problems with other kinds of clause than subordinate clause that need to be taken into account in evaluating a definition of the English clause. These are the non-basic clauses, the special operations clauses which were introduced earlier. They are part of my current work on the contextual semantics of clauses other than subordinate clause, particularly on independent clause, but it will suffice for me to outline, very briefly, some of their principal linguistic features as these may affect the parsing of their clauses.

10.3.2   A Brief Review of Special Operations Clauses

So far we have been dealing, by implication, with the stock or unmarked grammar of the basic clause in English. By basic, I mean that (a) the clause has no special operation of the kind to be described below, and (b), more important, the participants to their clause structure are *lexical participants*. Participants are the lexical items in subject, object, prepositional 'object', complement, object complement, etc., position. Lexical participant means such things as the subject in its role as performer or actor, the object as the performed upon or goal, the complement as the described, for example 'She is **nice**', and the identified, for example 'She is **the Bishop's wife**', and so on. A noun clause is also a lexical participant, for example 'He hated **what he saw**', where the noun clause **what he saw** plays the same role in the clause as the lexical head **the cruelty**, and has the lexical choices of subject = **he** and the verb = **saw**, with the **what**-object referring to the lexical choice outside its main clause structure. The same applies to adverbial clause; it too has the lexical choices of subject, predicate and adjunct.

Special operations clauses can be defined as those clauses which have *one or more non-lexical participants*, and by this I mean the grammatical operators of various kinds which signal the significant grammar of their clause in the context. These clauses are the well-known existential **There**, anticipatory **It**, cleft and pseudo-cleft clause, and the less well-known anaphoric matrix clauses which signal a clause relation with the preceding clause(s), for example **The reason is that**-clause, **The same is true of** X, the substitute matrix clause such as **This is that**-clause of (119) above, and so on. In these special S V C clauses, the subject is not a lexical participant; it is either relational (the reason, the truth, etc.) or grammatical (substitute **this**.) Such a subject signals the grammatical or relational nature of the lexical participants in their **that**-clause complements. The V is the grammatical verb **be** in its equative meaning of X = Y. The usual semantics of lexical verb transitivity do not apply here. The subject of this clause operates on the complement of this clause.

Special operations clauses can be divided into unmarked and marked operations on the basic clause. The unmarked group is existential **There**, anticipatory **It**, and anaphoric matrix clauses, for example **That is why**-clause, etc.; the marked group is cleft and pseudo-cleft clause. The grammatical significance of unmarked and marked is that we have a free choice according to whether we wish to mark the basic clause or not. In illustrating unmarked and marked special operations clauses, we illustrate them in principle by letting anticipatory **It** stand for the unmarked, and cleft clause stand for the marked.

10.3.3 The Unmarked Special Operations Clause

Anticipatory **It** has been noted by Quirk *et al.* (1972, p. 955) and others as a device for postponing the real subject, especially if it is long; it is described as the normal form of the clause. From a parsing point of view, we can view the item **It** as a signal that the real subject will be a noun clause of some kind which will follow the predication structure. (In contrast, existential **There** is a signal that the real subject will be a noun, a nominal group or a gerundial clause which will follow the verbal group.) We take a bolder view of this clause than Quirk *et al.* and say that anticipatory **It** as grammatical subject is the unmarked for which the noun clause in its normal subject position is the marked, though the degree of markedness would seem to depend upon the length and complexity of the noun clause. (See N. Edwards, 1980, for a study of the long subject in the clause as part of the notion of sentence complexity.)

The anticipatory **It** operation is the application of a grammatical subject to an otherwise basic clause consisting of lexical participants.

To mark the unmarked anticipatory **It** forms of (A) below, we simply rewrite them without the anticipatory **It** item, replacing the **It** item where it is with the noun clause which it signals, as in (B) below. This contrasts anticipatory **It** with˜cleft clause **It**, where the removal of the **It** would unmark the clause, besides requiring the removal of the rest of the grammatical matrix clause, **It is . . . who/that**, etc.

(147A)   It was peculiarly appropriate **that Durham should be a city of refuge**. (Scheurweghs, 1959, p. 118)

(147B)   **That Durham should be a city of refuge** was peculiarly appropriate.

(148A)   It helped a lot **not being able to speak French**. (Scheurweghs, 1959, p. 118)

(148B)   **Not being able to speak French** helped a lot.

The criterion for unmarked clause structure is whether it can be clefted. If we use the pseudo-cleft clause for anticipatory **It**, replacing the anticipatory **It** item with anticipatory **What** as in (147C) and (148C) below, we get:

(147C)   **What was peculiarly appropriate** was that Durham should be a city of refuge.

(148C)   **What helped a lot** was not being able to speak French.

Notice that the **what**-clauses are special operations subjects into which the previous predicate structure is shifted, thus signalling that the missing element of subject will appear as complement of the verb **be**. It is interesting that A. S. Hornby (1975, pp. 17–21) classifies anticipatory **It** as a basic clause pattern of English, but not the cleft clause **It**. We ignore the fact that the marking by the **What**-item of the pseudo-cleft clause, besides anticipating real subject, signals a corrective replacement of subject with the preceding sentence. Such a grammatical operation distinguishes pseudo from cleft clause **It**. (See Leech and Svartvik, 1975, p. 180, who treat both cleft and pseudo-cleft as cleft sentence).

10.3.4   *The Marked Special Operations Clause: Cleft Clause* **It**

It is in cleft clauses that we see a clause composed entirely of grammatical participants for S and C in the special S V C clause in which S signals the grammar of what is to be in C. Cleft clause **It** signals that the basic clause with its lexical participants will be clefted in two parts in its complement, the first of which contains the part of the basic clause that is to be emphasised, while the second contains the rest of the basic clause. One example will suffice for this much-trodden soil. In (149A) below, we have an independent clause pair co-ordinating two cleft clauses in the second sentence, followed by independent clauses co-ordinating another special operations clause of the S V C type, the two **This is why**-clauses which signal the clause relation of *reason* between its clause pair and the preceding one.

PEACE IN VIETNAM

(149A)   Sir, — May we take this opportunity to enlighten the nine of the 10 inaugural John F. Kennedy Memorial Scholars (June 1). **It was** John Kennedy **who** deepened the American commitment in Vietnam and **it was** he **who** spoke of America fighting any foe at any time in the defence of freedom. This is why America is in Vietnam today and why it has the support of the British Government.

Yours, &c.
Eric Koops
Philip Smart

University of Lancaster, Lancaster, Lancashire.
(Letter, *The Times*, 8 June 1967, p. 11)

The important thing to note is that, as clearly signalled by the verb **enlighten** in the first sentence, the information of all the basic clauses of the second and third sentences is widely known. (In the context, the verb **enlighten** = telling somebody something which they, as Scholars, ought to know). Anyone familiar with the extensive coverage of Kennedy in the papers at that time would have recognised the information of these clauses as known or already verbalised. The cleft clause stresses Kennedy's known role as subject in known clauses. The cleft's relative-like clause is, as is the pseudo-cleft's relative-like clause, very different in meaning from the normal relative clause for the normal subordination of the nominal group. Here it is not identifying Kennedy as the man who did these things but is saying that he and nobody else did these things which we, as readers, know about. If we regard the noun head of the normal relative clause as having focus in its clause, then in cleft clause it has marked focus, quite apart from the other differences in meaning. The dominant new information of the second sentence is the meaning of the grammatical signalling by the cleft clause itself. Finally, note that the next sentence is an evaluation of the significance of Kennedy's role as a performer in the preceding two clauses. It represents a **yes**-reply to the **yes/no**-question 'Is this why America is in Vietnam today and why it has the support of the British Government?' Again, the only new information is the meaning of the matrix clause **this is why**, affirming the reason as true. In the rewrite below, we remove the special operations matrix clauses, showing what the basic clauses look like underneath:

> (149B)   Sir,—May we take this opportunity to enlighten the nine of the 10 inaugural John F. Kennedy Memorial Scholars. John Kennedy deepened the American commitment in Vietnam and he spoke of America fighting any foe at any time in the defence of freedom. Consequently America is in Vietnam today and it has the support of the British Government.

Bearing in mind the anticipatory signalling of the first sentence of the assumed 'knownness' of the basic clauses, we have lost the 'spelling out' whose meanings explain why the writers bothered to 'repeat' these clauses and what significance their sequence and their groupings has for them in this context.

Summing up the special operations clauses, we have seen two kinds: the unmarked clause which has *one* grammatical participant in an otherwise basic clause, the item **It** which signals real subject as a noun clause to come in (147A) and (148A), and the marked clause whose participants are wholly grammatical, the cleft clause in (149A) and the pseudo-cleft clauses in (147C) and (148C), whose grammatical complement emphasises a significant part of the basic clause, for example in (147C) where we have the semantic paradox in which the **that**-clause is presented grammatically as a complement and semantically as subject. Thus, in the special matrix clause S **be** C, the **what**-clause anticipates real subject for its clause = S, was = V, C = the real subject of the **what**-clause which lexically realises the **what**-item and semantically completes its grammar as a basic clause. This is what I mean by grammatical participants at S and at C. It should be obvious from this syntactic behaviour that the S V O C A analysis is in need of some refinement, and that the subordination by the relative-like clauses in both kinds of cleft clause should be seen as special cases of subordination which share the confidence of normal subordination. I speak here of the confidence implied by the markedness of these clauses.

The Proposed Complementary Definitions of Sentence

11.1 General Introduction

Having cleared the question of the difference between the notion of a basic clause and special operations clause, we can now take up the problem of defining the sentence in the light of the description so far of independent clause and the various forms of subordinate clause, adding what is required for independent clause. To begin with, I suggest that we retain the term 'sentence' for two purposes – for discussions with the layman, and for applying to what is between full stops in written texts. Happily, most sentences between full stops consist of at least one independent clause so that the orthographic recognition works for much of the time. This everyday view of the sentence is captured in sense 6 of its definition in the *Shorter Oxford Dictionary* (third edition) below:

> A series of words in connected speech or writing, forming the grammatically complete expression of a single thought; in pop. use often, such a portion of a composition or utterance as extends from one full stop to another. In *Grammar*, the verbal expression of a proposition, a question, command, or request, containing normally a subject and a predicate.

Since we cannot expect the layman to distinguish between our technical use of clause and his everyday idea of sentence, it makes good sense to retain it in discussing language with him or her, providing we, as linguists, know what we mean by sentence. As it is, I have been using the term 'sentence' for what is between the full stops in the examples I use here. We now take up the 'In *Grammar*' part of the above definition.

Like Curme (1947, p. 97), who uses the question mark to show the question function overriding the grammar of independence, Bloomfield (1933, pp. 170–1) follows this definition of sentence closely, giving examples of independent clause, independent clause with question mark, and exclamatory clause to represent his three main sentence types. We remove question clause from our definition of sentence, retaining as sentence independent declarative clause and its marked form, exclamatory clause. We contrast these two kinds of independent clause with question clause in terms of 'given' and 'new' information. Independent clause is the *fait accompli* structure which people accept as communication in which they are being told something they don't know in terms of something which they do know. As we have noted, independent clause presents its unique clause as 'not hitherto known' while adverbial clause presents its clause as 'assumed known' or 'taken for granted as true'. In contrast, question clause presents its clause as 'given' or 'known' and specifies the grammatical form of the completion it demands by 'new' information. In short, the question tells us what we 'know' and demands something we don't know. Ignoring pushdown questions, what it demands is completion by independent clause.

We thus distinguish between two communicative executive functions of clause: independent clause which gives us the information we demand, and question clause which demands information. The priority of question over independent clause can be seen in the fact that if we want a particular relevant independent clause we ask a question to prevent ourselves being deluged with irrelevant independent clauses. Summing up, in sentence we include independent clause in its various forms, declarative clause, imperative clause and exclamatory clause. We see question clause as a demand for independent clause or its parts.

Speaking of independent clause, with or without subordinate clause, we take on trust the well established notions of subject, predicate and adjunct. For convenience, we ignore minor sentences (including verbless clause) and insist that for parsing purposes all independent clauses consist of at least a subject and a predicate. The imperative clause is the only exception to this; its lack of overt subject is a signal of command to the addressee and so the predicate alone suffices. We also take single word replies to questions as the independent clause we need for sentence, for example **John** for the **wh**-question 'Who ran away?', where we take **John** as the unmarked for which **John ran away** would be the marked form of reply. In principle, this applies equally to adverbial clauses as reply, for example 'Why did you go?' = **Because I wanted to.**

11.2   Assumptions about Context

We cannot directly consider definitions of sentence until we establish the notion of a linguistic context for sentence, but first we note what the sentence itself is a context for. Taking a word-based approach, we view the sentence as the minimum grammatical context for the word to have meaning as word. In this context of sentence, we take the clause as our primary unit for the 'paragraph' or utterance unit. We describe this context, moving from the word outwards to its surrounding structure of clause and to this clause's context with both its grammatically connected clauses and those (independent) clauses which adjoin it. In doing so, we are following up the implications of the claim I made earlier that the clause was our sole device of lexical selection from the larger linguistic whole. We take linguistic context in four stages.

The first stage is the word, lexical and non-lexical. The minimum context for the word, names and signs notwithstanding, to have meaning as a word is the grammar of clause. (This means exactly the same thing as the statement by Pike (1977, p. 482), who sees the clause as 'the minimum unit in which a proposition is stated'.) However, for this clause to have its full grammatical significance as clause in communication, it must have a definite grammatical status. It must either be independent or subordinated to an independent clause. For instance, the words **rats** and **bats** don't mean anything except what we can find in the dictionary until we put them into a clause which relates them significantly to each other. Let's take the immediate structure for the word **rats** in an actual example, **as well as rats**. This can either mean the subordinator **as well as**, as in **We killed cats as well as rats**, a structure which subordinates the noun **rats** to the noun **cats** and signals the noun **cats** as the new information. Or it can mean what it does in (150) below:

(150) SOME BATS SEE AS WELL AS RATS
       (Heading for short article which previews the semantic content for
       its topic, the sight of bats in (151) below)

We see that the minimum grammatical context for the comparative **as . . . as**-clause is an adjunct in end-position of its main clause **Some rats can see**. Here we have the words **bats** directly related as a compared subject with **rats** through its comparative clause which 'repeats' the predication **can see** by deletion. The important linguistic point is that the meaning of each word is in some way a function of all the other words in its clause as related by the verb **see**. For the purposes of discussion, we ignore the question of which words are indispensable to the meaning, though this could be established by a process of eliminating individual items in the clause.

Like the word, the clause gains further significance as clause through its semantic connection with the (independent) clauses which adjoin it. By adjoining it, I mean the clauses outside the grammatical boundary of the clause under study. The difference between the relations of words with words and the relations of independent clauses with adjoining independent clauses is that, while words have the very strictly predictable familiar structuring of clause and its parts, independent clauses have the less obviously rigid relations of *sequence* which is analogous to syntax but necessarily different in its organisation because of its different function in dealting with (independent) clauses as sequenced wholes.

We can now take C. C. Fries's (1952, pp. 21–6) point about spoken utterances as applying equally, if not more so, to written utterances: that we tend to communicate in utterances consisting of one or more independent clauses (including minor sentence), and add to this that we expect them to be significantly sequenced in these utterances and have their own unit boundaries. For instance, in the larger context of (151) below, the independent clause printed bold presented as sentence 1 is not physically connected with sentences 2 and 3 as it would be in subordination or co-ordination, but is connected to both of these sentences semantically by *its sequence with them in the same utterance unit*. The semantics of these units consists of the relations between its clauses outside the grammatical boundary of independent clause, and these relations are called clause relations, the definition of which I now rephrase as follows: 'A clause relation is the shared cognitive processes whereby we interpret the meaning of a clause or a group of clause in the light of their adjoining clause or group of clauses. Where the clauses are independent we can speak of "sentence relations".' (This revises Winter, 1971, 1974, 1977 and 1979, where clause is conflated with sentence.) Let us apply this notion to the utterance unit below.

SOME BATS SEE AS WELL AS RATS

(151)   (1) **The phrase 'blind as a bat'**, it appears, **grossly maligns that creature's optical system**. (2) Because the bat makes such superb use of the echo-location technique for hunting insects in the dark, we tend to think of its sight as relatively unimportant and under-developed. (3) Last year, however, zoologists from the University of Indiana found that bats which had been both temporarily deafened (by ear plugs) and blinded (with tiny blindfolds) were – perhaps not surprisingly – liable to touch pieces of cloth hung across their flight path; yet animals which were only deafened could avoid such obstacles. (*New Scientist*, 11 June 1970, p. 513)

We have here an utterance unit consisting of three members: sentence 1, a negative *evaluation* implying a *denial* of the idea that bats are blind; sentence 2, a *reason* why we tend to think of bats as blind; and sentence 3, a basis for the evaluation which corrects the implied denial of sentence 1, namely the finding that bats can see after all. This last sentence provides the basis for the evaluation of the idiom **blind as a bat** as grossly maligning the sight of bats, or more simply as wrong. The point here is that just as we understand the semantic relation of **bats** to **rats** through the syntax of the clause pair in the headline 'SOME BATS SEE AS WELL AS RATS', so too do we understand the meanings of sentences 2 and 3 in turn with respect to the leading sentence 1 through the significance of their sequential connections, with sentence 3 affirming the claim of the headline as true for some bats.

In this sequential pattern of evaluation of idiom implying a denial of idiom which predicts a reason for idiom and a corrective basis for the denial of idiom, we have an illustration of de Saussure's holistic notion: 'Language is a system of interdependent terms in which the value of each term results solely from the simultaneous presence of the others' (1907–13, pp. 114–15). The element evaluation predicts basis, the presence of basis predicts evaluation, the presence of denial predicts correction or basis, and so on. These are just some of the many patterns of meaning for sequential elements.

This brief discussion of the clause relations of the three sentences of (151) beings us to the second stage of context, and this is that the meaning of clause is a function of the other clauses of the utterance, at points of intersection and as a whole. The significance of this stage is that the meaning of each sentence in the utterance is completed by the other sentences. For instance, taking the clause pair connected by the clause connector *yet* in sentence 3 we can say that the lexical selection for this clause pair has in some way been predetermined by the lexical selection made for sentence 2 and particularly for sentence 1. What this completion of meaning means is that the significance of sentence 3 as basis depends upon our prior understanding of reason in sentence 2 and evaluation in sentence 1.

The third stage of context would be the other utterances of the larger whole as a development of the topic about the **sight of bats** where the same linguistic principle holds: the meaning of each utterance is a function of the other utterances. The fourth stage, which I can only sketch, is the specialist knowledge of the subject matter and the field of knowledge for which the article was written, and the audience for whom it was written. This would include the time of writing, the writer's purpose in writing the article and his awareness of what his readers could be expected to know and *not* to know if he is to tell them something they don't know in terms of something which they do – a primary requirement for efficient communication. All four have influence on the meaning of the clause used to select lexical information for communicating knowledge.

We can at our present stage of knowledge tackle the four stages with decreasing degrees of certainty according to our knowledge of how the language works. For the purpose of the definitions, we would ideally have to insist on all four stages being examined. The most nebulous stage, stage four can be approached indirectly through the evidence of the language: what the independent clauses or subordinate clauses tell us about the shared knowledge of the world by writer and audience.

With the four stages of our linguistic context sketched out, we can now move to the problem of the definitions of sentence.

11.3   The Proposed Complementary Definitions of Sentence

11.3.1   Introduction

I must acknowledge from the outset that just as I owe much of my approach towards English grammar (especially the parsing procedure) to C. C. Fries so too am I indebted to him for laying the foundations of my own attempt to define the sentence. I am going to depend upon his discussion of 'What is a Sentence?' (Fries 1952; 1957, pp. 9–28), and particularly on his discussion of the various definitions of sentence. I am not aware of any contemporary discussion of similar merit of this theoretical problem, and with minor reservations adopt his point of view as the basis for my extended definition.

My definition consists of two separate elements: (i) a grammatical definition and (ii) a set of three requirements that must be met either by the structure itself or by its context if it is to function as 'sentence'. Before I begin, I must sum up informally what I intend to cover for the purpose of the definitions. Sentence is independent clause or clause in its significant executive function of communicating a grammatically and semantically acceptable unit which *gives* information. We could call the grammatical status of independence the sentence function of clause. This opposes it to question function which *asks* for information or for confirmation of information offered. We keep the question function separate from the sentence function of clause, not ignoring changes of function, for example 'She left him and **who can blame her?**', where the question clause (and) **who can blame her?** is transactionally equivalent to the independent clause which is its implied answer: **nobody can blame her.**

The subject of 'What is a sentence', it appears, was once vast. Fries mentions John Ries (1894), who examined and criticised some 140 definitions and then created a new one of his own, which we take up below. As Fries and others have noted, one of the oldest (semantic) definitions going back past Priscian (AD 500) to Aristotle and Dionysius Thrax in Greece is still with us: 'A sentence is a group of words expressing a complete thought.' Ignoring the dictionary definition above, a fairly modern example of the 'thought' idea is to be found in Curme's otherwise solid work: 'A sentence is an expression of a thought or feeling by means of a word or words used in such a form as to convey the meaning intended' (Curme, 1947, p. 97).

We are in agreement with Nelson Francis (1958, p. 367) when he says that definitions of the sentence can wait until we have identified and described the basic syntactic structures (of English), but can only partially agree with him when he utterly dismisses the 'complete thought' idea as 'subjective and unscientific, hence outside the realm of linguistics'. The notion of a sentence being a complete thought is not as foolish as it looks if we redefine what is meant by a 'thought' and what is meant by 'complete'.

The idea of a 'thought' is right for the wrong reasons. I hope I have shown that the verb **think** itself is part of the potential semantics of the clause as already observed in the *ad hoc* super-adjunct interpolation. We noted that, in addition to interpolation clauses answering the question **What do you think of X?**, there are independent clauses devoted entirely to this question. These are the evaluation clauses such as **It was a wise policy** which, however, don't appear to be what the early definers of sentence had in mind. If we retain the notion of 'thought' for answers to think-questions, and if we replace 'thought' by 'topic' or 'proposition', we can then redefine the notion of completeness without reference to thought.

There must be two kinds of completeness in our definitions – grammatical completeness and semantic completeness. By semantic completeness I mean that the clause may be grammatically complete but not semantically complete and thus require an adjoining clause or clauses to complete its meaning as clause, for example, **There is a problem** is grammatically complete but cannot be understood without the next (independent) clause: it raises the obligatory question 'What is this problem?'

Having cleared the idea of a thought and the notion of completeness, we can now take up the composite definitions. I find that we require three complementary requirements to explain the communicative function of independent clause:

(i) a requirement for grammatical and semantic completeness,

(ii) a requirement to be told what you don't know in terms of what you do know, and

(iii) a requirement to take the sentence on trust as true unless otherwise signalled.

11.4 Definition 1 in Two Parts

11.4.1 Introduction

As already stated, the definition of sentence is a definition of independent clause. As such it is also a definition of subordinate clause since subordinate clause is a basic function of its (main) clause, which means it cannot exist as a clause without the (main) clause to which it is subordinated. At its simplest, this first definition requires that a sentence be both grammatically complete and semantically complete within the bounds of their propositional notions about the topic (clause relational units) as these are signalled by the clause. In this two-part definition, the intelligibility of the second part is a function of the first.

11.4.2 Definition 1.1: Requirement for Grammatical Completion

This part requires that the clause not merely be grammatically complete but have the grammatical status of independence so that we would expect the sentence to consist of one or more clauses, one of which is at least independent. We see independent clause as the semantic and grammatical unit of utterance, not sentence, since sentence can by definition be more than one clause grammatically grouped together by co-ordination or subordination.

Fries's well-known examples of the similarity between **the barking dog** and **the dog is barking** will do perfectly well to illustrate what is and what is not a sentence, providing we distinguish between the semantics of the two structures in respect of the notion of **barking**. He notes that **the barking dog** is not a sentence unless it is part of some larger structure such as the (independent) **the barking dog protected the house**. If **the barking dog** did belong to this clause, the then premodifier **barking** is 'given' in a clause where the predication is the 'new' information. It answers the pushdown question 'What kind of dog?' before the top (main) question is asked: 'What did the barking dog do (for his master)?' Needless to add, Fries showed his awareness of the question criterion here, and elsewhere, by implying that 'the barking dog' as answer to the question 'What frightened the burglar away?' was acceptable as a (spoken) sentence, though he failed to note that **the barking dog** was the unmarked form of the reply 'the barking dog **did**, etc.', which is what gives **the barking dog** independent clause status. The point about **the barking dog** in isolation is not that it is not a sentence, but rather that it is not an independent clause and hence not a sentence. Similarly, if we see the example **the dog is barking** as the answer to the **wh**-question 'What is the dog doing (now)?', then as a reply to a question for independence it is independent and hence has sentence function. Thus we see that the premodifier **barking** and the finite present participle **barking** differ in structural meaning according to the questions which they are answering.

We can conclude from the above discussion of Fries that to communicate successfully we must do so in independent units which are grammatically complete in that we are able to recognise the start and the finish of their structural boundaries. We can now attempt a definition of the grammatical completion in terms of the parsing procedure derived from C. C. Fries, which we apply to sentences in use: *when we have fulfilled all the predictive signals of autonomous grammar for the clause*, we have grammatical completion or independence for this clause. For instance, in the incomplete structure **she is incredibly** . . . there are at least three grammatical cues of autonomous grammar: the subject **she** and the verb **is** which require a predictable predicate structure, and the morphology **ly** of the adverb **incredibly** which reinforces the prediction of a complement by adjective. When we have fulfilled all these signals by something like **She is incredibly naive**, and there are no further autonomous cues of postmodifier (for example 'in her dealings with men') or connection with another clause by subordinator or co-ordinator, etc., then we have a one-clause sentence. So we see that grammatical completion and independent clause are the same thing.

To cover the notion of grammatical completion all we need is the first of the following three definitions. Fries notes that the Jespersen and the Bloomfield definitions are based upon the Meillet definition. Judging by the dates and by the very close similarity of the three definitions, there is no reason to dispute this. The reader can decide which of the three he likes or make a synthesis of all three.

(i)   the sentence can be defined [as follows]: a group of words joined together by grammatical agreement [relating devices] and which, not grammatically dependent on any other group, are complete in themselves. (Meillet (1903) translation in Fries, 1952; 1957, p. 20)

(ii)   A sentence is a (relatively) complete and independent human utterance – the completeness and independence being shown by its standing alone, i.e. *of being uttered by itself*. (My emphasis of Jespersen, 1924, p. 307.)

(iii)   It is evident that the sentences in any utterances are marked off by the mere fact that each sentence is an independent linguistic form, not included by virtue of any grammatical construction in any larger linguistic form.
(Bloomfield's 1933 version of the 1926 version quoted by C. C. Fries: 'A sentence is a construction (or form) which, in the given utterance, is not part of any larger construction.')

If we want a definition of grammatical completion only, including the one-word self-standing clauses such as 'John' in reply to the question 'Who has just come in?' or the 'minor sentence' 'Fire!', a composite of the above three definitions will do. We must conclude that the requirement for grammatical completion as independent clause is a requirement for a semantically autonomous structure which makes a minimum of sense in terms of its parts; that is, a structure that makes sense to us when it is complete and does not make sense to us when it is not. This structural sense is at once the most trivial and the most important requirement for the sentence, and we have now to distinguish between a grammatical and a notional sense of completion in order to understand where grammatical completion is not enough for the clause to be fully understood as clause. Taking it for granted that the structure **He took the** . . . is grammatically incomplete, we note that it is both grammatically and notionally incomplete. It is grammatically incomplete because its verb **took** does not have its grammatically expected object and the article **the** does not have the noun head it signals to come; it is notionally incomplete because there is no lexical object to make sense of the verb **took** and to fulfil the lexicality signalled by the article **the**. Providing this structure with a lexical object solves the problem of its making sense to us as a clause, for example **He took the easy way out**.

We now come to the crucial point which I regard as the central weakness of the above purely grammatical definition. Providing the structure **He took the** with an object like the **easy way out** does indeed resolve the grammatical and its associated notional problem *as a clause*, but it does not resolve the larger notional problem of the clause as a grammatically completed structure. Under well-defined circumstances, we may not understand concretely what is meant by taking the easy way out though we may understand the abstract meaning of the cliché. This requires explanation. If we haven't already heard the detail of what the easy way out is, then we do not fully understand the significance of this clause until we see the next clause, for example 'He took the easy way out – **he deserted her**.' If we already knew that he had deserted her, then the clause could be a fitting comment clause, for example 'So he took the easy way out after all!' The affirmation by **So** signals that we already know what the detail of the easy way out is. This sentence is now not notionally incomplete.

We have now reached the limits of the autonomous meaning for the out-of-context clause **He took the easy way out** and require at least the notional or semantic completion of this clause next to supplement the notion of grammatical completion.

11.4.3 Definition 1.2: Requirement for Semantic Completion

Having achieved grammatical completion as clause, there is a supplementary requirement for semantic completion. What this means is that we must fulfil our non-grammatical cues, for example the lexical realisation required for the abstract nominal group **the easy way out** of the clause **He took the easy way out**. We must now look more closely at what Fries complained about when he criticised Bloomfield's definition as being unclear about what a linguistic form was. His suspicion that it should be an utterance and not a sentence was well grounded. What we are talking about here is the unit immediately larger than the sentence. If an independent clause lacks the fulfilment of its lexical cues when its clause is grammatically complete, then this clause is semantically incomplete and requires semantic completion by another clause, for example **he deserted her** for the cue **the easy way out** in **He took the easy way out**. This is now further explained with textual examples.

In Winter, 1977, pp. 67–74, I speak of clauses which are grammatically well formed but nevertheless inadequate as information, for example the clause **There is a problem**, noting that until these clauses are lexically realised by an adjoining clause or clauses they remain incomprehensible, though perfectly grammatical. Not merely does existential **There** signal a coming identification of the word **problem** but the next clause has to answer the question 'What is this problem?'

The technical term we adopted here for this kind of clause is *unspecific clause*. For an unspecific clause to be semantically complete in respect of its lexical cues (for example **problem**, the easy **way** out, etc.) it must have lexical realisation by the next clause(s). We term these next clauses *specific clauses*. We can now rephrase the requirement for semantic completion as: for each *unspecific clause*, we the decoders require lexical realisation by specific clause. What this requirement means is that where we have unspecific sentence its minimum linguistic structure is an utterance which contains it and at least one specific sentence. We now look more closely at the notion of lexical realisation.

11.4.4 Lexical Realisation as Basic Semantic Organisation

We now consider the linguistic significance of lexical realisation underlying the relation of unspecific to specific clause. First we note that the relation of unspecific to specific is a common semantic feature within the internal grammatical organisation of the clause itself. For instance, we all recognise abstract from concrete nouns by the fact that they require obligatory lexical realisation. An example of this is the unspecific nouns **technology** and **service** in the following rewrite from which I have removed the specific elements: **The technology has benefits for the service.** If we don't already know what technology or what service is meant, we have a meaningless sentence which raises the questions 'What technology and what service?' In the actual example, we observe a typical obligatory function of pre- and postmodifier to noun heads in which we have to specify the particulars of the noun heads:

> (152)   The technology **of the space age** has benefits for the **merchant shipping** service. Bob Crew looks at how even the dirty British coaster could dodge a salt cake on its smokestack. (*Guardian*, 11 September 1980, p. 12)

We have lexically fulfilled the noun **technology** as **the technology of the space age,** and the noun **service** as **the merchant shipping service,** and now fully grasp what is meant by the nouns **technology** and **service.** However, where the demand for lexical realisation is not met within the structure of the clause, this then becomes the function of the adjoining clause, especially if the whole clause is devoted to expressing it as a topic. For instance, although we have met the need for internal lexical realisation, the clause remains an *unspecific clause* because its topic, **having benefits,** demands lexical realisation: 'What benefits are meant?' Even if we don't understand what 'dodging a salt cake on its smokestack' means – and I don't – we know that it must mean some kind of benefit to the merchant shipping service. This next sentence is the specific clause which completes the meaning of its unspecific clause, so that we complete its notional meaning as clause.

There are many kinds of unspecific clause. All we can do here is to look at a few examples which illustrate the principle of lexical fulfilment or lexical realisation.

If unspecific clause is not preceded by its specific clause, it is followed by it. In these instances, we speak of unspecific clause anticipating the semantics of its specific clause(s), as in (152) above, where the predication **having benefits for the merchant shipping service** anticipates the specific clause that follows it. A common kind of unspecific clause is also a *connective clause* (Winter, 1974, p. 561); that is, a clause which functions entirely as a semantic conjunction between its adjoining independent clauses, as in (153) below, where we have a characteristic example of existential **There**-clause.

> (153)   If Conservative leaders are now having second thoughts, they should explain why; if not, it is equally incumbent upon them to re-iterate their arguments. This is a case in which silence can be as influential upon affairs as speech and, in some circumstances, could

be more dangerous. The Conservative attitude to Rhodesia in the days to come is a matter of the greatest interest to the Rhodesian Government, and they also have a right to know where they stand.
There is another point. The Tory Party in Parliament and out has been divided on Central African policy for years. (Leading article, *The Times*, 13 October 1965, p. 13)

The existential **There**-clause here refers anaphorically and cataphorically to adjoining clauses; it refers to the preceding sentence as one **point** and the next as another **point**. Connective clauses like these are by definition unspecific clauses because they cannot operate as sentences without their adjoining sentences.

11.4.5   Summary and Conclusions about Definition 1

We have noted that before we can consider the communicative property of clause it must be grammatically complete in two senses, its structural parts must be complete and it or the clause to which belongs must be independent. However, grammatical completeness does not necessarily mean semantic completeness. There are clauses which are semantically incomplete and which have linguistic features which we can pin down, for example the lexical items **having benefits**, etc., in (152) and (another) **point** of (153) above. Such clauses require lexical realisation by adjoining specific clause(s), and so we speak of a two-part utterance of unspecific and specific clause as the minimum linguistic context.

We have ignored another kind of semantic completion in which specific clauses have their notional semantics completed, such as the evaluation clause implying a denial in sentence 1 of (151) above, whose meanings are completed by sentence 3 which offers both a basis for the evaluation and a correction for its implied denial.

Summing up, a sentence must not merely be grammatically complete; it must be semantically complete. Just what semantically completes the sentence has yet to be fully described, but there is no doubt that where the sentence is semantically incomplete we require the adjoining orthographic sentence(s) to complete it semantically. The first definition thus covers grammatical and semantic completeness, but it does not cover the contextual semantics of independence and subordination. This is the subject of the next definition.

11.5   Definition 2: Communicating What Is Not Known in Terms of What Is

11.5.1   Introduction

The main point of focusing attention on the subordinate clause in

English, particularly the adverbial clause, was to provide the reader
with a clear idea of the difference in contextual semantics between the
grammar of independence and the grammar of subordination. In
discussing their differences of context, it was made clear that we were
simply developing further the well-known notions of 'given' and 'new'
of the Prague School. The differences of context were differences of
'given' and 'new' *of the whole clauses.* It was proposed that adverbial
clause which we take as representative of the subordinate clause in
general, presents its information as 'assumed known' or 'taken for
granted as true' while independent clause presents its information as
'not hitherto assumed known'. Since the adverbial clause cannot exist
without its main clause, this means that it provides what is known or
taken for granted as true as a clause for its main clause's *not* hitherto
assumed known.

The common-sense observable point we now make is that when we
tell people something we try to tell them something they don't know or
don't know in the form in which it is told, but this is too simple to
account for the balance between expressing what we don't know
against what we do know. We noted that independent clause itself was
a synthesis of 'given' and 'new' in which the repetition of the
participants and the presupposed development of the topic were the
'given' elements of the question which we used to elicit the new
information of the main clause. For instance, the sentence which
follows the sentence **There is another point** in (153) has the following
given and new components. First, the **there**-clause signals a change of
subtopic. The given topic is **the Tory attitude to Rhodesia**; the new
part of the topic is the Tory attitude **in Parliament and out** towards
Central African Policy. The new information for the change of
subtopic is the verb **divided on** and the time duration **for years** in the
predication has been divided on Central African policy for years.

The mere existence of subordinate clause is a powerful indication
that we also communicate what is known, what is taken for granted as
true, or what is taken for granted as a possibility. Our listener needs to
know this to reconcile it with what he already knows. We return to our
assumptions about context, and note now that the consequence of
insisting on the adjoining context, for a sentence to have its full
meaning is that the preceding sentences provide its given information,
so that we cannot repeat the preceding clauses without explicitly
acknowledging the repeated clause. In Winter (1974, 1977 and 1979) I
note that we do in fact repeat clauses a good deal of the time, and that
substitute clauses in new grammatical environments such as **if they do**,
etc., are our special clauses for adding new information to the known
by repeated clause, so that the repeated clause preserves its lexical
uniqueness. This adding of new information I have called

replacement; the second sentence from (154) below is another example: 'Everyone is against it: everyone **assumes** it **is inevitable**.' Note that the replacement here is a function of the repeated elements of its clause.

Next, we are concerned with the nature of the fundamental information offered in either subordinate clause or independent clause. In discussing the semantics of interpolation as evaluation of its host clause, I proposed that 'know' information is the unmarked state of communication for normal clause and that 'think' information is the marked. We now formalise all this in the following two complementary definitions of which the first is the 'know' information as the unmarked, and the second is the 'think' information as the marked.

11.5.2 The 'Know' and 'Think' Definition of Sentence

We separate the definitions to indicate the staging of the questions for the whole clause as topic: 'Tell me what you know and then tell me what you think about what you know'. Building upon the requirements of Definition 1 for grammatical and semantic completeness, the following definition requires that the sentence have either of two kinds of fundamental information, 'know' information as fact, and 'think' information as evaluation. it is very important to note that the definition assumes that we have a definite knowledge to communicate to our decoder.

> A sentence is the communicative device we use to tell somebody something they *don't know* in terms of something which they *do know*, and *where it is relevant*, to tell them what we *think* of what we have just given them to know, or what we *think* of what is already known.

The point that you can only communicate the unknown in terms of the known is a hoary cliché in the communications-teaching business. It is one of those self-evident truths to anybody who has investigated how we communicate. What has been difficult has been how to apply this knowledge about language to language. I am taking it for granted that it is true, with the following reminder. If we try to tell somebody about how to programme a computer and they have not the faintest knowledge of computer programming, then they will not follow us, even though they 'understand' the grammar of our clauses.

The key linguistic items in the definition are the verbs **know** and **think**. Take the item **know** first and consider this. If somebody asks you 'What did he do with his money?' and you reply 'I don't know', you are formalising the kind of **do**-information you lack in formulating a reply. There is a major distinction between 'know' and 'think' information. This is to be observed in the familiar objection we make to people who don't give us facts but their conclusions: 'Don't tell me what you think – tell me what you know!' This distinction between 'know' and 'think' information is ignored by the traditional definitions of independent declarative clause as 'stating a fact' (for example Curme, 1947, p. 97). It either states a 'fact' or it states what we think or feel; both kinds of information are presented by independent clause.

It will be recalled that intepolation by independent clause was treated as self-evaluation of the host clause. By self-evaluation I meant that the interpolating clause evaluated the host clause or that part which it interrupted. In this interruptive relation, the host clause was the *situation* for which the interpolating clause was its *evaluation*. We also contrasted the interpolating independent clause with evaluation clause in (141A and B) on p. 158, where the former inter-polating clause becomes evaluation clause.

11.5.3 *The Basic Text Structure of Situation and Evaluation*

There is a basic text relation whose fundamental semantics of clause is represented by the lexical items **situation** and **evaluation**. Where the whole topic of the clause is devoted to 'know' information, this is potentially interpreted as situation; where the whole topic of the clause is devoted to 'think' information about this situation clause, we have an evaluation clause or comment clause. We call the relation situation and evaluation. These are the marked forms of 'know' and 'think', and their lexical items **situation** and **evaluation** are used to refer anaphorically or cataphorically to the semantic nature of the lexical realisation of the clauses to which they refer in their immediate context. It is my claim that situation and evaluation is one of the larger clause relations which organises the other clause relations in messages, short articles, stories, arguments, etc. The fuller structure of this larger relation can be internally structured by problem or problem and solution as aspects of situation. For a more detailed description of the variety of short texts which illustrate these relations, see the companion works by my colleagues M. P. Hoey (forthcoming) and M. P. Jordan (forthcoming).

In (154) below, the lexical item situation is lexically realised by the information of its main clause, which in turn refers to the information of the previous larger clause relation of the interpretation of the division of Germany as being rather like sin. The situation is the spectacle of two hostile and heavily armed states glaring at each other across the Berlin Wall.

(154)   The division of Germany is rather like sin. Everyone is against it;
        everyone assumes it is inevitable. Indeed, so accustomed have we
        become to the spectacle of two hostile and heavily armed states
        glaring at each other across the Berlin Wall, that we tend to forget
        how unnatural and explosive a **situation** this is. Even if the Vietnam
        war were to be settled tomorrow, the issue of Germany would
        continue to block further progress to Soviet – American under-
        standing. In particular . . . (*Observer*, 2 January 1966, p. 10)

Notice that the **that**-clause of the **so-that** clause evaluates the situation
as unnatural and explosive ('think' information), and because it is
evaluating the situation we speak of this clause as being evaluation
clause. Notice too that the last sentence evaluates this evaluation of
situation further.

In (155), we have a simpler unmarked example of situation and
evaluation (of situation) in which the first sentence presents the 'facts'
(know) and the clause pair in the second sentence presents the
assessment of these facts (think).

(155)   The nation's only existing test stand for the S-11 stage of the giant
        Saturn-V rocket which will propel Americans to the Moon was
        damaged when the S-11 stage burst. Luckily the stage had finished
        its test series; luckily too the damage was minimal. (*New Scientist*, 9
        June 1966, p. 635)

Finally, we consider an example of unspecific clause which is also
evaluation clause. In (156) below, the first sentence is an anticipatory
evaluation of the specific clauses which presents the situation in the
next two sentences. We sum up Definition 2 with this example.

(156)   The whole point of my writing this now is to say that what happened
        was totally different, totally unexpected. In something like 85 per
        cent of the encounters the steam had gone out of the challenge and
        the chips from the shoulder; hostility was replaced with serious
        enquiry; suspicion with courtesy, resentment with something that
        was almost enthusiasm. Those who had demanded: 'Who the hell
        are you to tell us?' now said: 'What do you suppose can be done?'
            The recent series of debacles in South Vietnam have shocked so
        many Americans into a complete reversal of attitude. It seemed to
        me that the mood of the country had changed more radically than I
        would have believed possible. (*New Statesman*, 17 June 1966, p.
        873)

There are three points to be noted. First, we see the motivation for the
'telling you something you don't know' part of the definition explicitly
expressed in the first sentence. Paraphrasing this in terms of our
definition we have 'The whole point of my writing this now is to tell

you that what happened to me was very different, and totally unexpected from what was known to have happened before (to critics).' The item **totally unexpected** signals an unexpected outcome for this previous happening and becomes part of the semantics of **difference**. Second, the lexical item **different** in the first sentence signals the coming contrasts between the two happenings. This relation of contrast is paraphrased by the three-clause co-ordination clause **X was replaced with Y**, where X represents the previously known happenings and Y represents the 'new' happenings to be made known, that hostility was replaced with serious enquiry, suspicion with courtesy, resentment with something that was almost like enthusiasm. This contrast is retrospectively signalled by the notion of being **shocked into a complete reversal** in the second paragraph. Finally, we note that the significance of the 'think' information of the first (unspecific clause) sentence is a function of the supportive contrast between the two 'knows' expressed by sentences 2 and 3: what was known to have happened before then and what had just happened (to the critics). Thus, we see an instance of how the information of 'know' and 'think' work together in composing a notionally complete 'paragraph' unit.

11.5.4   Summary and Conclusions about Definition 2

Following up the definition, we briefly examined the difference between 'know' and 'think' information as these two are manifested in the larger clause relation of situation and evaluation, pointing out earlier that this relation is the same as interpolation by independent clause. In discussing 'know' and 'think' information, it was noted that we confined ourselves to clauses whose whole topic was devoted to 'know' or 'think' information. By doing so, we have ignored the minor think-evaluation which is a stock part of the adjective premodifier to the noun head in the nominal group of the clause whose topic is devoted to something other than 'think' information, for example the role of the premodifier element **very nice** in the clause **I met a very nice girl yesterday**, where the clause topic is **meeting somebody yesterday**, with the evaluation as **very nice** as its unmarked evaluation. (The grammatical point being made here is that for the adjective **very nice** the premodifier slot is the unmarked for which complement in a **be** clause is the marked.)

So far we have assumed that we have some definite facts (know) to communicate and that we give the 'know' clauses significance by saying what we 'think' about them. However, we are often ignorant about some things or have only a partial knowledge of them. When this happens *situation* become the assumed, invented, or supposed situation (hypothetical member), and *evaluation* becomes an evaluation of a likely reality for which we try to find 'facts' to fit the hypothetical member. This evaluation of a likely reality I call the real member. The hypothetical and real relation is our next basic text structure. It is the subject of the third and last complementary definition.

11.6   Definition 3: Taking the Sentence on Trust as True

11.6.1   Introduction to Definition 3

So far the definition has been built up on the requirement for grammatical and semantic completion, the requirement to communicate what is not known in terms of what is, reconciling two kinds of semantics, the contextual semantics of subordination and independence and the semantics of the verbs 'know' and 'think'. What we lack to complete our definition of sentence is the basic signalling properties of its clause(s); that is, we have to account for what the grammatical choices of the clause tell us about how we should receive the clause as message.

We now have to supplement the signalled meaning of independence and subordination, especially adverbial clause subordination. Independence is where the unique clause presents its information as 'not hitherto assumed known', whether this information is 'think' or 'know' information; subordination is where the unique clause presents its information as 'assumed known' or 'taken for granted as true', and in this way serves as the 'known' clause for the 'new' of its main clause. However, in signalling their clauses as either independent or subordinate, the cues of grammatical status also signal something else. This is that the encoder believes that what he is presenting as 'known' is known, and what he is presenting as 'new' is new. In short, his clause betrays his belief system, *if he is not deliberately lying*.

However, this kind of signalling does not cover the inevitable contingency of ignorance; often we lack the knowledge to communicate or we are uncertain as to how definite our knowledge is, with shades in between these two. So we frame our definition to cover this contingency on the efficiency principle of 'least effort', bearing in mind that we are describing the signalling role of both independent clause and subordinate clause in sentence function. Above all, we note that this definition must cover the sentence *as it is presented*, the sentence in actual use.

What now follows is a definition of grammar as the serious signalling of the encoder's intent to communicate as received by the decoder. It is partly based upon two earlier related definitions of the sentence which are cited by C. C. Fries (1952; 1957, pp. 17-18). We cite these two definitions and then follow it with the proposed complementary Definition 3:

(1)   A sentence is a grammatically constructed smallest unit of speech which expresses its content with respect to *this content's relation to reality*. (John Ries, 1894, and revised in 1931)

(2)   A sentence is a portion of speech that is putting forward to the listener a state of things (a thing meant) as having validity, i.e. *as being true*. (Karl Sunden, 1941)

I have *underlined* the parts of these definitions which I have picked up below. Of the two definitions, Karl Sunden's comes closest to the notion of presented as true. Note that the proposed definition, like my Definition 2 earlier, is framed from the decoder's point of view, thus acknowledging its involuntary nature and that it depends on trust.

The proposed (complementary) definition
Where there is trust, the natural instinct of the decoder is to take on trust as true the sentence *as presented, unless it is otherwise signalled*.

As I see it, the Sunden definition is much the same as my definition, except that it lacks the riders for when we don't take the sentence on trust as true.

First we note that this definition is a definition of the decoder's trust in the encoder; that is, it is more convenient for the decoder to believe in everything than to doubt or to challenge everything. The drawback acknowledged in the definition is that, where the decoder distrusts the encoder or the truthfulness of the encoder, the system breaks down and they no longer communicate; nobody is as deaf as those who will not hear.

The definition with the riders enables us to account for the fact that in written English texts sentences are overwhelmingly positive declarative (independent) clause. In the Osti Programme (reported in R. D. Huddleston *et al.* 1968, p. 606), we noted that only 4·5 per cent of all clauses were grammatically negative. The rider *'unless it is otherwise signalled'* enables us to account for (i) the function of the modal auxiliary verbs and their lexical paraphrases (for example **might** = **possible**), where we have doubts about the definiteness of the clause, and (ii) the function of the hypothetical and real relation, where we have no 'facts' to go by. We now consider the definition with the rider under the heading of 'Positive and Negative Clause', and then consider the rider itself under the heading of 'The Basic Text Structure of Hypothetical and Real', below.

11.6.2   *Positive and Negative Clause*

Taking the overwhelming numbers of positive clauses in written English (95·5 per cent in the Osti Programme), we note that positive clause does not simply mean the converse of negative clause. What we should be concerned with is whether the negative or the positive clause is significant in its semantic function in its relation to its adjoining clauses. By significant, I mean those independent clauses or noun clauses which are answers to **yes/no**-questions. A positive reply is called an *affirmation clause*; a negative reply is called a *denial clause*. A very likely explanation why most clauses in texts are positive is that most sentences would seem to represent answers to **wh**-questions. Answers to these open-ended questions can be either positive or negative, with a strong tendency for positive replies or replies which match the polarity of the **wh**-question. A negative answer to a **wh**-question (which is not a **yes/no**-question) is not a denial clause, for example 'Why did he go there?' = (because) he **didn't** want to miss the fun. A denial clause would be the answer to a **yes/no**-question: 'Did he want to miss the fun?' = 'No, he **didn't** want to miss it.' In written texts, such significant positive and negative clauses are rare.

Accordingly, we distinguish between two kinds of independent declarative clause: (i) those which answer **wh**-questions and are not significant as either positive or negative clause, and (ii) those which answer **yes/no**-questions, the affirmation and the denial clause. We assign group (i) to the normal run-of-the-mill sentences, and group (ii), affirmation and denial clause, to the real member of the hypothetical and real relation below. Affirmation and denial clause are discussed by Zandvoort (1962, pp. 230–1) as confirmative and denial statements. He speaks of these statements as being 'modelled on the preceding sentence' (in our terms on the hypothetical member).

Before we can leave independent declarative clause, I wish briefly to note the well established function of modal verbs in which a modal verb signals doubt or indefiniteness of the 'think' or 'know' information of its clause. This is the difference between the otherwise unmarked 'know' clause **he has gone** versus the marked 'know as think' clause **he may have gone**, where we mark its truth status as probably true with the modal verb **may**. Some modal verbs, however, do not always signal indefiniteness or doubt. Consider the following sentence which is both situation and evaluation combined in the same clause: **You should not have gone**. The modal verb **should** is deductive here, and the clause is not a denial clause because **you have**, in fact, **gone**; the clause is an evaluation of the fact that you did go. For a real world example of this, notice how an advertiser in (157) below uses the modal verb **should** in an advertisement for body deodorant which is aimed at the antisocial male reader who is assumed *not* to take offence at perspiration. This assumption is presented as 'fact' by the modal verb **should** in the second sentence, where it was italicised to indicate the strong stress it would get in speech.

> (157) ARE YOU MAN ENOUGH TO USE A DEODORANT?
> Perspiration offends others. It **should** offend you, too. Ignoring it won't cure it. Not will soap and water. For to beat perspiration odours you would have to bath every 6 hours.
> Can you bath that often?
> No.
> The answer? Old Spice Stick Deodorant.
> (*Daily Mail*, 20 July 1965, p. 1)

Notice that in the next sentence the gerundial clause subject **Ignoring it** (*not* taking notice of perspiration) is a compatible denial which affirms the implied denial clause of the second sentence: **it does not offend you**. This denial clause is further reflected by the compatibly matched denial clauses of the third and fourth sentences whose clauses are co-ordinated by the co-ordinator **Nor**.

We have noted the basic text relation of situation and evaluation as the central aspect of Definition 2. This is to be seen in contrast with the basic text relation of hypothetical and real as the central aspect of Definition 3. It is in the real member of this last relation that the contextual role of affirmation and denial clause will become apparent.

11.6.3 The Basic Text Structure of Hypothetical and Real

Here we take up the most important part of the definition from a signalling point of view, the rider *unless it is otherwise signalled.* We have already discussed the use of modal verbs for signalling indefiniteness as one kind of signalling otherwise, but we cannot dismiss the hypothetical and real relation so easily because it is less known than modal verbs. In Definition 2, we had the relation of 'know' and 'think' information in the larger clause relation of situation and evaluation, where the situation element represents 'know' and the evaluation element represents 'think'. However, where we do not have facts or 'know' information, *situation* becomes hypothetical situation, and the evaluation element has to investigate the possibility of finding the true situation, with the purpose of converting hypothetical situation to real situation. The linguistically important point about hypothetical situation is that we are signalling the clause as neither true nor false, and that this relation has to be signalled overtly.

For the purposes of analysis, the hypothetical situation is abbreviated to *hypothetical member*, and the evaluation of a likely reality for this hypothetical member is abbreviated to *real member*. The vocabulary-3 items which are superordinate signals of this membership are the lexical items **hypothetical** as in the contrast to be seen in the typical question 'Are you asking me a hypothetical question or are you asking me for facts?', and **real** as in the typical question about a reason: 'I wonder what his real reason is?' Perhaps the contextual meaning of **hypothetical** is best seen in its use in the following sentence taken out of an address given to the staff of a college by their principal which I report in (158) below. This is the principal's concluding sentence in which he comments on the possibility of enforced staff redundancies:

(158) It's **all very hypothetical** — I don't know — nobody knows.

Notice the role of the paired clauses that follow as providing the basis for the evaluation as **all very hypothetical**; in particular, notice the meaning of **hypothetical** as 'I don't know – nobody knows'.

Hypothetical situation raises an interesting question: how do we talk about something which we know nothing about? The answer is that we invent or assume something to be true and then investigate it as a candidate for the truth. As already noted, the investigation is called the real member. It is in the real member that affirmation clause and denial clause play their significant roles, especially if we take real to mean an evaluation of the (likely) reality for the hypothetical clause. Thus, linguistically, the hypothetical means neither true nor false but a candidate for the truth; the real means 'evaluating what is true' (see Winter, 1974, pp. 272–301, where I call this the truth relation). The operation of this relation is best grasped by considering the role of affirmation and denial clauses within their larger clause relations.

In fitting the affirmation clause and the denial clause into the hypothetical and real relation, it is necessary to give two kinds of linguistic cue which characterise the relation. First, affirmation and denial clause are answers to **yes/no**-questions where the question is 'Is it true?' It is the stock question for the real member, and if it remains unanswered it remains hypothetical. It is thus by definition the hypothetical for which its reply clause is its real.

Secondly, there is a range of lexical items of all kinds whose semantics is subordinate to the superordinate lexical paraphrase items of **hypothetical** and **real**. We can take the lexical items which signal hypotheticality and reality in turn. Those which signal hypotheticality are **argument, assumption, belief, claim, conclusion, expect, feel, guess, illusion, imagine, proposition, rumour, speculate, suggestion, suppose, theory, think**, etc. The lexical items which signal real are divided into affirmation and denial. Affirmation items are **affirm, agree, confirm, concur, evidence, fact (know), reality, right, true**, etc. Denial items are **contradict, correct, deny, dismiss, disagree, dispute, false, lie, mistake, object to, opposite, rebut, repudiate, wrong**, etc. The important point about these denial items is that their presence signals retrospectively that the clause to which they refer is *hypothetical*. (See also Winter, 1977, p. 20, Vocabulary-3 Items.) As to the complementary role of modal verbs and their lexical paraphrases, we might note here that they overlap from indefiniteness where the concern is not so much for the truth as for the definiteness of their clause to hypotheticality where the concern is for the truth of the clause as such, for example the modal verb **would** (have) and **could** (have) in (161) below.

Having sketched out some of the representative items of the hypothetical and real relation, we can now fit the affirmation and denial clause into its framework. It is important to note *how* affirmation or denial are initiated. Affirmation or denial clause are not simply **yes** or **no** answers to the truth question being applied to the hypothetical clause. 'Is it true or is it correct, etc.?' They are 'know' questions as opposed to the hypothetical clause which is a 'think' question if we think of 'think' as imagining or supposing something. What could initiate affirmation or denial clause is a two-part question in which the 'know' question is a preambling lead into the true-question: 'What do you know about it?' (the hypothetical clause): 'Is it true, etc?' A **yes-** or a **no**-answer predicts 'know' clauses in its support: for **yes**, we can have *reason* or *basis* clause; for **no**, we can have *correction* and/or *basis* clause and/or *reason* clause. We take affirmation clause first and then follow with denial clause. The notion of significant positive or significant negative clause will now become clearer.

11.6.4 Some Examples of Affirmation Clause and Denial Clause

To understand the social interaction point about the hypothetical and real relation, we note that it is a central function in reporting somebody else's clause(s). The reporter as decoder interprets somebody else's clause as hypothetical and then provides his real version of what it means. From a rhetorical point of view, this reporter can reinterpret somebody else's 'fact' or real and provide his own real for it.

In (159) below, the hypothetical is signalled by **a merited tribute** and further by the source, **he said**. The writer here uses the marked affirmation **so it is**, following it up with an evaluation (think) as a basis for the affirmation.

(159)   Soon after taking office the Prime Minister paid a merited tribute to the Civil Service. **It was**, he said, **one of the best administrative machines in the world**. And **so it is**, British civil servants have every right to be proud of their achievement and their reputation. But even the best can be improved. (*Guardian*, 17 February 1966, p. 10)

In (160) below, the words within quotation marks are taken from a book about women agents in France during the War. The cue for hypotheticality is the quotation marks showing somebody else's clause, and in the fact that the reviewer affirms the clause: 'Is it true that they don't receive special treatment?' = **Yes**. The affirmation is also an evaluation clause: **mercifully**.

(160)   'The present state of the French and English press is such that some of these women [agents] have received a great deal of attention, much of it ill-informed and some of it ill-intentioned. **They will receive no special treatment** [in my book].' **They don't**, mercifully. (Book review, *Guardian*, 12 April 1966, p. 12)

In (161) below, the first sentence speculates about a spy's escape route. This is the cue for two rival hypotheses about the actual means of escape. Note the role of the modal verbs throughout **would have, could have**, etc. If we can't affirm or deny a hypothesis we can either agree or disagree with it. Here the writer notes an agreement with the first hypothesis by the police, referring to it as a **theory**.

(161)   Once over the prison wall, Blake's escape route to Eastern Europe would not have been difficult. **A small plane could have picked him up in a lonely field**; this was a **theory** strongly considered by the police when Charles Wilson, one of the Great Train Robbers, escaped from Winson Green prison in Birmingham. Equally, he could have been taken on board a small, innocent-looking fishing boat to meet another ship in the Channel. (*Observer*, 30 October 1966, p. 11)

Next, we consider two examples of denial clause. These negatived clauses would probably form less than half of the 4·5 per cent negatived clauses cited by the Osti Programme. The thing to note is that denial denies the truth of the hypothetical clause. Here we have significant negative clause.

In (162) below, sentence 1 signals hypothetical by wishing to 'correct the wrong impression'. The quotation marks contain the hypothetical statements. Sentence 3 contains the denial clause.

(162)   PSYCHIATRIC EVIDENCE
        Sir, (1) May I emerge from the medical anonymity for which I was

very grateful, to correct the wrong impression left by your headlines (October 8): **'Psychiatrist quits court, Protest at remark by Judge.'** (2) I understand that several national newspapers carried similar headlines. (3) This I regret because **I did not quit in protest.**

(4) What actually happened was that I had just been dismissed by the President and stood up to leave, expressing my surprise, as reported in your columns. (5) The role of the medical witness in courts where the future of young children is being decided is too important a matter for petty protest and walk-out . . . (Letter, *The ⸗ Times*, 12 October 1966, p. 12)

Note that sentence 4 offers the correction clause which sentence 1 anticipates; it answers the truth question 'If you did not quit in protest, what actually happened to you in court?' Sentence 5 evaluates the correction clause from the medical witness's point of view.

Finally, in (163) below, the hypothetical member is signalled by the verb **suppose** whose **that**-clause object contains the hypothetical clause. Notice that this clause is partially denied by the special operations clause **this was not always the case,** whose nominal subject **this** repeats the hypothetical clause by substitution.

(163) The modern generation of young women, proud of their uninhibited impulses, are apt to **suppose** that **Edwardian girls were timid, coy and lacking in exciting inclinations.** I soon learned that **this was not always the case.** Late one night the bell rang and on the step were a young woman, her face muffled up, and a sheepish young man.

When I came to examine her in a good light I observed her eyes flashing with fury while he explained that they had merely been saying 'goodnight' when 'this happened'.

The young lady was unable to utter a sound for in attempting to devour each other with kisses she had dislocated her jaw. (Dr C. Willett Cunnington on his experience as a doctor)

Notice that the rest of the text offers a basis for the partial denial clause in the form of 'story' to the contrary of the hypothetical clause. Notice also that it is structured as situation implying problem (third sentence) unspecific problem (fourth sentence), and, finally, specific problem or identification and evaluation of problem (doctor's diagnosis).

11.6.5 *Summary and Conclusion*

We have noted that the natural instinct of the decoder is to take a sentence on trust as true as presented unless otherwise warned. We noted that without any such rider the grammar of either positive or negative (independent) clause is taken on trust as true. This is what the grammatical choice of clause means. These positive and negative clauses were not significant as positive or negative clause; they were seen as answers to **wh**-questions. We noted that statistically most clauses in written texts were positive.

We noted two kinds of rider warning the decoder not to take the sentence on trust as true. The first was the use of modal verbs to signal indefiniteness or doubt, and from doubt we move to the second of the warnings to the reader, the warning of hypotheticality. This second warning accounted for the hypothetical and real relation. Within the hypothetical member, in addition to the retrospective signalling of 'hypothetical' by affirmation or denial clause, we found that the 'hypothetical' was signalled in various ways: by the notion of quoting a 'merited tribute' in (159); the quotation marks of somebody else's statement in (160); speculative evaluation of the ease of Blake's escape route as a *general* idea anticipates the *particular* hypotheses of about how it **could have been** done, and this is retrospectively signalled as hypothesis by the noun **theory**: in (161); the notion of 'correcting a mistaken impression' in (162); and finally the verb **suppose** in (163).

Within the real member of this relation, we find that significant positive and significant negative clause are significant because they are 'yes' and 'no' answers to **yes/no**-questions: 'Is it true?' We found affirmation clause in (159) and (160), noting that in (160) the affirmation clause was negative; we found denial clause in (162) and (163), noting the predicted structures of the real which followed the denial clause, for example the correction and the evaluation of the correction in (162) and the contrary instance of the hypothesis as a correction and basis for the denial in (163). There was the minor snag of finding a negative clause as affirmation clause in (160); if you affirm a denial clause, the affirmation must match it as another denial clause.

We can draw two related conclusions from the foregoing description of the two riders to the definition, namely from the modality of the verb and its lexical paraphrases and the existence of the hypothetical and real relation. The first is that we need the riders to the definition because the sentence must cater for a lack of knowledge and the degrees of uncertainty all speakers have. The second is that affirmation clause and denial clause are significant as positive and as negative clause because they are 'know' information or initiate 'know' information for the 'think' information of the hypothetical member. As a larger clause relation, the fundamental semantics of hypothetical and real is a 'matching' of the 'think' information of the hypothetical element with the 'know' information of the real element; if they match, we have affirmation as true; if they don't match we have denial as true. The linguistic purpose of real is to establish the hypothetical as a new situation; that is, as new 'fact'.

The conclusion which the reader will by now be drawing is that signalling the truth is the marked form for which otherwise taking the sentence on trust as true is the unmarked. One criterion of markedness is whether the signal predicts a strong contrast by a co-ordinator like **but**, as in (164) below, where the lexical item **true** signals the real member. Here the special operations clause **All this is true** is the real member which affirms the truth of the hypothetical member, which is printed bold. The hypotheticality of the preceding **that**-clause is signalled as something which is overlooked. The co-ordination by **But** is also predicted by the evaluation of the hypothesis as a foregone conclusion; this is the presence of the disjunct **of course**. The **But**-clause continues the real member.

(164) Of course, it is easy for a minority out of office to overlook **that compromise is the inevitable companion of responsibility. Idealism and transacting political business don't go well together. All this is true**. But then, this is precisely why a minority party is needed: to be the flag-carrier of idealism and of intellectual innovation. Under Grimond, the Liberals have performed this role admirably – while resisting the temptations which their irresponsible position offers. (*Observer*, 22 January 1967, p. 10)

Having completed our complementary definitions, it requires little imagination to see where a definition of question clause might fit in. A question is the device in which we present what we already know or presuppose as true, and ask for what we don't know to be supplied in reply. A **wh**-question asks for lexical realisation of some kind; a **yes/no**-question asks for confirmation of a hypothetical clause; it initiates the real member of the hypothetical and real relation.

For further description of the hypothetical and real relation in texts, see Winter (1979, pp. 109–10 and 126–7), Hoey and Winter (forthcoming) and Jordan (1978, pp. 163–70).

11.7 Rephrasing and Definitions in Terms of Requirements on the Encoder

11.7.1 Introduction

We now summarise the three definitions and draw conclusions from them, rephrasing the complementary parts of the definitions in composite terms of three requirements which the decoder makes of the encoder when being communicated with. All of these requirements take for granted the requirements of clause relations as described earlier in 11.2, namely that the word makes sense in its clause and the clause makes sense in its context of adjoining clauses in particular ways. The requirements assume the vantage point of a sentence in context; that is, the sentence either has a situational context or a context of immediately preceding sentences. For instance, a substitute clause has at least a context of an immediately preceding sentence. A substitute clause is by definition an unspecific clause; that is, it becomes an unspecific clause if it is taken out of its context because it loses the specific clause which has immediately preceded it. We have already noted the linguistic principle of context that unspecific clause demands semantic completion by specific clause which lexically fulfils it. In the case of substitute clause as unspecific clause, we simply note that it represents what we already 'know' about the clause from the immediately preceding context as in (165) below, where we have two instances of substitute clause in turn: **So it should** and (before he) **does this sort of thing again**. Their preceding lexical fulfilment is printed bold.

(165) Moreover, servicemen are Government employees and **the Government** must presumably **set a good firm example to other employers**.
So it should, but not if this means **dishonouring an agreement**. Mr Brown should also consider (before he **does this sort of thing again**) the problem he is setting the Prices and Incomes Board. (*Guardian*, 26 November 1965, p. 12)

The substitute clause repeats the clause **The Government . . . set a good firm example to other employers**, and the substitute clause **does this sort of thing again** repeats the non-finite clause **dishonouring an agreement** and provides it with an explicit subject. Here repetition of the clause is synonomous with 'known' for the substitute clause. In the requirements below, the notions of 'given' or 'known' can mean what is given or known from the preceding context along the principles of the substitute clause function here.

The principle of stepping outside the sentence boundary applies equally to specific clause where an item of its clause signals another similar meaning specific clause. Consider the signalling cue in the notion of **once** and the past tense of its clause signalling a comparison with the notion of **now** and the present tense to come in (166) below.

(166) Then the whole operation is reversed through all its stages until the pump is reattached to the plant. **The operation was once performed by a minimum of six men. Now** it is done by **one electrician**. (*New Society*, 7 April 1966, p. 6)

In Prague School terms of 'given' and 'new', we can say that in both (165) and (166) above the preceding clause becomes the 'given' for the next clause's 'new', that is, the preceding specific clauses have become the 'given' for the 'new' substitute clauses in (165) and the first member of the comparison, **once**, becomes the 'given' for the second member's **now** as the 'new'. We took for granted this 'given' and 'newness' of the independent clause in Definition 2. It is part of the larger relation of 'given' and 'new', where 'given' is what is known and 'new' is what is *not* known *at that point of the context where a particular sentence appears*. We are also taking for granted the repetition of the participants of the clause as part of the grammatically 'given' information of this clause in context, whether it is subordinate or independent, and whatever the relation the clause bears with its preceding clauses.

So in our three requirements below, we are assuming a preceding context for the sentence when we rephrase the definitions in terms of the kind of requirement which the encoder might make when he wishes to be communicated with.

11.7.2   Requirement 1

The encoder must achieve independence for the clause of his sentence by fulfilling all the grammatical cues it presents, and when he has done this he must fulfil all the lexical cues, especially the anticipatory ones, for example unspecific clause must be lexically fulfilled (realised) by specific clause or clauses. He must also fulfil all notional requirements, for example the clause-relational requirements such as an evaluation clause followed by its situation or basis clause where these clauses have not already preceded evaluation clause. Summing up Definition 1, independence is the first requirement for sentence, but it is not enough to account for its semantics. We can say that semantic completeness accounts for what is immediately beyond grammatical completeness and is an inescapable part of it. The linguistic significance of the notion of unspecific clause is that its minimum linguistic context is that it must be in some kind of semantic relation with a specific clause which makes sense of it in particular ways. In lay terms, we need another sentence or two to 'explain' the particular sentence which has been presented to us. This is what the study of clause relations is about.

11.7.3   Requirement 2

The encoder must communicate to the decoder what is *not* known to the decoder in terms of what is (already) known, distinguishing between what the decoder knows and what others know. Where relevant, having communicated what is not known, he communicates what he *thinks* about what is known or just made known. Here the decoder wants two kinds of information, 'know' information and 'think' information, and he wants to be told what information is not known in terms of what information is already known or presupposed. This accounts for the distinction between independent clause and subordinate clause. It also accounts for the 'given' and the 'new' information of the independent clause itself other than its subordinate clause information.

The linguistic significance of this requirement when it complements the first requirement of grammatical and semantic completeness is that it explains the semantic relations between adjoining clauses and sentences in terms of The Prague School's contextual notion of 'given' and 'new', which has long been seen as explaining the information system behind intonation and stress. (See Brazil *et al.*, 1980, for a compatible approach.)

We can illustrate the linguistic requirement for prior knowledge by looking at a particular sequenced utterance according to what sentences precede it and what sentences follow it. The clauses of the sentences which precede it provide what is to be known or given for its new information, so that the proper understanding of this sentence demands the prior knowledge of its preceding sentences, and such prior knowledge is to be found subordinated when the clause itself has already appeared in the context. If, however, we look ahead of this sentence to the sentences that follow it, we know that we cannot repeat the sentence without explicit acknowledgement or semantic change by replacement with new information. That is, we either acknowledge that we are repeating an independent clause by signalling it, by **as you know, as I have just said**, etc., or we acknowledge that the clause has already appeared or is already known by subordinating it in any of three ways: (i) as *adverbial clause* to paraphrase its clause relation with the new (main) clause; (ii) as *noun clause* to 'talk about' the known clause or the known question-clause as we would any other noun item of the clause; or (iii) as *relative clause* where we use the lexical uniqueness of the known clause in order to identify the noun head by its role in this known clause. Finally, we have noted the difference in linguistic 'confidence' between the 'new' clause by independence and the same clause as a 'known' clause by subordination, particularly adverbial clause subordination.

We have also noted that 'know' and 'think' clauses are the fundamental semantics of the situation and evaluation relation, and earlier we noted the situation and evaluation relation explains the interpolation function, especially interpolation by independent clause as the evaluation of situation in which the host clause itself is its linguistic situation.

11.7.4   Requirement 3

The encoder must tell the truth, taking care to warn us by the appropriate signalling where we cannot take it for granted that the clause of his sentence is true or not true. Notice that this requirement from the encoder is an acknowledgement of its largely involuntary nature in the response by the decoder: the decoder can do no other than take the sentence as presented as true unless otherwise signalled. Notice also the implication of trust in the use of the modal verb **must** in this requirement from the encoder.

The study of how we signal that the truth cannot be taken for granted should have an important place in English grammar. Take the description of the hypothetical and real relation which we saw as a special relation in which the 'think' information of the hypothetical member is evaluatively matched with the 'know' information of the real member. We might study, for instance, how the hypotheticality signal of the hypothetical members suspends the finiteness or 'factness' of the hypothetical clause, for example the difference between **She has died** where the clause is presented as a 'fact' or 'real' versus **They think she has died** where the clause is not presented as 'fact' but as a speculation of possible 'fact'. All this would be only incidental to the study of the various lexical items which could signal hypotheticality. We might study the significant negative and the significant positive clauses of denial clause and affirmation clause as replies to the 'know' question 'What do you know about it? More specifically, is it true?' A study of negation which examines this aspect of negation is long overdue. Such a study of negation would contrast denial (as true) with affirmation in contexts.

11.7.5   Conclusions about the Requirements on the Encoder

We see from the discussion of the requirements that the requirement for grammatical completeness and independence is basic before we can communicate in sentences, but that grammatical completeness, etc., does not necessarily mean semantic completeness. We accordingly see the contextual meaning of the sentence as a function of its adjoining sentences.

The second and third requirement between them account for how we handle the semantic unit of clause in sentence and groups of sentences (utterances) in terms of basic 'know' and 'think' information. The implication of these two requirements is that the basis of our entire communication system depends upon the complementarity of 'know' and 'think' information.

Much work has still to be done on English utterances, spoken as well as written, to corroborate or refute the claims implicit in the definitions. For instance, the 'given' and 'new' system of the independent clause itself has been taken for granted in our concentration upon adverbial clause subordination. It will be remembered that we treated the information in the adverbial clause and its main clause as whole clause 'givens' and 'news' respectively. Perhaps there may be further complementary definitions to account for the assumptions about context that the meaning of an utterance is the function of its adjoining utterances, especially its preceding utterances since these will affect the grammatical status of its 'given' information. Perhaps most urgent of all is the problem of defining the question function so that it is complementary to the definitions of sentence. We have already noted that a question is a demand for 'new' information to be supplied to the 'known' information of the question clause, for example the question **Who did she see?** signals that she has indeed seen somebody but we don't know whom. The **yes/no**-question 'Did he ever arrive there?' is a fully lexically realised clause which asks for the truth, whether the answer is 'Yes, he did' or 'No, he didn't'. Any description of English grammar must take into account the linguistic contrast between the hypothetical clause 'Did he ever arrive there?' and the real clause 'No, he didn't' in respect of their contextual differences.

We have gone some of the way towards the goal of defining the question function in our use of the question criterion, which I have noted earlier follows the approach proposed by A. G. Hatcher (1956), and of Fries's work on spoken utterances in which he notes the role of questions in eliciting sentences. The value of the question criterion is unquestionable. Implicit in all the analyses in the present work is the assumption that for every clause there must be a question which it is answering.

11.8 An Application of the Requirements to a Made-Up Sentence

It now remains for us to consider how we might apply the composite requirements for 'sentence' function to an aspect of linguistic description. We could, for instance, consider the use of the convenient and simple made-up examples of sentence in present-day linguistic analysis. The use of made-up or 'idealised' sentences has a very long history in linguistic discussion, and goes back to the Middle Ages when there was a change in the ways of looking at the grammar of the sentence. Up to then, the study of grammar was a study of the writers of classical literature. Now, as Robins (1967, p. 89) notes, there was a change from the data-oriented grammars to the theory-oriented approach of the *modistae* who 'made up their examples almost formulaicly without regard to actual utterances or to situational plausibility; being only concerned with exemplifying a particular structure, they frequently produced sentences that could scarcely have occurred in any other context of situation'.

It should be noted that nearly all the made-up sentences one sees in the literature are specific clauses, not unspecific clauses. J. Lyons (1977, p. 29) distinguishes between two kinds of 'sentence': the 'system-sentence', the idealised one which linguists use for the purposes of analysis, and the 'text-sentence', the sentence in actual spoken or written use. The whole point of the present study is to describe the 'text-sentence' in dual terms of independent clause and subordinate clause and their contrast with question clause.

Let us now consider the 'system-sentence' **John hit Mary** as illustrating the transtivity of the verb **hit** in an independent clause. How much of the composite requirement will this sentence meet? The particular linguistic point about most 'system-sentences' like these is that they are specific clauses. There are, of course, good reasons why they are not unspecific clauses because of their very obvious need for adjoining clauses (for example 'There are difficulties'), but how far might such theoretical speculations about grammar have proceeded on an unremitting diet of unspecific clause?

Applying the requirements, we find that the sentence **John hit Mary** only meets half of one of them, the first part of Definition 1, which requires a grammatical completeness with independence that makes a minimum sense in terms of the words of the clause itself. It only partly meets the second part of Definition 1, which requires semantic completeness for the items of its clause. What we have here is dictionary completeness; that is, we have a sentence which illustrates the use of the verb **hit** in a sentence which makes sense because its words are semantically self-consistent with respect to their relation to the verb **hit**, that is to say there are two human participants in an action which we know human beings do each other. What we don't have is the *specifics* of the verb **hit** in its contextual significance as an action. This is to be seen in the questions which it raises for specifics: **How** did he hit her? With a poker? With his open hand? With a pillow? And **where** did he hit her? On the head? In the face? On the arm? In what circumstances (situation) is the action of hitting significant? Was it provoked, or unprovoked? What consequences were there?, etc. Such contextual questions which ask for the significance of the action blend into Definitions 2 and 3.

It fails Definition 2; it does not tell us something we don't know in terms of something which we do know. Nothing in this sentence connects with any John or Mary we know. In particular, we do not have the 'given' or 'known' information supplied by the preceding context of sentences, or a shared knowledge about the development of human relations between John and Mary. Worse, out of context, the written sentence can have three contextual meanings according to which part of the clause is the new information by independent clause for its 'given' information.

To mean something to us as communication, part of the clause must be known to us. We might know both the participants in a particular kind of relation in which the verb **hit** could be a predictable part of the behaviour of one of the participants. For example, John and Mary quarrelled bitterly about Jane − He lost his temper when she reproached him about his affair with Jane − **He hit her**. Here the verb **hit** is the new information. The meaning of the sentence is 'How did losing his temper affect his behaviour towards her? − more specifically, what did he do to her?' Notice the role of the pronouns **he** and **she** showing that we 'know' **John** and **Mary** in this context.

If, however, we don't know **John**; that is, if **John** is the new information, then we have a different context: 'Who hit Mary?' Similarly, if **Mary** is the new information, then we have yet another context: 'Who did John hit?' As previously noted, the lexical parts of the **wh**-question in each case show what is presupposed to be true, for example the **wh**-question 'Who hit Mary?' presupposes that somebody did in fact hit Mary, but we don't know who. In short, the sentence does not have any meaningful 'given' or 'new' information and does not meet the Prague School's requirements for a functional sentence perspective. It is also perhaps worthy of note that it is impossible to say **John hit Mary** aloud without conveying one of the potential meanings by stress or intonation.

Finally, the sentence **John hit Mary** fails Definition 3, even though it presents its clause to be taken on trust as true in the unmarked state, *without any riders of doubt*, and its information is 'know' information presented as 'fact'. 'Know' information is the clause which answers a 'do'-question, for example 'What did John do to Mary?'; presentation as 'fact' is signalled by the finiteness of the verb and its simple past tense. If we suppose that the encoder of this sentence presents his sentence to be taken on trust as true, unless otherwise signalled, then the grammatical signalling of independent clause here is meaningless as signal because (i) there is no such person as John and Mary here and no such event as this John hitting this Mary for the encoder to present, and (ii) there is consequently no intent to mean by grammatical choice for lexical items other than for a dictionary-type purpose. In short, Definition 3 does not apply.

It should, however, be noted that if we insist upon the encoder meeting requirement 3, to say nothing of requirement 2, we encounter a theoretical problem with fairy stories and fiction. Insisting upon requirements 2 and 3 being met in their full rigour means that we can have no fiction or fairy stories. All we can say here as readers of fiction or fairy stories is that we consciously suspend our belief system as this is embodied in the meaning of our grammatical signalling cues, and simply re-take or double-take the lot on trust as true, enjoying the suspension of belief for its own sake. We can still study the individual sentences in these works because they have a linguistic context of adjoining sentences which the made-up **John hits Mary** does not have.

Bibliography

Bloomfield, L. (1926), 'A set of postulates for the science of language', *Language*, vol. 2, p. 156.

Bloomfield, L. (1933), *Language* (London: Allen & Unwin).

Bolinger, D. (1968), *Aspects of Language* (New York: Harcourt, Brace & World; rev. edn 1980).

Brazil, D., Coulthard, M., and Johns, C. (1980), *Discourse Intonation and Language Teaching* (London: Longman).

Chomsky, N. (1965), *Aspects of the Theory of Syntax* (Cambridge, Mass.: MIT Press).

Curme, G. O. (1947), *English Grammar* (New York: Barnes & Noble).

Danes, F. (1974), 'Functional sentence perspective and the organization of the text', in F. Danes (ed.) *Papers on Functional Sentence Perspective* (The Hague: Mouton).

Dillon, G. L. (1978), *Language Processing and the Reading of Literature* (London and Bloomington, Ind.: Indiana University Press).

Eckersley, E. C., and Eckersley, J. M. (1960), *A Comprehensive English Grammar for Foreign Students* (London: Longman).

Edwards, N. (1980), 'Difficulty in text as a function of syntactic complexity', M.Phil. dissertation, Open University, March.

Francis, W. N. (1958), *The Structure of American English* (New York: Ronald Press).

Fries, C. C. (1952; 1957), *The Structure of English* (London: Longman).

Greenbaum, S. (1969), *Studies in Adverbial Usage* (London: Longman).

Halliday, M. A. K. (1961), 'Categories of the theory of grammar', *Word*, vol. 17, no. 3, pp. 241-94.

Halliday, M. A. K. (1967), 'Notes on transitivity and theme in English', *Journal of Linguistics*, vol. 12, pp. 206-44.

Hatcher, A. G. (1956), 'Syntax and the sentence', *Word*, vol. 12, pp. 234-50.

Hatcher, A. G. (1956), 'Theme and underlying question', *Word*, vol. 12, monograph 3.

Hill, A. A. (1958), *Introduction to Linguistic Structures* (New York: Harcourt, Brace & Co.).

Hockett, C. F. (1956), *A Course in Modern Linguistics* (New York: Macmillan).

Hoey, M. P. (1979), Signalling in Discourse, Discourse Analysis Monograph No. 6. (Birmingham, University of Birmingham).

Hoey, M. P., and Winter, E. O. (forthcoming), 'Believe me for mine honour', *Language and Style*.

Hoey, M. P. (forthcoming), *On the Surface of Discourse* (London: Allen & Unwin).

Hornby, A. S. (1975), *Guide to Patterns and Usage in English* (London: Oxford University Press; 1st edn 1954).

Huddleston, R. D., Hudson, R. A., Winter, E. O., and Henrici, A. (1968), 'Sentence and clause in scientific English', Osti Report 5030, University College, London.

Hudson, R. A. (1968), 'The clause complex', in Huddleston *et al.* (1968), pp. 289–559.

Hudson, R. A. (1969), 'Types of co-ordination relation in English', mimeo., University College, London, March.

Hudson, R. A. (1971), *English Complex Sentences: An Introduction to Systemic Grammar* (Amsterdam: North-Holland).

Jacobs, R. A., and Rosenbaum, P. S. (1968), *English Transformational Grammar* (Lexington, Mass.: Xerox College Publishing).

Jacobsen, Bent (1977), *Transformational Generative Grammar* (Amsterdam: North-Holland).

Jacobson, S. (1964), *Adverbial Positions in English*, (Stockholm: A. B. Studentbok).

Jespersen, O. (1924), *The Philosophy of Grammar* (New York: Henry Holt & Co.).

Jespersen, O. (1937), *Analytic Syntax* (New York: Holt, Rinehart & Winston).

Jespersen, O. (1940), *A Modern English Grammar* (London: Allen & Unwin), pt 5, 'Syntax'.

Jordan, M. P. (1978), 'The principal semantics of the nominals "this" and "that" in contemporary English writing', PhD dissertation, Hatfield Polytechnic, April.

Jordan, M. P. (forthcoming), *Prose Structures of Everyday English Use* (London: Allen & Unwin).

Karlsen, R. (1959), *Studies in the Connection of Clauses in Current English: Zero Ellipsis and Explicit Forms* (Bergen: J. W. Eides Bokstrykkeri S.S.).

Keenan, E. L. (1971), 'Two kinds of presupposition in natural language', in C. J. Fillmore and D. T. Langendoen (eds), *Studies in Linguistic Semantics* (New York: Holt, Rinehart & Winston), pp. 44–52.

Kiparsky, P., and Kiparsky, C. (1970), 'Fact', in M. Bierwisch and K. E. Heidolph (eds), *Semantics: An Interdisciplinary Reader in Philosophy, Linguistics and Psychology* (Cambridge: Cambridge University Press), pp. 345–69.

Leech, G. N., and Svartvik, J. (1975), *A Communicative Grammar of English* (London: Longman).

Longacre, R. (1972), *Hierarchy and Universality of Discourse Constituents in New Guinea Languages* (Washington, DC: Georgetown University Press).

Lyons, J. (1977), *Semantics* (Cambridge: Cambridge University Press).

Makkai, Adam (1972), *Idiom Structure in English* (The Hague: Mouton).

Meillet, A. (1903), *Introduction à l'étude des langues indo-européenes* (Paris).

Pike, K. L. (1977), *Grammatical Analysis* (Austin, Texas: University of Texas).

Poutsma, H. (1926–9), A Grammar of Late Modern English (Gröningen: Nordhoff).

Quirk, R. (1954), *The Concessive Relation in Old English Poetry* (New Haven, Conn.: Yale University Press).

Quirk, R. (1962; revised 1968), *The Use of English* (London: Longman).

Quirk, R., Greenbaum, S., Leech, G. N., and Svartvik, J. (1972), *A Grammar of Contemporary English* (London: Longman).

Robins, R. H. (1967), *A Short History of Linguistics* (London: Longman).

Saussure, F. de (1907–13), *A Course in General Linguistics* (London: Fontana/Collins).

Scheurweghs, G. C. (1959), *Present-day English Syntax* (London: Longman).

Sinclair, J. McH. (1972), *A Course in Spoken English* (London: Oxford University Press).

Sweet, H. (1881–98), *A New English Grammar* (London: Oxford University Press).

Winter, E. O. (1968), 'Anaphoric sentence adjuncts', in Huddleston *et al.* (1968), pp. 560–604.

Winter, E. O. (1971), Connection in science material: a proposition about the semantics of clause relations', in CILT Reports and Papers 7, *Science and Technology in a Second Language* (London: Centre for Information on Language Teaching and Research), pp. 41–52.

Winter, E. O. (1974), 'Replacement as a function of repetition: a study of its principal features in the clause relations of contemporary English', PhD thesis, University of London.

Winter, E. O. (1977), 'A clause-relational approach to English texts', *Instructional Science* (Amsterdam), vol. 6, no. 1, special issue.

Winter, E. O. (1979), 'Replacement as a fundamental function of the sentence in context', *Forum Linguisticum*, vol. 4, no. 2 (December), pp. 95–133.

Zandvoort, R. W. (1962), *A Handbook of English Grammar* (London: Longman).

Index

The convention for finding examples is as follows. **Bold** type is used for the alphabetical symbols or the numbers which indicate the example, and the ordinary numbering that immediately follows each example is its page number. Thus, **78**, 104 is example (78) on page 104. All other numbers are page numbers.